Sweet Girl

Sweet Girl
♥ *Heartbeats of a Special Life*

Kurt Ritchie

Copyright © 2015 by Kurt Ritchie

All rights reserved.
No portion of this book may be reproduced in any form without written permission of the publisher.

Published by RKR Books, Arlington, Texas, USA
www.rkrbooks.com

ISBN: 978-1-888943-00-9

Cover & book spine photos by Anne Dixon
Back cover photos by Carol Ritchie

The information contained in this book related to pet health, including diet, medicine, and veterinary care, is offered for educational and entertainment purposes. Individuals are advised to consult a veterinarian before administering to pets any diet, medication, or health supplements referred to in this book. The author and the publisher assume no responsibility or liability for personal, pet, or other injury, loss, or damage caused (or alleged to have been caused, directly or indirectly) by suggestions or information in this publication.

www.sweetgirlsasha.com

For Mom,
who instilled in me, by example and grace,
perpetual love and respect for the pets in my life

> My little dog ...
>   a heartbeat at my feet.
>
> *– Edith Wharton*
> *a founder of the ASPCA*

introduction • 1

one • memoirs • 9

two • home • 33

three • sweet girl • 59

four • siblings • 85

five • companionship • 117

six • health • 147

seven • heartbeats • 175

eight • communion • 203

nine • faith • 237

ten • signs • 265

eleven • hope • 295

postscript • 309

epilogue • 319

> "Do not go where the path may lead,
> go instead where there is no path
> and leave a trail.
>
> – *Ralph Waldo Emerson*

introduction

Sweet Girl

Introduction

WHEN I WAS IN THE SIXTH GRADE at Verona School, just weeks before graduating to junior high, my final English assignment showed promise to captivate untamed youthful spirit. It was an ultimate exercise in self-indulgence, irresistible to inquisitive and fanciful fresh minds.

My teacher instructed us each to write our autobiography.

I maintained good grades in every subject, but English strayed far from my favorite. (I did, however, like spelling.) Math, science, and music were much more exciting to me, but writing the story of *my* life grabbed my undivided attention. There were no rules about how to collect thoughts or gather ideas; just tell my own story.

School homework like this did not seem like work at all. I longed for projects of this sort, assignments that allowed me to explore the depths of my creativity and cheer with wild abandon. No textbooks. Freedom of imagination. Of course, proper grammar, spelling, and punctuation would contribute to determining how my "book" would be graded. By and large, these details seemed secondary and were the least of my worries.

I had a story to tell.

THROUGHOUT MY LIFE, any unhindered original project, given what I felt expressed a fascinating topic, has always generated the same enthusiastic response and dedication. I cannot wait to tackle a subject of interest in the most innovative ways.

Earlier in my sixth-grade year, the school had hosted a creative arts and science "Mini Youth Talent Fair." Students could submit entries in several categories. Ribbons would be awarded for each grade level and category. The mayor of our city would also choose one entry from the entire school for a grand prize, the "Mayor's Trophy."

One of my seven entries was a science project. I presented facts about the human body, constructing a plywood jigsaw puzzle with removable pieces cut into the shapes of internal organs, a homemade representation of a doctor's model. I featured the five senses, crafting a Styrofoam ear canal with a seashell cochlea, a ping-pong eyeball with a blue cat's-eye marble for the iris, and a red felt tongue that had been stuffed with cotton, sewn, and marked to point out taste buds.

I enjoyed creating my human body project (my career choice at that age—after "Major League" baseball player—was doctor), but my favorite entry for the fair yearned for life in the creative arts category. I designed and fabricated a ventriloquist's dummy, using a large wooden cube for the head. I painted hair and a face on it and the mouth opened and closed using string, thumb tacks, and rubber bands. I thought "Blockhead" spoke genius. I would lay awake in bed many nights articulating a classic ventriloquist shtick to entertain the audience as Blockhead and I accepted the grand prize.

Introduction

I felt proud of my projects, entered in every category, and created using only my eleven-year-old imagination and meager resources for construction. My chosen themes captured my spirit, each subject stirring great interest as I completed my work, focused and on a mission to do my very best. But I remained certain that my most inventive entry temporarily sat speechless as a silly entertainer's puppet.

On the day of judgment, my work activities in the classroom were interrupted when, startlingly enough, I was called to the principal's office. Unless there had been a family emergency, I knew of no other reason to be removed from class. I was nervous, fearing what had prompted the summons. Much to my surprise, I was told that my talent fair project had won the Mayor's Trophy.

I was shocked, trembling in electrified disbelief.

I had spent many laborious hours on my ingenious ventriloquism project *and my dreams had come true!*

Just one caveat—the grand prize had been awarded for my seashell, ping-pong, and plywood science project.

Standing as tall as my ventriloquist's puppet, my resplendent angel-topped trophy shines as a testament and reminder that we are often pulled in directions we least expect. Nevertheless, they are often rewarding, highly regarded, and perhaps our proper path.

I HAVE NEVER BEEN ONE to follow a path, however, much less a proper one. Seldom secure, but endlessly interesting, I have always let the universe blaze my unique trail, composing my own rhythm, marching to my own drum. Perhaps by free will, perhaps by destiny, but certainly not by my calculation,

I find myself unpredictably drawn into unlikely, yet increasingly sublime and meaningful missions.

This book is one of them.

When I sat down to write my sixth-grade autobiography, outlining each year as a separate chapter in my nineteen-page, construction paper-bound book, I never could have guessed that the topics briefly highlighted within—primarily medical emergencies and my childhood pets—would contribute to the telling of a little dog's story four decades later.

This little dog would come into my life spontaneously, during a time of transition, in a decade of thrilling adventures and tumultuous crises. My tiny companion would courageously stand strong at the core of chaos, radiating pure love and joy to all who were gripped by her gravitational pull. Her life force, vast beyond this world, would promise reason and order, faith and hope. Her lifetime, alas, would be cut much too short.

At the time of the inevitable loss of my beloved friend, during my free fall into the bottomless pit of sorrow, I was rescued by a long forgotten, yet familiar grade school thought: *I have a story to tell.* It was an epiphany, a life assignment. I had never contemplated writing a memoir of sorts, but at that moment, instantaneously, it became paramount. It seemed like the proper thing to do, a new trail to blaze, straightaway.

So ONCE AGAIN, I am piecing together chapters of my life, this time to share the story of an inspirational life force, a canine companion arriving in my life and bringing forth the greatest love, joy, faith, and wisdom. It is my hope that if this story expresses at least a fraction of the depth of these qualities she bestowed upon me, I might once again make my passing grade. This project may exceed my sixth-grade teacher's expectations, but I believe the assignment is roughly the same: no rules, just tell my story.

Kurt Ritchie
January 2015

Sweet Girl

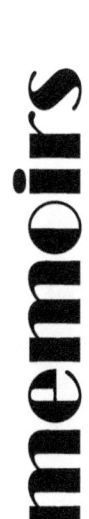

chapter one

Sweet Girl

SHE SAT QUIETLY, devoted and faithful, her deep brown eyes focused, while I could no longer contain my sorrow. Our dialogue was brief. The message was unmistakable. It was a heartrending confirmation of the inevitable; a clock-stopping validation that the time had come. Within minutes, the profundity and immediacy of our understanding became devastatingly clear.

Sasha was gone.

My constant companion would leave me in a deep hole from which it would be hard to escape. The emotional pain would be difficult to endure. For she had been a good friend and a master of anticipation, never judging, longing to participate, and living to share a lifetime of love and happiness. Her loss was too much to bear. My mind was full of questions.

How do I go on? Why did this happen? What could I have done differently to change this outcome?

OF ALL THE PATHS I could have chosen, only one could have led to this heartbreak. Always blazing new trails, with no expectations, I could have done nothing differently. The path was correct, but there would be repercussions—the pain, the loss, the grief—and it would take time to understand. Out of darkness, I would begin to receive messages of inspiration. There were life lessons to learn.

In order to move forward, I had to look back.

Recalling a lifetime of special pet memories gave me strength and confidence that—although sadly ill-fated—I was on the right track. My long history with pets had prepared me for this path—the only path I was destined to take—the uncharted trail to Sasha and her extraordinary journey.

FORTY YEARS BEFORE SASHA, our spirited little Maltese puppy, came bouncing into our lives, I was the youngster bouncing around in the lives of many family pets. I never knew a home without a four-legged friend. It's only been a few rare years that I have lived without a dog in the house. And those years were merely by design, not by choice. From the moment I shared a roof with my parents (and later, my younger sister), a loyal canine companion has always been there to entertain, love, and protect me and my family.

Through the course of fifty-plus years, I have been blessed to know and share my time and living spaces with several terrific dogs. And cats. And rabbits, hamsters, guinea pigs, mice, turtles, goldfish, doves, and even a failed attempt at sea monkeys. (I was so disappointed when the eggs never hatched. I really wanted to see that caricature community of tiny sea people living in the fish bowl on our kitchen countertop. Never mind that they were actually brine shrimp.)

My formative years were always filled with a household of furry friends. I was fortunate to have parents that not only allowed these pets, but usually encouraged them and wholeheartedly participated in the selection process. Our pets were indeed members of our family, and in every instance, lived a full life in our household. Even the more unconventional varieties of creatures were with us for the long haul. We only adopted out a litter each of puppies and kittens when they simply numbered too many to keep.

Dogs and cats, and a few species, such as hamsters or guinea pigs, were chosen (without parental resistance and with great anticipation) merely to become pets. But for many others that we hoped could join our household, we needed a plan of action to supplicate our parents. I never lacked fair reasoning or a full justification to support these necessary additions. I quickly learned to make good on my promises and committed to consistent daily care to ensure a quality lifetime for these pets. I was justly obliged for choosing to satisfy spontaneous childhood creature comforts.

I rescued turtles from the wilderness of our neighborhood city block. How they survived all the way to our street in the first place seemed miraculous. We lived several blocks from the nearest natural water source and a main thoroughfare crossed every snail-paced path in our direction.

A junior high science project provided a great excuse to bring a pet mouse—which led to dozens—into the house. Oh, the joys of weekly Habitrail mouse-house cleaning sessions, just to witness daily scurrying rat-race chases through a maze of plastic tubes and passageways. But in all honesty, that science class mouse (of the dozens that occupied our rodent amusement park at one time or another) became a special pet that stood high above the simple, demeaning title of pesky vermin.

Goldfish were prizes at our annual elementary school mixer—a carnival-like fund-raising school fair with multifarious games and events for kids to win treats to take home, including the barbaric ring toss for goldfish. Attempting to lob wooden loops over wide-eyed water pets was undoubtedly the most popular mixer attraction. You could hear the *clink clank* of dancing rings on glass bowls well before entering this classroom midway sideshow.

Unfortunately, winners could usually guarantee a journey through the city sewer system for most of the unlucky and unwitting golden trophy pets. Our goldfish never had the opportunity to attempt the treacherous swim to freedom, as they all survived happily in their well-nurtured countertop aqua-environs, often for many months, until the sad day they floated belly-up. Even at that point, they were given a respectful burial in our backyard rather than the notorious final flush, to the subterranean tunnels of the unknown.

Backyard funerals were the norm for our pets. Growing up in Michigan on land rich with dark fertile topsoil accommodated this process, even though the pet burial procedure most likely challenged city ordinances. Nevertheless, over the years, the area behind the garage of my childhood home became sacred ground for our unorthodox pet cemetery and I imagine, is host to many animal remains to this day.

From the tiniest goldfish and pet mouse, to our sixty-pound much-adored Boxer, each deceased pet was lovingly settled into an appropriately fitting cardboard box and entombed at the bottom of a suitably-sized hole in the ground, which my father would plot and prepare. Our service was ceremonial, yet informal. We all gathered around as the box was covered with dirt and our dear family pet was given a proper final resting place.

THE LOVE FOR PETS in my family passed down from earlier generations. My grandparents always embraced pets while raising my mother. When my mom married, the tradition of household pets continued with my parents. My sister, Lynne, and I grew up knowing pets to be commonplace in our family, whether at home or at Grandma's.

My grandparents were integral to my early years, regularly participating in many of our family affairs. They lived around the block from us—I spied the back of their house easily from my bedroom window. I spent much time in my grandparents' home, playing with Binky, their Basenji-type hound, and innocently enjoying their household duties. I observed the typical ways of their retired lifestyle. From the basics of living, like breakfast cereals they enjoyed, to daily chores and hobbies, such as Grandma's cooking and sewing or Grandpa's home movies and handyman tasks, their regular routines became relevant to my life. These activities eventually came together to develop and benefit an interest that began at seven years of age and continued through my high school years. A magical new hobby that further cemented a connection I could share with my grandparents for the rest of their lives.

It all started with breakfast.

Breakfast cereals have always been important in my life. Not because my hometown is Battle Creek, Michigan, the home of Kellogg's, Post, and Ralston, breakfast food manufacturers that proclaimed Battle Creek the "Cereal City." But simply, I have enjoyed a bowl of cereal most mornings for as long as I can remember. It was nice, however, to grow up in a place presenting a pleasant welcome to the world, where you could step outside to pure imagination—the aroma of toasted Froot Loops in the air.

While my family contributed to Kellogg's success, always keeping the typical sugar-laden, kid-favorite boxes of Frosted Flakes and Cocoa Krispies in our pantry, my grandparents kept Post in business with boxes of sensible unsweetened Grape-Nuts and Shredded Wheat lining their kitchen cupboard. Although the treasured nuggets at home were ridiculously sweet, it was always a treat to eat breakfast at Grandma's, to taste-test the rare cereals seldom seen in our kitchen (with spoonfuls of sugar, of course!).

As a curious youngster trying to make sense of enticing advertisements on Grandma's cereal boxes, my excitement bubbled over and imagination soared when one day I discovered an ad for a "Squarecrow FREE Magic Kit." For only seven Chex box tops (and likely a few pennies for shipping and handling), this wondrous collection of magical paraphernalia could be on its way to our house from those magnificent cereal makers. It didn't take much encouragement to persuade my grandparents to collect the necessary cereal box tops to order that splendiferous set of "nine amazing magic tricks" that could change our lives forever in the most miraculous ways.

The magic bug had bitten hard and there was no antidote.

The seemingly infinite shipping time for the magic kit was the longest wait of my life. My mind blistered with enchantment as I suffered in the agony of impatience. Every night in bed, as moonlight through my window cast enigmatic shadows of phantasmagoria that slowly crept up the wall, my head filled with hopeful anticipation and wizardly dreams of the fantastical things I would do when I'd have a real magic wand to create anything I'd like.

Yes, the amazing magic kit included a real magic wand! Anything was now possible!

Sure, there were several other items of conjuring equipment, but nothing else could possibly hold true powers like the magic wand.

Oh, how it would change our lives!

When the eagerly-anticipated mysterious checkerboard package finally arrived, my giant juvenile hopes of true magic were crushed by a small box of preposterously un-magical simple plastic props.

The magic wand was all wand and no magic.

This eye-opening realization that magic did not naturally *happen* with the wave of a wand was disappointing to say the least. Even so, learning and creating magic *tricks* still interested me; a spark that ignited the pursuit of bigger and more spectacular illusions for the better part of the next decade.

Geography played an important role in this continued interest since we lived only a half hour from the "Magic Capital of the World," Colon, Michigan. With continued encouragement, my grandfather was my biggest supporter, regularly joining me for local magic club meetings. Because my interest in magic developed before I could drive, Grandpa also gladly attended annual magic conventions with me and patiently waited for hours as I paced the creaky wooden floor, studying every piece of magic equipment on display beyond the black-box-with-floating-skeletons façade of Abbott's Magic Company.

My magic act gradually became a larger production that showcased more mystical equipment—dancing canes, levitating silver balls, flourishing bouquets of feather flowers, rainbow silks perpetually changing colors, a Houdini-style trunk escape, the vertical cutting of a girl into thirds—and sleight-of-hand assistance, including Lynne (the "lucky" Zig-Zag victim) and a few friends. I often employed my mom and grandparents as behind-the-scenes helpers, utilizing their sewing and woodworking skills to create amazing props of illusion for an award-winning stage show we presented locally throughout my high school years. To expand and build a bigger show was my goal, and working with live animals was the obvious and exciting next step.

This growing performance of prestidigitation was the catalyst for me to become the delighted owner of several rabbits and a large family of white doves. Although they were adopted as thrilling live props in my ever-expanding illusion show, these woodland creatures (like the other animals that shared our home) were first and foremost our pets.

They became stars of magic, often crouched and covered in small spaces waiting for their time in the spotlight, but mostly they were cuddled and coddled, living in magnificent indoor-outdoor cages Dad and I constructed. I enjoyed raising rabbits and training doves. I quickly learned that just like dogs and cats, every animal and bird had a unique personality. Most lived long happy lives as proud performers and much-beloved pets.

OUR DOGS AND CATS were *family* pets; however, Lynne and I were able to claim the host of other random species that graced our household as strictly *our* pets. With that claim, it became clear that the responsibility to care for each guinea pig, hamster, mouse, rabbit, and dove was also *ours*. While Mom assumed the task of daily feedings for the dog and cat, and Dad changed the kitty litter and did the canine pooper-scooper chores, Lynne and I took care of our little critters, feeding, watering, and cleaning their cages. (From a typical kid's standpoint, I reluctantly accepted this role. It seemed more of a chore than it seemed a true responsibility. But that soon changed.)

These regular chores ranged from basement sink scrubbings of the ever-expanding mouse condos to the weekly newspaper round-up of dove-dropping stalagmites in our small walk-in bird sanctuary.

During many Michigan winters, I made evening treks to the garage through drifts of snow—lettuce and carrots in hand—for our rabbits in their cozy, hay-filled cages. It wasn't *that* far to go, but sub-zero temperatures and arctic winds were ready to sting my eyes and burn my cheeks within seconds of exposure. It called for head-to-toe protection prep—a spacewalk suit-up—complete with winter parka, boots, wool cap, scarf, and gloves. I took an extra carrot or two for life support should I temporarily veer off course, lost in space until the spring thaw.

The year-round routine included scoops of rabbit food

pellets and water refills. During the freezing winter season, it also meant a round-trip to the hot water faucet to melt the slow-forming cylinder of ice in their water bottle. This daily care was more than merely routine, it *was* a big responsibility—*my* responsibility.

These pets depended on me.

I took this important role to heart, keeping them safe, clean, nourished, and healthy. Their well-being depended on it and I never took that responsibility lightly. These were not just animals in cages, they were our *friends*.

And I don't take that title lightly, either.

Calling our pets "friends" is not just for kids. At any age our pets are our friends, likely our best friends. After all, it is well known and presumed that "a dog is man's *best* friend." I indubitably concur; however, many "friends" have shared my family home over the years, and the best were not always dogs.

From the moment I took my first breath to the time I moved out on my own, my family had dogs. We had one dog at a time, but we always had a cat as well.

One dog and one cat.

That was the canine-feline ratio for the first seventeen years of my life. Add to that, all the other creatures that came to share our home. Living with these caged pets never became an issue for our dog and cat. On many occasions the instinctive predator-versus-prey adversaries met nose-to-nose (supervised, of course) without harmful consequences. As much as we loved our canine and feline companions, Lynne and I grew close to our other animals as well.

My connection was clear—a "sixth sense"—with three unique pets. I loved and nurtured all our pets, but I held special regard for one rabbit, one mouse, and one dove. They each had strong personalities with a seemingly extrasensory adeptness that helped form their undeniable bonds with me.

MY FIRST RABBIT, named (not surprisingly) Hocus Pocus—Hokey for short—was white with black ears. She was a tame, good-natured bunny that took to the entertainment business right from the start. Easy to train, she relished the opportunity to be the star of my magic act. She was a true magician's assistant—the ubiquitous and hackneyed, yet genuine, "white rabbit in the black top hat."

She tolerated inconspicuous transport and backstage preparations, seeming to understand the need to stay hidden from curious eyes until "Abracadabra!" signaled her spontaneous reveal to cheerful applause. Because she fit into my magic routine so aptly, I felt a true rapport with her that didn't compare to my relationship with our other pets.

That is until Heidi came along.

Rabbits are easily trained. They show affection and display emotions, much like cats and dogs. Hokey was a good friend who lived a nice long life, literally enjoying time in the spotlight, bringing happiness and joy to not only myself, but to awe-inspired audiences.

A warm-hearted relationship with a rabbit is reasonable. But what about a warm-hearted relationship with a mouse?

HEIDI WAS THE NAME bestowed upon an astonishingly affectionate and intelligent brown mouse I adopted from my junior high science class.

A few months before the adoption, I decided that building a maze to demonstrate a mouse's ability to learn and remember patterns would be a great science project. I'm not sure how, but I convinced my parents that this was a good idea, so we were off to the local pet store to pick out a cute little white mouse I named Sam. (And a black-and-white pet mouse for Lynne. The store clerk assured us that both were male. Right.)

Sam, as it turned out, was actually Samantha. A large family of mice soon followed. Nevertheless, they were fun pets to keep in the rodent-friendly aquarium environment we had created for them—fun to look at, that is. They were not easy to tame, which caused much frustration when we tried to catch and hold them. Instinctive feral ways held them in arrested development. There was little hope for domestication. Except for Sam. She gradually became docile and accepted our handlings, but she never did become the amazing pet that our little Heidi was.

When Heidi came home from the school science lab at the end of the school year, she taught us many lessons. She was the antithesis of what we had come to learn about pet mice. She had no apprehensions about being held or meeting our other pets. She awaited every opportunity to be the center of attention, whether crawling up and down our arms, or stealing a spot from the other mice to run endlessly in the exercise wheel. Although the others cowered in the corners, Heidi could not wait for me to open the cage—by then, what were the ever-expanding cubes and tubes of a Habitrail system—so she could investigate territories outside her usual confines. She loved to be held and did everything in her power to communicate with me.

She looked into my eyes.

She listened.

She understood.

She demonstrated amazing comprehension—considering how unintelligent the other mice seemed to be. She enjoyed time with us outside the cage and willingly returned when instructed to. Her attempt to form an emotional tie with me was extraordinary; however, her adventurous spirit could not be harnessed.

'TWAS THE NIGHT BEFORE an important function, and all through our house, something *was* stirring—it was Heidi, my mouse. The surprise present she delivered came wrapped in a frightening morning scenario.

Before I awoke that morning, Mom saw our cat, Tippy, sitting on the corner of my parents' bed, his eyes fixated toward the ceiling.

"What are you looking at?"

Following the cat's gaze, Mom noticed he was staring at the top of the window curtain. Calm and attentive, there sat a little brown field mouse.

Startled and concerned, Mom thought, *Oh no, we've got a mouse in the house!*

Then it dawned on her, *Yes, we've got a mouse in the house—we've got several mice—but they should be in a cage!*

As Mom ran downstairs to our family room where we kept our pet mice, she remembered in horror that she was hosting a ladies board meeting in our home—in just a few hours. And now there were mice on the loose in our house!

Sure enough, when she got to the cage, one of the Habitrail exit caps was open. Apparently, it had not been secured properly the night before. (Heidi had likely taken advantage of this oversight and popped it loose.) Sam was still running around inside the cage, frantic that the others had left, although most were close by and promptly returned to the cage. Of course, the ever-audacious Heidi was nowhere to be found.

Returning to images of Tippy salivating over the mouse sitting on the curtain, Mom ran back upstairs to wake me.

"You'd better get up. Your mouse is loose in the house—Heidi's in the bedroom."

Heidi and Tippy had met several times under friendly circumstances; however, without supervision Tippy probably would not have been so kind. This little brown mouse had become our friend. It was distressing to think what we might encounter in an unsupervised situation like this.

Still half asleep, my heart was racing faster than my footsteps as I ran to my parents' bedroom, hoping this was a bad dream. I was afraid this sudden wake-up call was not going to end well.

Wiping the sleep from my eyes, I exhaled in relief when I got to the bedroom and saw Tippy patiently waiting, keeping our little roommate corralled. Heidi was still sitting on the curtain, watching the search activities. I was able to return her to her secured home. She was unfazed and surely full of stories from her overnight adventure that took her from one end of the house to the other, including dog-and-cat-evading maneuvers and the mountain-cliff stair-scaling to the bedroom. Mom also breathed a huge sigh of relief. She could rest assured her soon-to-be-arriving guests would not descry a ghastly surprise running across the tray of hors d'oeuvres.

Our cat found Heidi for us, luckily from a safe distance, only to illustrate how intelligent and mischievous that little mouse could be. Heidi loved the attention and valued the connection she had with me. I felt the same toward her. She was a special little pet that seemed to understand and communicate in ways that inspired and affected me more than I could comprehend.

Heidi was another good friend.

ABOUT THE TIME I started high school, I entered my final pet plea to my parents, another round of reasoning to persuade them I needed to incorporate live doves into my magic act. It wasn't too difficult, though. The idea was appealing, since my interest in magic had developed into a lucrative hobby (relatively speaking, for a jobless teenager). Eventually, we kept up to eight doves at one time; however, like the mice, it started with two.

George was the male and Chenoa was the female. They became illustrious entertainers, like Hokey, and they each had a distinctive personality. Chenoa was docile, easily trained, and well behaved. George, on the other hand, was a show-off. But he was also smart. He anticipated my every move, instinctively knowing what I expected of him. He became another close relationship over the years, not just as a performing "show bird," shuffled from palm to perch on the stage, but as an inspirational, wonderful pet.

George was the first of many white doves to join our family and lived nearly twenty years. He outlived every other dove that graced our home. Along with Hokey and Heidi,

George shared a seemingly strong telepathic connection, different from the typical loving ways of our other pets.

I took great pride in this unusual miscellanea of pets that I loved and nurtured. They proved throughout their lives how important and emotional our relationships with animals—not just dogs and cats—can be.

So, what about the dogs and cats?

There were *always* dogs and cats.

Our house was not a home without our dog and cat.

KIM, OUR FAMILY PET BOXER, preceded my entrance into this world. She was just a few months older than me and the first dog my parents adopted after they were married. She was a protective companion through my toddler years and well into Lynne's early years. It was a sad day when Kim succumbed to a brain tumor and we had to find the ideal burial plot for her final resting place in our backyard.

Although Kim was our only dog during those early years, we also adopted a black and white cat named Tinkerbell. She was a frisky kitty who revered our large canine companion.

Kim and Tinkerbell played with us and chased each other around the house, always respecting the youthful nature of my toddler self and my baby sister. They were terrific children's playmates who knew playful limits before becoming too rough. When we lost Tinkerbell as well, it was not long before a new dog and cat would arrive in our home.

A SERENDIPITOUS DISCOVERY on the steps of my elementary school introduced us to an apparently abandoned kitten. He was a tiny gray tabby with a little white tip on his tail. He could not have been more than six weeks old, and he needed a home—our home.

This was the beginning of a nineteen-year relationship with Tippy, our big and tough, but lovable tomcat. He claimed title to longest-living family pet Lynne and I grew up with; he was unmistakably one-in-a-million and our best friend throughout our school years.

Once upon a time, life with Tippy filled volumes of storybook memories, but one holiday tale glimmered happily ever after.

The Christmas season has always been reason for decorations and celebration in my family's household. Typical preparations were customary, especially the Christmas tree and trimmings. Our pets also enjoyed holidays, so when it came time to decorate, Tippy sat near to witness and "help" with ornaments and lights. (He equally enjoyed a few climbing adventures up and down the fragrant unadorned living room pine.)

Once the tree was swathed in lights, ornaments, and garland, Mom trimmed the ends of the branches with tinsel, shimmering strands of silver foil, emulating icicles. Tippy was usually well-behaved, seldom bothering a fully-decorated tree, but when temptation beckoned and he could not resist, proof of guilt trailed him.

"Tippy's been into the tinsel again!"

The evidence was always irrefutable.

The icicles were always a glistening delight to see, sparkling in the colorful lights on the Christmas tree. It wasn't exactly the same dazzling vision when they were hanging out of Tippy's rear end.

SEVEN MONTHS after Kim passed, we went looking to adopt Mickey. Little did we know how remarkable this fluffy little pup would become in our family. Just as Tippy was *the* cat of my adolescent years, Mickey was *the* dog.

Tippy's canine buddy was a hyperactive, but sweet, Shetland Sheepdog puppy. Mickey bore the common sable, white, and tan Sheltie markings. He ranked high among the terrific dogs I've known, only the second dog I had ever lived with by the time I turned ten.

A few weeks into welcoming our newest family member home, the school year came to an end and summertime was upon us. My sister and I eagerly anticipated those days, when Michigan afternoons would gently warm our skin under true blue skies scattered with plumose animal-like clouds. And we would play in the lush green grass of our backyard, running and tumbling with our new puppy jumping all over us.

A day could last forever. Time lingered so slowly, allowing us to savor every moment.

A feast for the senses.

The evening sun always seemed to suspend motionlessly for hours in the indigo western sky. The fragrance of fresh cut lawns mingled with the aromas of Dad's charcoal-grilled steaks and burgers riding a breeze through the neighborhood. In the background, destined-to-be pop music classics strained in treble tones from our AM transistor radio. Above all, our precious pup became the passion of those long dog days as he filled our family with newfound joy.

Those were summer days to remember; days meant for kids and puppies to be just that, and nothing else.

No worries.

Heaven on Earth.

Our newest gift from heaven was such a great family pet—fun and playful and smart and obedient. Although Mickey was a good friend to us all, he was undeniably Mom's dog. Of course, Lynne and I were young, and Mom was "the hand that fed him," but she was also his trainer extraordinaire. She established the rules and Mickey was quick to learn and accept.

Mickey easily understood the common commands to sit, stay, lie down, and so on (we taught him to shake hands, too!), but around the perimeter of our home, "stay" demonstrated Mickey's studious comprehension. No matter what happened along our street, Mickey never moved one paw beyond the curb or property line of our yard. Our neighbors were flabbergasted by his obedience. There was no fence. There was no hedge. There was just the explicit knowledge—thanks to Mom's patience and diligent teaching—not to breach that border under any circumstance.

Once Mickey knew where he was supposed to stay, he obeyed without reminders. He knew his boundaries so well. We could let him outside unsupervised and remain confident that he would not chase other animals or dart into traffic. And he never did. (Ironic, considering his spontaneous race that took place with continuous laps around the dining room table every time the telephone rang.)

Mickey's outdoor decorum was simply amazing.

It was also simply "normal."

I grew up believing this was typical behavior for pet dogs. My experience a decade later would disprove my belief, but as a sixth-grade entertainer-wannabe science expert writing about a new family pet, I blissfully took great dog etiquette for granted.

Albeit he had hyperactive tendencies, Mickey was an intelligent, loving, happy dog and a much-adored member of our family for nearly ten years.

He, too, was our best friend.

WE NEVER DID HAVE more than one dog at a time, but Tippy did get a kitty companion later in his life. Another stray brought our cat count to two with the addition of a tiny, shy black kitten we named Babe. By the time Babe came along, I was about to graduate high school and move on to college life and beyond. Lynne was entering high school and had a few years left at home, so Babe started her life with us as my sister's cat. At about half the size of Tippy, and having an even smaller percentage of self-confidence, she remained a small kitty and was timid around strangers. She always stayed indoors, terrified to go anywhere near the outside world. Though filled with irrational fear, Babe was another loving family pet.

The collective of misfit critters that regularly brought joy to our lives did not exist without occasional mishaps or health issues. Our home suffered the pain and consequences of many unforgettable pet problems. Babe often lost large patches of hair, apparently from agoraphobic stress. The doorbell (and telephone) invariably sent Mickey into sudden neurotic flits. Plus, there was the hamster that went blind, the rabbit that chewed phone wires, the doves with bird lice, the puppy that plucked a feather duster clean throughout the house, the cat that sprayed urine in furnace vents during the heating season, and the dog that ate an entire birthday cake (and the box) after snatching it from the dining room buffet, just to mention a few matters—but not the names, to protect the innocent—that come to mind. Living with pets wasn't always a sunny occasion, but overall, life was always better having these pets than had it been without them.

While our family pets—for better *and* worse—stood by my transition to life on my own, I started to think of days beyond my family home, and adopting pets of my own inevitably crossed my mind.

MERE BLOCKS AWAY, during all the years of pet adventures in my family's home, Carol, my future wife, lived in a home which had been mostly free of pets. There were a few exceptions: the occasional pet gerbils or mice, and one special Barrington Bunny, a rabbit adopted by Carol's father and named after the main character of a pensive parable (by the same name) that he would often read to their family at Christmastime.

Other interests and family allergies precluded the adoption of dogs or cats in her home. Carol, however, did enjoy visiting a menagerie of pets through frequent jaunts to her friend's home in the country. Upon joining the 4-H Club, she also became the proud owner of a gray Arabian horse named Jayzon Rafhannan.

Spending many hours each week on the farm allowed time with lots of cats, dogs, barnyard fowl, and small farm animals. She showed Hannan (and once, a trophy-winning goat) at local county fairs, earning a plethora of ribbons for her efforts. Childhood days on the farm and teenage adventures in 4-H and at horse shows remain very happy memories for Carol.

Although Carol enjoyed visiting dogs and cats on the farm, living without these pets in her family home established a specific sense of what a family pet was for her. That compared much differently to my ongoing experiences with family pets. Of course, we hadn't met during that time in our lives, so what difference would that make to either one of us?

It wasn't until our paths crossed, the direction of our lives coincided, and we were on our way to a new life together, that we would soon discover what having a family pet really meant to each of us.

♪♫

chapter two

home

Sweet Girl

Home

THE PURSUIT OF MY DREAMS and goals, and the eight-year transition from impulsive high school teenager to conciliatory husband, would definitively shape the future course for my personal family of pets. It would be a jarring journey, full of twists and turns, but I held on to my pet ideals as new pups eventually came aboard for the bumpy ride.

Pets had become an important fact of my life growing up, intertwined with our daily routine and family activities. I had grown close to these animal friends, connecting and communicating in ways difficult to comprehend, but rich in spirit and emotion. No matter what plans I had for my future, I always intended to continue friendships with pets in my own home.

Of course, there would be many other interests requiring my attention, so although important, new pets would have to take a back seat as I meandered through years of trying to find my way. A cadence of heartbeats and drumbeats accompanied me on this arduous ride—the soundtrack and rhythms of my life. There soon would be pups, but first there were drums.

BANGING ON ANYTHING, driving my family crazy, came early in my life. Not that making noise or causing parental frustration was intentional, though. It was the inevitable effect of an early appreciation for rhythm and the sound of percussion. Although my parents may have objected, a red-rimmed metal toy drum (a toddler gift from my grandparents) clearly did not help their cause. My endless fascination did not stop there—it likely began there. Pot-and-pan lids crashed spectacularly as cymbals. Empty oatmeal boxes and coffee cans thrashed marvelously as tom-toms. I always tried to imagine the magnificent drum that was surely hiding in a mysterious round hat box in Grandma's attic. I attempted—with less than effective results—to "build" a drum, using scraps of leather, wood, and metal, garage and basement relics of abandoned projects past. By then, my parents could see that my passion for anything percussive was determinedly genuine.

My life as a drummer officially began in the fifth grade, the year typically designated for beginning band students. I almost got stuck playing the violin (not a bad thing, just not *my* thing), an orchestra voice the music teacher needed to fill. Through my mom's insistence with the school principal that I play the musical instrument *I* wanted to play, I continued on my felicitous lifelong journey to becoming a percussionist.

From the simple Gladstone rubber drum pad, to a vintage Ludwig red-sparkle wooden snare drum, and eventually to a pieced-together garage sale drum kit, I practiced my drums and studied percussion throughout my school years. Marching band was a big part of my junior high and high school life. Forming a rock band with my buddies was a thrill during my high school years. By then, I was able to acquire a proper five-piece Pearl drum set through the local music shop—the same store whose owner would offer me a full-time job after high school graduation. I soon moved on to other bands, eventually landing work with several country-rock bands, gigging at local bars and restaurants. I also continued working with music students during local marching band percussion sectionals and weekly private drum lessons.

When I started college at Western Michigan University, I planned to continue my music education; however, I also had a keen interest in television production and expected to study Broadcast Communications. When I found that many communications courses were closed to freshmen and sophomores, I filled my schedule with music studies. It was no surprise that everything in my late-teenage life began to revolve around music.

My full class schedule at WMU entailed hours of daily interstate highway commutes each week in my recently acquired, but brashly selected, slightly rusted, nauseatingly yellow Chevy Vega (with black racing stripes). My music album interests have always encompassed a myriad of styles and genres; however, the soundtrack of my college-bound journeys was predominately the horn-driven melodies of the pop-jazz-rock group Chicago. Syncopated rhythms blazed my path, blaring through the surface-mounted box speakers of my brand new personally-installed Pioneer Super Tuner.

To afford my first, very own used car, music albums, and state-of-the-art mobile stereo system, I was working full-time at the local music store, playing drums in my band several nights a week, and teaching private drum lessons to a dozen students, all while trying to keep up with my undergraduate studies. How I found enough hours in a day, or in a week for that matter, is a mystery to me.

I managed to continue that schedule for a couple of years, occasionally switching out the audio cassette-based driving entertainment from Chicago tracks to the country-rock harmonies of Nashville favorite, Alabama, or the time-signature-contested progressive chords and rhythms of the Canadian rock band, Rush. I irrefutably rocked the limits of daily mileage and drum-load capacity my fully-ripened lemon hatchback was able to endure. Plenty of musical activities satisfied and occupied my time, but I guess my jam-packed agenda just wasn't quite fully composed.

When a friend wanted to sell his house (he made me an offer I couldn't refuse), I barely hesitated to accept his proposal. The small single-story dwelling was a fixer-upper, so I added handyman house renovations—including a drum studio in the basement—to my already saturated schedule. Moving from my family home to a house of my own seemed to happen quickly, but thoughts of potential four-legged friends to join me in my new abode had been crossing my mind the entire time.

DURING THE HOLIDAY semester break, just one month before I became the proud possessor of my eight hundred-square-foot personal palace, I traveled to Rio de Janeiro to visit my girlfriend. Her family lived there during a temporary teacher exchange program. This was my first time flying—from Detroit to New York, and then on to Rio, on a Pan Am 747. I was anxious about the flights, a bit nervous, but with auspicious anticipation.

When in-flight beverages were offered, I proudly ordered a screwdriver. Not for anxiety. Primarily to collect the tiny bottle, a vogue serving of vodka, but also, having recently come of legal age, simply because I could.

This trip, my first travel overseas, stirred excitement and an overwhelming desire to learn about my destination. With samba drumbeats, flavors of *feijoada* (the national dish of Brazil), and scenic postcard visions of Cristo Redentor-topped Corcovado and Pão de Açúcar (Sugarloaf) mountains weighing heavily on my anticipatory psyche, I learned some Portuguese to feel a closer connection with this heretofore unfamiliar culture I was longing to experience. My trusty Berlitz Rio pocket travel guide provided just enough words and short phrases to put into practice during my brief stay in paradise. Connecting the words with people, places, things, events, music, and food only whet my appetite to continue learning about and incorporating parts of this culture into my life back home.

My two-week adventure exploring exotic natural vistas and bountiful boutiques along heavily trodden metropolitan miles of mosaic tile sidewalks through the crowded city streets and white sandy beaches of Ipanema and Copacabana faded into the sunset and came to a close much too quickly. Lingering memories and the sweet samba melody of "Garota de Ipanema" remained fresh on my mind during my reluctant return to routine.

With my abrupt move into home ownership, and—drum roll please—my adoption of a new puppy, I couldn't keep myself from choosing the perfect Rio-inspired name for my own—at least in spirit—girl from Ipanema.

"AÇÚCAR" [ah-SOO-kah] is the word for *sugar* in Brazil. It was also the new name for the darling, yet rambunctious little sugar-white pup I found listed in the local want-ads back home. Açúcar grew to slightly resemble a Border Collie, but she was a mutt.

Açúcar was a good-natured dog and receptive to training, but I was a terrible dog trainer. Oh, I could get her to "sit" and act fairly obediently in the house and fenced-in backyard, but that was about it.

"Do not let her get out the front door!"

This frequent exclamation echoed throughout the house as Açúcar positioned herself near the door and waited with bated breath.

She was a reluctant jailbird looking for any opportunity to slip past an unsuspecting door guard and fly the coop, running as fast and as far away as her quick and nimble legs would allow.

Aarrgh! Good grief.

My mom was so good at training our family dogs to stay in the yard—without fences—but I could hardly keep my dog in the house without regular attempted escapes from Alcatraz, surely to embark on endless expeditions to search for the source for which she had become the namesake, all the way to Brazil, no less.

Açúcar would eventually return home as the thrill of unbarred freedom waned, with likely a notion of hunger if she stayed away too long. Attempts to expedite her return became a fun game to play—for her. Trying to catch her played out as a pointless ritual of avoid-and-seek.

I was doing all the seeking.

She always won.

Home

It ended as a waiting game. We played this game very few times. Açúcar ran a cunning sport once she slipped past the front door, but I quickly became more astute at preventing that from happening.

The score was changing.

Although I had surrendered pursuit during these few escapes, on one occasion, my girlfriend gave chase on foot up the street, and by some bizarre turn of luck, caught Açúcar. Feeling proud of her atypical success in apprehending my fugitive Fido, she doggedly held tight to the menacing mutt. Grasping a front paw in each hand, she walked backward all the way home, enrapt in a rather deranged dog dance, Açúcar toddling on two legs and firmly in tow (a pre-YouTube video destined only for imagination). I watched in amazement, doubled-over and crying with laughter.

A truly great renegade dog capture indeed.

Thanks to my reaction, though, Açúcar wasn't the only one in the doghouse.

IT WAS NOT LONG before Açúcar had a canine companion in the household. I had never lived with more than one pet dog at a time, but it only took a couple of months to determine that with the schedule I was keeping and in my absence, it would be a lot less stressful for Açúcar if I adopted another dog to keep her company.

Opportunely, my girlfriend's family Keeshond had taken an intimate interest in a neighbor's German Shepherd and had given birth to a litter of pups. We could not resist keeping the cutest fluffy little boy dog with exaggeratedly pointed ears.

We named Açúcar's new companion Yoda.

(Okay, not so original, but era appropriate—and he did slightly resemble that iconic Jedi Master from *The Empire Strikes Back*.)

When he became full grown, Yoda was essentially a small German Shepherd—with a curled tail. He had an affable personality and was unequivocally obedient. Well, let's just say Yoda was everything that Açúcar was not.

My family pet dogs had been wonderful. Kim, the Boxer, and largest of all, was a loving, family protector. Mickey, the Sheltie, was hyperactive, but sweet and faithful. Açúcar was a good dog most of the time, just misunderstood (by her assessment).

But Yoda was the best dog I had ever lived with up to that point.

He just did everything right, all the time.

He never tried to run away as his "sister" did. He was a gentle loving dog and got along well with people and other animals. When summoned, he bolted to sit patiently in front of me, his disproportionately large ears always at attention, waiting to obey any command.

Yoda and Açúcar were the "odd couple" pups that had been living with me for several years when Carol and I started dating.

YODA WAS A MEDIUM-SIZE DOG, but he had a big dog bark. I'm sure many solicitors ran past my house when he had a few things to say. He didn't bark often, though. He reserved that deep intimidating tone for just the right occasion.

One such occasion happened several years after Carol and I were married, when Yoda was our only pet. I was traveling out of town, so Carol decided to stay overnight with our good friends, Spence and Lora. They encouraged Carol to bring Yoda along, even though they shared their home with three pet Dachshunds. Shortly after Carol and Yoda arrived and were settled in the living room, the smooth-coat copper-tones were let into the house, a split-level with the living room on the upper floor. When they came running up the stairs, long noses barely clearing the top step, Yoda let out one big "WOOF!"

The wiener dogs stopped flat in their tracks before tumbling and bouncing backward head-over-tail in a Slinky-like race to the landing. The poor little guys were not ready for that shockingly reverberating, Wizard-of-Oz welcome in their own home!

WHEN CAROL AND I MET, she was a lighthearted hair stylist by day and an enthusiastic amateur singer by night. Upon hearing her spot-on rendition of Stevie Nicks's "After the Glitter Fades," I invited her to sing a few times with my band. That led to her learning to play bass guitar and joining the band, and eventually, becoming my life partner.

During the first year after we met, Carol and I started dating, became engaged, and then married. Until that time, Carol had lived her entire life without dogs in her home. She started to see how life *with* dogs compared to life *without* dogs. But, in the blink of an eye, everything changed for us again and we had a year to determine whether we would be a family with dogs or without dogs.

Drastic changes were in store for the busy month of our wedding. In the middle of June, we were single and living in Michigan and I owned two dogs. By the end of June, we were married and living in Texas and I owned two dogs, but they were still living in the Great Lakes State.

Through a series of strange, curious, ridiculous, fantastic, and questionable, albeit fortunate events, we packed a recently purchased, heavily road-worn hippie van, and my Camaro, with all the belongings we could squeeze in (mainly music equipment), and hit the wagon train trail to the American frontier with little more than a few hundred dollars.

We moved into a third-floor apartment with a balcony, overlooking a courtyard comprising an exercise room gazebo, four swimming pools, and the largest hot tub we had ever seen—it alone could easily have passed for a pool. (Everything *is* bigger in Texas!) This Lone Star utopia was an irresistible attraction for a young, free-spirited couple deciding to make an outrageous move of this sort in the first place.

Earlier in the year, before we knew of this paradise awaiting us, we traveled to Texas with visions of Southfork and the theme to *Dallas* playing heavily on our minds. We were visiting friends from Michigan who were living in our unbeknownst-to-us future apartment. Beyond our discovery of suite Xanadu, we were fascinated by the metropolitan expanse of opportunity, so we researched encyclopedic telephone books and newspaper-advertised work options for our burgeoning music career (at least that's what we thought at the time). When we found out that our friends were moving in June, we practically begged them to take over their lease. They said yes. We went home to plan for our move and prepare for our wedding. They moved. We got married.

We loaded up the van and we moved to DFW, Dallas–Fort Worth that is, swimming pools, music stars.

Cue the banjo music.

While this crazy adventure was an ideal dream for us, a couple of early twenty-something musician wannabes, it was our parents' worst nightmare. Although there was never resistance, they were scared to death for us and fully expected our return in a matter of months, with heads down and tails between our legs, like Açúcar returning home from an afternoon pleasure run through the far reaches of the neighborhood.

The move was spontaneous, but the timing and arrangements were ingenious. Our overloaded hippie-van-and-car caravan across the country began early one morning during the first part of June, with the help of a friend and Carol's sister, Anne. We headed southbound along a zigzag web of interstate highways. With a hint of forethought, we had packed a portable CB radio in case of emergency—or by the looks of our bargain jalopy, for *the inevitable*.

The van broke down only once, fortuitously near an exit, and with the aid and assistance of a gracious trucker, we were back on the road again heading south until we miraculously arrived at our destination twenty-four hours after our departure. We moved everything into the apartment, left the vehicles in Texas, and flew back to Michigan for our mid-June wedding. We were soon off to Florida for a week-long honeymoon, and then back to our new home on the range before we could flip the calendar to July.

No jobs, no money, newly wedded … now what?
And no pets. What about Yoda and Açúcar?

A YEAR-LONG STRUGGLE with our musical aspirations led Carol on a circuitous path to beginning a career in food. This was the '80s, the advent of keyboard samplers, sequencers, and drum machines, and we were on the leading edge of this technology. But it became difficult to hold on as opportunities shook from our grip. We had to expand our reach toward stability.

While I spent every waking hour sequencing and recording songs for our hotel lounge act, Carol faced reality and took on a part-time job, across the street from our faded utopia, at a quick-serve Tex-Mex restaurant chain that made much of their food from scratch. Carol learned the intricacies of making great Tex-Mex basics: refried beans, guacamole, and salsa. She already had a love for Mexican food, so dripping in grease and perpetually smelling of last night's munchies-run was really heaven-scent.

The highlight of the year occurred when these work efforts coincided, collided, and culminated in the musical appearance of Minx (our flirtatious moniker as a music duo) at Taco Bueno—a first (and probably the last) for fast-food taco tunes.

Except for our version of Madonna's "La Isla Bonita," live pop music from a corner booth in a pop-Mex eatery wasn't the best pop mix. Our friends made up most of the sparse audience as others paused in puzzlement. We had fun (and free tacos!), so it was all good.

And over twenty-five years later, it's all *bueno* to tell.

WE AGREED THAT a one-year apartment lease was our "trial period" in Texas to see what we could make of it. After all, I still had two dogs living in Michigan, and although it sometimes felt like it, I never once intended to abandon my pets. Fortunately, our relocation was a matter of fortuitous timing and dog-sitting arrangements.

When we decided to move, Carol's good friend (from her 4-H days) rented my house and took care of Yoda and Açúcar so they could continue to live in a stable, familiar home. Carol's friend had grown up on a farm, so she knew life with animals in her home. I liked this plan. Our extended hiatus from the dogs, however, was still a concern. We had a life-changing decision to make.

Should we take or break this opportunity?

We had to go for it.

Our job prospects in Michigan were not happening in ways we had hoped, so this change was a matter of perfect timing. We could realize our goals in a larger metropolitan area, and it wouldn't hurt to escape the snowy winters of the Mighty Mitten. Our sights were set on Texas and all the arrangements had fallen into place.

But just for one year.

I wasn't prepared to walk away from my dogs forever. They were still my responsibility, my family, but we had to have time to find ways to make a better life for us, and for them, in Texas.

One year.

We had a tough and trying time ahead. Music opportunities—beyond our taco-palooza—were few and far between, but we remained hopeful. Married life was something new and exciting, yet under the circumstances, quite stressful. We looked life right in the face.

Did we do the right thing?
Can we continue to struggle to make this work?
What do we do after our "one-year trial period"?

My dogs were living a thousand miles away. Either we would return to them, or they were going to move to Texas—but not to live in an apartment. We were compelled to decide the next step in our lives. The decision came more easily and much more quickly than we expected.

On our first trip to Texas, I learned that my cousin lived in the Dallas–Fort Worth area. As it turned out, by some unusual twist of fate, her house was only a mile from the apartment we would soon inhabit. During our year of trials and tribulations, we spent time becoming reacquainted with my cousin and her son. When she became aware of our year-end issue and pending move, she offered a solution to satisfy our quandary and her desire to return to Arizona: move into her house.

Securing work was a challenge, but the sheer excitement of having our own place and bringing the dogs to live with us outweighed any reservations we might have had about finding our way in Texas. At least *I* was excited about finally reuniting with Yoda and Açúcar.

The year in the apartment without pets did not help the dogs' cause. Although Carol tolerated the dogs before our move, it seemed that she did it as a courtesy to me. Yoda and Açúcar had been my pets for several years before Carol and I met. She didn't share the puppy bond with them as I had, and they only served as a reminder of my life before we met. I could see there was detachment, but I had always hoped that when Carol spent more time around the dogs, pets in the house would become as natural to her as they had always been for me. I mistakenly assumed that a year removed from my pets would give us the quality time we needed to establish our life together *and* prepare for the inevitable pet reunion. Time only distanced her connection with the dogs. It would be a rough road to build our new "family life"—our new "home"—in Texas.

We were practically starting over. We were a year married with random job opportunities, about to move into a new living situation with my dogs joining us in a house a long way from their home. When we returned to pick them up, they were excited to go. Carol's friend had taken good care of them, although during a brief stay at her family's farm, a scary incident might have taken a terrible turn.

Considering Açúcar's track record, it was ironic that Yoda strayed away from the country house and was hit by a car. Fortunately, he did not suffer serious injuries and appeared to be in great health when we once again loaded up more stuff, *and my dogs*, to travel south across the country to our new home—this time in a low-mileage Dodge Caravan we arranged to buy from my dad.

It wasn't going to be long before Carol and I finally discovered what having pets in our still-newlywed life would really mean to each of us.

WE HAD EXPERIENCED life without dogs; the time had come for life *with* dogs. While I could not wait to show the dogs our new home in Texas, I don't think Carol was quite so enthusiastic. Easing this potentially painful transition was the invitation to Carol's friend to accompany us on the trip home. She welcomed a much-needed vacation to see where we lived and be with the dogs for a while longer (after all, she did take care of them for an entire year). And Carol could enjoy a distraction while the dogs became accustomed to the home where they would live for the rest of their lives.

The fenced-in areas of both homes were similar with large grassy yards and several shade trees. The houses were also of similar size, so it wasn't much of a change for the dogs. Adapting to the weather was by far the biggest difference. While it could get uncomfortably warm during a Michigan summer, the Texas heat told a much different, sizzling story.

In older Texas houses—ours included—outside walls without insulation and no central air conditioning were common. This lack of amenities accounted for many agonizing days of sweltering heat during the summer and temperately chilly days during the winter. The dogs adapted (panting more often than before), but they missed romping around in the Michigan snow during the winters. The few times we'd have a small accumulation of snow in our Texas backyard became big play days for them. But regardless of temperature and precipitation, they had fun times in the yard year-round. The covered back porch faced east, so hot summer afternoons and evenings were much more tolerable for enjoying time outside.

All the dogs and cats in my family have been indoor pets. Although many enjoyed hours outside, they all always lived in the house and were never kept outdoors for an extended length of time. I continued this trend with my pets; however, my dogs have conveniently had access to fenced-in backyards.

My family cats were free to roam, though most stayed close to home. Tippy liked to go outside—to answer the call of the wild—but when nature was calling, he would scratch furiously on the door for us to let him *inside* where he'd hit the basement stairs running. We'd soon hear kitty litter spattering against the side of the furnace. He would spend an afternoon in the great outdoors, but could only do his bathroom business indoors, in his private litter box.

Considering we always had dogs and cats while I was growing up, and I continued that tendency on my own, it's surprising that we had never installed a dog door in my family home. When that changed recently, it made me wonder how we had managed without one all those years.

Yoda and Açúcar never had the opportunity to use the "doggie door of free will." That required us to let them out, or let them in. Equally important as "cookie" or "squirrel," "outside" is a word the dogs knew instinctively from the first time we opened the backdoor. Letting the dogs outside became a routine, repeated many times throughout the day.

While at first, sharing the house was enough of an adjustment, Carol became accustomed to the daily rituals of dogs out, dogs in, and soon began to build a limited relationship with the dogs through this uncomplicated, yet regular routine. Those first years in the house saw the beginnings of our cooking business, giving rise to more opportunities for Carol to connect with the dogs—they loved to sample what she was cooking in the kitchen.

OUR STRUGGLES in the music business continued for several of the first years we were married. We transitioned in and out of various bands and played a scant hotel circuit in the Dallas–Fort Worth area, but we could not stay booked consistently.

We were literally "starving artists."

Living on a strict, small budget for food, we learned to cut costs, from scrimping on grocery purchases and using lots of coupons, to deleting the dining-out occasions. And since we were not eating out, knowing how to cook at home became more than just a good idea.

Relying on her brief experience in the Tex-Mex restaurant kitchen, and consulting with our families for recipe ideas, Carol began to cook from scratch every day. During those lean days, Carol approached a kitchen shop in a local mall and was hired for a part-time job. It wasn't long before the store manager persuaded Carol to start teaching cooking classes at the store, since ironically, she was the only employee who knew how to cook! When her classes expanded to other locations throughout Dallas and Fort Worth, we decided that maybe the music business should be put on hold—the food business was calling.

This marked the beginning of our cooking enterprise, "Cookin' with Carol."

The transition from playing music five nights a week, to teaching cooking classes five nights a week, was quick and promising. It was also a lot of work. Where I had previously spent my days organizing songs into performance sets, I transitioned to organizing recipes into cooking classes. While Carol developed the recipes and presented the classes, I published the recipes in cookbooks for her cooking class students. Each week we'd come up with new themes, topics, and recipes for the classes, everything from homemade bread and desserts to international cuisines, such as French, Italian, Tex-Mex, and Chinese. Our new business was always a challenge, but a lot of fun.

Plus, we were no longer starving artists.

Frequent recipe testing determined the recipes for the cooking classes. One favorite culinary lesson demonstrated making pasta from scratch. Preparing for class was always an interactive experience for the dogs at home.

When it came time to stretch the pasta dough and cut it into noodles, the dogs were always ready to slurp the spaghetti like Lady and the Tramp. A favorite photo shows Açúcar with head held high, ready to snatch a long strand of freshly formed pasta hovering overhead from my stepdad's outstretched arm during a family visit.

Carol's cooking and the dogs' never-ending willingness to taste-test the recipes continued to solidify a newfound connection that Carol was beginning to share with our "new" family members.

Not unlike our music playing days, the cooking class work schedule usually allowed some free hours during the daytime. This became yet another opportunity for Carol to share "quality" time with the dogs—she took them on walks. Açúcar loved this since her prison escape days were behind her by then. She never once ran out the front door during the several years she lived in Texas, but she eagerly looked forward to seeing us bring her leash out of the closet.

Yoda also enjoyed his walks. He actually could be *walked*, whereas Açúcar liked to take *us* for walks, or more aptly, sprints, nearly choking herself in the process. After Açúcar passed (at nine years old), I occasionally coordinated Yoda's walks with Spence and his Dachshunds. They strolled in confidence with Yoda the bodyguard along for the outing. Whenever their bold vocalizations along the neighborhood path became presumptuous, it was yet another proper occasion for Yoda's single "SILENCE!" to instantly tie their tongues, freezing all forward motion until clocks could be reset.

ONE OF OUR RETURN TRIPS to Michigan came unexpectedly just one month after our wedding. My grandmother had been in failing health and sadly succumbed to her illness. This left my grandfather alone in a large house. He and my grandmother had never traveled by plane, but in her absence, and with our encouragement, Grandpa eventually decided to take to the air for a new experience and valuable family time. He wanted to visit us in our new home.

After we settled in our Texas house with the dogs, Grandpa came to spend a few weeks with us on two occasions. He always liked seeing Yoda and Açúcar at my house in Michigan, but these trips to Texas provided countless hours for him to enjoy concentrated time with the dogs.

He adored Yoda.

Who wouldn't have?

Yoda was the perfect dog—the perfect pet.

They spent many hours together just enjoying time on the back porch or an afternoon at leisure in the living room. Whenever we traveled to Michigan (after Açúcar's passing), we stayed with my grandfather and he always encouraged us to bring Yoda along.

Yoda always liked to travel. He was comfortable

stretched across the rear bench seat of our minivan for the long journey. Of course, there were times (business trips, local travels, or long work days) when it was not convenient for him to go. Rarely did our absence involve more than a standard work shift away from home, but he readily resigned himself to any situation.

On one occasion when no other arrangements could be made, he waited at home alone for us while we flew to New Orleans (for "food appointments") and back, all in the same day. I doubt that he moved from the same spot all day. At that point, he was a senior dog and much less active.

Less than a year later, in 1996, when Yoda was thirteen years old, a sudden illness took him from us. Our world became empty, our sadness endured. Our daily routine was no longer routine. His death was a huge loss to our lives that only time could attempt to heal. After all, he was our buddy, our housemate, our companion, and our best friend.

Yoda was a great dog.

In 1992, we had been planning a December holiday trip to Michigan to spend time with family when Grandpa became ill just after Thanksgiving. His illness came on quickly and within a matter of days, he was gone. Our plans for a holiday visit sadly turned to plans for his funeral. We had arranged, once again, to stay with him, and Yoda was to come along as usual. Although the thought of staying in my grandparents' empty home was disheartening, we decided to keep to those plans. As it turned out, the quiet ambiance and household memories were emotionally easier to bear than expected.

And spiritually revelatory.

After a couple "normal" nights in the house without incident, Carol decided to stay a night with her friends on the farm (where she had continued to board her horse). Feeling comfortable, and having no reason to expect anything unusual, Yoda and I were left alone overnight in my grandparents' house for the first time.

I stayed in the bedroom across the hall from my grandfather's bedroom, leaving my door open. Yoda lay nearby on the floor. I was sound asleep and there were no disturbances to cause Yoda to wake me, when I suddenly awoke with abrupt shock on the edge of a vivid dream. My instant recollection of an implicit vision startled, and then comforted me.

That was the only night I had stayed in the house alone—well, with Yoda. No other people. What I experienced was uniquely selective; a message for me at a time and place explicitly isolated, yet familiar.

Was it merely coincidence or purely opportunistic?

Or was it just a figment of my own dreamscape imagination?

The image was much too real and felt unlike any other dream I had ever experienced in my entire life. This "vision" was dramatically powerful beyond my own creative thought processes. Although Yoda was not an element of this otherworldly display, if only by name, his presence was apposite.

Not until recently, oddly enough, when I recalled this memory, did I consider the similarity between Yoda's Star Wars eponym during the final "reunion" scene in *Return of the Jedi*, with what I "witnessed" that night.

In my extraordinary vision, I walked across the hall to my

grandfather's bedroom door, looked inside, and saw Grandpa standing next to Grandma, who was seated in the rocking chair at the foot of his bed. Their presence was vivid and radiant, surrounded by an aura-like glow. The golden rays instantly branded the detailed features of my grandfather's face—a mature expression of an enduring, yet highly satisfying life—into my vulnerable, yet receptive semiconsciousness.

The message was unspoken, yet ever so clear.

They were together once again—healthy, happy, and at peace. This vision was a pure manifestation of love and serenity, enveloping my senses, offering confident reassurance that everything was okay. The image remains crystal clear and the message profound.

It would not be until two decades later, during the events surrounding Sasha's passing, when such a strong spiritual message would once again be presented to me in a similar philosophical and contemplative manner.

AT THE TIME of Yoda's passing, Carol and I were approaching our tenth wedding anniversary. Through an adjusted way of living to which she had never been accustomed—living with dogs, that is (five years with Yoda as our only pet)—Carol grew fond of *our* pets and shared my grief and sadness when our home became much more quiet and lonely.

While indeed a time of sorrow, we were also elated about business opportunities that preoccupied our minds and time, precluding us from seriously considering new pets for several years.

In the years following, Carol continued to teach cooking classes and appeared regularly on TV, cooking on the Dallas–Fort Worth NBC-affiliate news program. We produced a reputable local cable television cooking show, welcoming public television culinary royalty, including Martin Yan, Nathalie Dupree, Jacques Pépin, and the legendary Julia Child. We traveled to France and Australia, returning several times. We oversaw the construction of a new home. I designed and built a state-of-the-art kitchen set for *Cookin' with Carol* (our cooking show), we were nominated for a James Beard Award (the Oscars of the food business), and we traveled often throughout the U.S.

We didn't have time to consider growing our family, so we kept working—for six years—without any pets in the house. This was the longest time in my family, in all my homes, I had ever been without a dog.

Little did we know that the birth of a tiny white pup with apricot ears in December 2002 was about to change our lives forever.

♪♫

chapter three

sweet girl

Sweet Girl

Sweet Girl

WINTERS IN TEXAS are consistently unpredictable. Temperatures can suggest spring-like weather with sunshine days, or sweep in a surprise snowstorm, blanketing a frozen landscape. In early February 2003, we had eluded the snow cover, although the thermometer reminded us that we were not yet beyond that possibility.

Carol was preparing to leave to present a cooking demo during the news that chilly first Saturday morning when something rattled the house. I was still in bed and waking to an odd sense that something strange had happened. We could not determine what caused the sudden uneasiness; however, once Carol arrived at the news station, the explanation became clear and it remained the breaking news story for the rest of the month. What had startled our senses was a shock wave from the tragic Space Shuttle Columbia disintegration over East Texas. That weekend marked a terribly sad day in our nation's history and an unforgettable date on the calendar.

That date also marked a new direction in our family history.

A FEW MONTHS EARLIER, we had experienced our own personal tragedy when my father passed away after a decades-long battle with heart disease. In December, we had traveled to Florida for his memorial service, then on to Michigan to spend time with family for the holidays. During the time between grief and celebration, we were having serious discussions about adopting a puppy. It had been six years since Yoda died. We had been traveling often during those years and we had been in our new home for three years. Taking into consideration our work schedule and routine, and our intention to limit our travels, we felt it was a good time to welcome a pet into our household.

Clearly, our new pet would be a dog. That was never in question. Carol and I agreed that a small dog would be the best choice for our family. If we did continue to travel, a small dog in a pet carrier could conveniently join us.

My first experience with a tiny pet dog came shortly after I moved into my own place. It was an indirect connection, but close enough for loving inspiration, through random visits to my mom's house. While I struggled with managing two medium-sized polar-opposite pups at home, Mom was back to taintless training exercises with a newly adopted precious black Toy Poodle tot.

Beau quickly became a family favorite, warming every heart in his presence. He shed light on everything to expect when living with pocket-size pups. He paved the way and set a brand new standard for pet dogs in my family. His affectionate spirit and traits of companionship influenced future dog considerations.

With small dogs in mind (and having had the benefit of knowing Beau for over a decade), we began searching the

Internet and researching toy dog breeds to see which might be most appropriate for our home. We each had a favorite choice in mind.

My choice was fairly simple.

After Beau passed, Mom's next dog, Sophie, was a cute little Maltese. We had had the privilege of spending time with her during every trip to Michigan since 1995. Sophie loved to be held and never missed an opportunity to sit with me, including any social gathering around the dinner table. She would sit patiently on my lap, facing the table, while I teasingly tied her ears together over her head. Her hair was often trimmed short and wavy—a "puppy cut"—although her tail and ears remained long, so a loose, floppy knot over her head was often the style while she sat with me. She never minded that I messed with her hair, as long as she could have a front row seat at the table. Sophie's friendly and playful, yet serene personality endeared her (and the Maltese breed) to me.

When we were ready to adopt a dog, it had to be a Maltese … "Ye Ancient Dogge of Malta."

With origins tracing back over two thousand years to the tiny, remote Mediterranean archipelago nation of Malta, the Maltese is an aristocrat of the canine world. Attractive, clever, and highly devoted to its owners, it is a small lap dog, weighing less than ten pounds. It has dark eyes, long silky white hair (similar to human hair because it does not shed and rarely causes allergic reactions), and a plume-like tail. The Maltese is lively and energetic, affectionate, inquisitive, and easily trained; this ancient purebred companion is known for its good temperament and gentle, loving, yet stalwart nature.[1]

Carol also adored Sophie and shared in learning as much as we could about Maltese dogs. But for her pet consideration, she had been studying another breed.

Since our first trip to Australia in 1997, we have been dedicated fans of "The Land Down Under." Anything about Australia is quick to catch our attention. Cookbooks, memorabilia, wine, art, music, photos, and videos fill our list of favorite Australian keepsakes, while images of spectacular sights, tasting indigenous foods in mouth-watering recipes, and fun-filled visits with Aussie friends top our list of precious travel memories. Whenever we discover an Australian connection at home in Texas, it's a welcome surprise we do not want to miss. Piecing these parts together brought the pleasant discovery that there was a toy dog breed hailing from … where else? Australia!

The Australian Silky Terrier is the recognized breed of dog originally resulting from the crossbreeding of the Australian Terrier and the Yorkshire Terrier. Much the same as the Maltese, the Silky Terrier is also a small, yet stout, energetic dog with long silky hair (also similar to human hair, and hypoallergenic). It is known for its joyful, vivacious spirit. Although not a highly common breed in the U.S., out of curiosity and after Internet research, Carol found that a respected and award-winning Silky Terrier dog breeder lived near Houston. In our newly decided quest to find the perfect pet, this fact could not be ignored.

Through a few e-mail and phone correspondences with this Silky breeder, we were surprised and delighted to find out that a litter of pups had been born in mid-December. If interested, we could adopt one of the puppies in late February, contingent upon our meeting the breeder's approval, which was based on particular "adoptive parents" criteria. After all, these pups were whelped from a long line of show dogs. While the thought of owning a "show dog" was exciting, it had never occurred to us. It raised our new pet ownership decision to an exclusive—and potentially much more expensive—level.

I really had no interest in becoming the owner of a show dog. I just wanted a new pet to share our life. While on the surface, raising a show dog in our family sounded enlivening and seemed to be marked with distinction, my biggest concern was that it would be time- and cost-prohibitive.

Carol looked to her past experience in the horse show ring, bringing sentimentality to her decision.

"It would be so much fun to get back into that arena," she'd say, sharing her primary thought.

And beyond that, we were talking about an *Australian* Silky Terrier.

The more we became entrenched in the particulars of a Silky Terrier pup, the further away we moved from discussing Maltese pups. The Silky pup's availability seemed like perfect timing, and upon further correspondence, the cost and potential, yet undemanding, opportunities in the show ring became much clearer to us. The breeder would allow us to adopt one of her pups as a pet; additionally, if we did decide to participate in dog shows, we would have her guidance and full support.

The circumstances of this adoption seemed to be falling into place quite conveniently.

So it was decided.

Australian sentimentality won the blue ribbon; Maltese endearment didn't make the cut.

As we continued to correspond with the Silky breeder and began to make necessary arrangements to welcome our new puppy home in a matter of weeks, I could not forget that our once-in-a-six-year decision had caused us to forfeit the opportunity to adopt a Maltese pup.

When we first decided to look for a pup, we were set on adopting a female. As it turned out, the Silky puppies were male. With everything else about the adoption seemingly ideal, this was not going to be the deal breaker. A little boy Silky pup would soon bring overwhelming joy to our home. But I still had an underlying determination to find a Maltese pup. A female Maltese pup.

We surely wouldn't be able to afford two puppies (especially since one was a "show dog"), but at some point—akin to the saturation of sentimentality in Carol's captivation with the show dog Silky—the cost and every other consideration just flew out the window. Emotion took over and sensibility was gone with the wind.

Finding a Maltese puppy never became a change of plans. Our intent to adopt an Australian Silky Terrier in February never wavered. But that did not keep me from searching the newspaper want ads throughout January, hoping for just one bite from an unsuspecting female Maltese pup needing a home. While options were not lacking, most were barks with no bites. Nothing warranted a closer look past the black-and-white newsprint.

On that fateful early February weekend, however, I ran across a few promising prospects. The Sunday paper classifieds described a litter of Maltese puppies about twenty minutes away, and a single white female in need of a home: an eight-week-old Maltese an hour drive due north.

Temptation and opportunity got the best of us, so on a chilly winter Monday, overcast with drizzling rain, Carol and I set off to take a look at several Maltese pups waiting for adoption.

We had just two destinations on the agenda. Both were suburban homes with Maltese pets and incidents of puppies resulting from owners blatantly ignoring Bob Barker's oft-recited pet reproductive-altering advice. Clearly, these were not Maltese breeders by profession. But it was also clear that they were not likely to spay or neuter their pets anytime soon.

The first stop was not ideal. There were four cute, playful puppies, but the ill-kept premises seemed more unfortunate than promising, so we decided to move on. These situations prompt the need for spay-and-neutering preaching. Sadly, those pups needed to be rescued rather than sold at a premium for the short-term windfall the seller surely hoped to gain.

Big profits openly encourage abusers to continue this unsavory behavior in pet procreation. It's truly a dilemma. The puppies exist. They need a home. But paying prices excessively above practical costs incurred for care until adoption only perpetuates the problem. If the pups are not sold, they risk highly unfortunate fates at the hands of irresponsible and uncaring sellers. Pay unjust prices to save the pups and the sellers win. Reject the price, spurn the sellers, and the pups lose. It's a double-edged price tag.

Pay the price or count the cost.

We felt for those four puppies. They were barely weaned from their mother, they were without a first vet exam, and they were toddling around in a tiny fenced-off floor space that the owner did not seem to care about cleaning too often (not to mention the rest of the house). Just sad. Our hearts wanted to rescue a pup, but we simply were not willing to pay its "caretaker" a nonnegotiable, irrational fee for the lack of caretaking and probable poor-puppy-health ramifications.

In one stop, our hopes seemed dashed.

"Should we even go to the other house?" I asked Carol as I became discouraged and began to wonder if this pursuit was a heartbreaking waste of time.

"We've come this far. We might as well go look," she offered without much confidence, but with just enough conviction to tip the scale to *yes*.

But I already knew the answer. We could not be defeated so easily. We had to go to the other house, to follow up on the other ad. It was especially important now, as this visit would most likely be our only chance to consider a Maltese puppy. As we drove north, little did we know there was no turning back. For we had an appointment with destiny.

Our family was about to change forever.

THE DREARY AFTERNOON became much brighter with our next stop. It had become breezy, windy I suppose, as the threat of rain continued throughout the day. Gray clouds flooded the sky, moving briskly as if to avoid the very weather they were bringing.

When we arrived at a fairly new, small brick house, it became evident that we were at the right address. We could see several Maltese dogs running around in the backyard. Upon ringing the doorbell, we heard a fair share of barking coming from beyond the closed door. We were greeted by a nice, middle-aged woman who promptly invited us in, explaining that there was just one puppy for adoption. Before we had time to respond, the most adorable tiny white pup came running into view, partly to see who had come to visit, but mainly in a playful chase with the other dogs running around the room.

The house was littered with moving boxes—coming or going, I'm not certain which it was—and an equal number of adult Maltese dogs, with a Yorkie thrown in for good measure. There was no mistake that this woman really liked Maltese dogs. They were not raised to participate in dog shows. They were plainly pets and there were a lot of them. For every dog we saw in the house, there were probably twice as many in the backyard. And then there was the busy, cute little puppy running around the furniture and boxes stacked in the living room.

Actually, there were two puppies. Two single white females. The second was slightly larger than the first playful pup we met. We quickly learned that another family had already claimed the larger pup for adoption. So the selection was already determined. If we decided to go home with a Maltese pup, it would be the spunky little darling we first laid eyes on when we arrived.

She was a trinket of sunshine—dancing in our arms—disguised as the tiniest toy doggie, soft as a cotton ball, white feather tail waving as if to take flight, a black button nose taking scrupulous notes, and her most mirthful brown eyes shining deep into our hearts. Carol and I shared a relentless welcome of sweet puppy kisses.

The choice was easy.

How could we resist?

Honestly, we couldn't resist. We did try to remain stoic,

although we were barely able to contain our excitement while we sat down to discuss the reasonable purchase agreement and complete the adoption.

Late in the afternoon, we became the official parents of our little girl puppy and settled back into the car for our hour-plus drive home. We trudged along in the Dallas rush-hour traffic, people slowing and speeding, swerving and merging to get home from work. We weren't sure how our petite pup would react to such a long time in the car. But she showed us right from the start that she would not retreat from imminent threat. With a cold rain dotting the windshield, the wide-swiping wipers prompted several fierce growls from our tiny defender. Once she determined the raging squeegee would remain at a safe distance outside the window, she quickly became comfortable and cozy, no whining or whimpering, while she nestled in a large, soft towel on Carol's lap. By the time we were cruising down the highway, she had settled into a nice, lasting nap for the journey home.

From the moment I carried her to the car, our peerless passenger placed complete trust in us and she never looked back. She did not long for her mother dog or puppy playmate or a person from her brief past. Without apprehension, Carol and I instantaneously became her familiar human touch—her family. She had no reservations about the course her life would be taking.

As she slept comfortably, dreaming of the wonders awaiting her, we marveled at her aplomb.

She knew she was where she was meant to be.

So young, so small, so innocent, so confident.

So perfect.

We were lost in perfection, lost in love, falling headfirst

into protective and nurturing faithfulness. The world around us disappeared as our precious puppy unwittingly engaged our undivided attention. She would soon wake to a brand new family, a brand new home, and a brand new name. Our lucky path to adopt this tiny angel happened so fast, we hadn't even considered names. But as we drove home, as if by instinct (or premonition), a name came to me. We barely knew our new pup, but without hesitation or a specific reason, the name fit perfectly. So I suggested it to Carol and she agreed we would name our newly adopted baby Maltese, Sasha.

Our sweet girl Sasha.

WE ARRIVED HOME early in the evening, just after what would have been a southern sky winter sunset, on that cold gray night. We were excited to see how Sasha would explore and enjoy her new home. We brought her into the house and set her gently on the living room floor while she was still sound asleep, lovingly swaddled in her cozy travel towel. When we coaxed her awake, she began to take a look around at her new surroundings.

An energetic spirit unlike any our home had ever known began to seep into every crack and crevice as Sasha followed our footsteps from one room to another with a tiny bouncing trot. Our family grew in a heartbeat, by a tiny bundle of heartbeats, by the greatest leaps and bounds.

We smiled.

Sasha smiled.

And she would continue to smile with great intensity, forever warming our hearts and our home.

Her adoption was spontaneous (and weeks before our planned Silky adoption), so we hadn't previously purchased dog supplies. However, the seller gave us a small bag of kibble to last a week or so. We designated a proper space on the kitchen floor for makeshift food and water bowls, pointed these out to our curious and adventurous explorer, and took her to the backyard to become acquainted with her new "toilet."

While Sasha became familiar with the layout of her new residence, she was also becoming familiar with us. It did not take more than that first night snuggling between us in bed to forever become "Mama" and "Daddy." She also accepted her name straightaway and recognized words and phrases like "let's go outside," "dinner," "cookie," "toy," "bedtime," "potty," and "time to tinkle." This was just the beginning; she would build volumes of vocabulary never to forget.

Within a few days, Sasha had her own stylish dinner and water bowls, several plush puppy toys, chew bones and training treats, a cozy dog bed, a matching red collar and leash, a small hard-shell pet carrier, a large bag of high-quality puppy chow that would last into the spring, and a bottle of Nature's Miracle—the leakproof insurance policy covering inevitable indoor puppy-potty mishaps.

We also bought a medium-sized cage with a plush bed, her personal space when we had to leave her alone in the house. She willingly entered this safe sanctuary whenever we commanded her to "Kennel up."

To avoid spills, I attached a large hamster-style water bottle to the side of the cage (the kind familiar to my childhood pet rabbits). Designed for small dogs, it became a favorite water dispenser for Sasha throughout her life. Her thirst relief was always a source of surprise and amazement for our guests. The discussion would usually begin after hearing a few ball-bearing-in-metal *clink clink clink* sounds emanating near our dining room table.

"What is that noise?" most would ask.

We could never resist answering with a straight face, "That's our gerbil."

"What?"

And then we'd break composure, "It's Sasha's water bottle. She's drinking her water."

We'd explain, to our guests' astonishment, how she was raised on that bottle, preferring it to her water bowl.

WHILE SAD NEWS filled world headlines that first week of Sasha's adoption, we, sadly, had little time to notice. We had our hands full and minds preoccupied, our hearts happily in love with Sasha. We were elated with the new direction our lives were taking. The six-year pet hiatus was over and we were once again starting from scratch—feeding schedule, potty training, play time, nap time, bath time, vet examinations and vaccinations, dog walks, car rides, constant attention around our feet, and introductions to new people, places, things, and the outdoor elements—namely thunderstorms and rain.

Loud claps of thunder are scary to many people. It's understandable that these giant rumbles that rattle the house, with accompanying flashes of bright white light in every window, would be frightening to a little puppy. Although we would be safe and sound inside the house, Sasha would always seek us out for protection from the storm.

Ironically, however, Sasha would never hesitate to head out to the backyard during an unrelenting storm when she needed to potty. She learned this when I had no choice but to take her out and stand with her (with or without an umbrella) during days of heavy rain that just would not subside. Somehow, the storms became much less intimidating to her when she was literally soaking it all in. What made this okay was the welcome to a warm towel back inside.

When a rainstorm wasn't on the horizon, Sasha soon found another way to guarantee a warm towel embrace during an afternoon with Mama.

Carol's first opportunity to babysit our new pup proved to be a true test of doggie motherhood. Living with Yoda, a mature easygoing dog, was hardly a challenge, not to mention that we were six years removed from that time. The antics of a rambunctious puppy would be a brand new experience for Carol, with plenty of challenges to meet head-on. The first of many incidents did not disappoint.

Our backyard was scarcely a lawn when we adopted Sasha. Grasses and weeds had gradually moved into our sandy lot over a few years' time while we postponed landscaping. Our plan to design a yard with trees, bushes, decks, flagstones, pergolas, and gardens was beginning to evolve and would see completion in a few years, but until then, Sasha had full run of the wide-open weedy lot with only one obstacle.

I had already begun the first effort of our landscaping plans, painstakingly digging by spade and pitchfork, a four- by six- by two-foot-deep hole in the black clay topsoil. This would eventually be our goldfish pond, but it started out as a temporary mud pit. Rainwater usually kept the bottom few inches filled, but it was not pretty.

I was away at work one sunny afternoon, while Carol kept a watchful eye on our curious pup. This, of course, included trips to the backyard. While Sasha enjoyed running to every corner of the yard, Carol walked along in playful pursuit. She hesitated toward the back of the lot, looking away for merely a moment—but long enough for Sasha to escape all peripheral view and scurry halfway across the clearing, through Texas wildflowers and noxious weeds, with only one destination in mind. She was heading straight for the kiddie pool.

"Sasha, noooo! Not the pond!"

Carol started running after her, but was clearly out of the race.

With a head start, and leaping in headlong flight toward the abyss, our little white pup went headfirst into the black lagoon. Carol rescued the cute creature before submersion, though, and a first bath became imminent for our chocolate-dipped marshmallow.

Carol quickly learned that our new little handful would indeed be all that and more.

FOR THE FIRST FEW DAYS while Sasha was becoming comfortable in her new home, I was able to stay with her so she would not be left alone in the house. And she never was—even while I was there.

Wherever I went, I had a tiny white shadow.

When she wasn't following me, Sasha was in my arms, cuddled close for as long as I liked. Maltese love to be held and Sasha was no exception. Not only did she appreciate a better perspective above tables and counters, more importantly, she wanted to share her love through the warm embrace, a simple act exemplifying the symbiotic relationship we would share for the rest of her life.

The only place she could not go (in my footsteps or in my arms)—and she always let me know it was not nice to abandon her—was the shower. (Considering the thunderstorms and the pond episode, a shower would have been trifling in comparison.) Sasha sat just outside on the bath mat, whimpering and crying for me to come back.

Daddy! Where did you go? Come back! Why did you leave me here alone?

It was adorable and heartbreaking at the same time.

"Girl, don't cry. I'm right here. I'll be out in just a minute."

I would try to ease her worries, but my waterlogged words were drowned out by her downpour of tears.

Eventually, she realized I always came back from that strange wet nook, so it wasn't necessary to vocalize her concern. She did, however, continue to wait quietly adjacent to the shower stall through each showering session, unless there were other distractions to keep her occupied.

Toys could keep her busy and entertained for dozens of minutes at a time. Her first toy, a plush orange dog with brown floppy ears, was bigger than she was. She would drag it around, tripping all through the house, biting, tugging, shaking, tossing, and tumbling when she needed self-entertainment. Naps were so much more comfortable when she snuggled up to her big nappy orange buddy. It remained her favorite toy throughout her first year, until she literally outgrew it, and transferred her interests to many other options from the erupting volcano of dog toys in our living room.

Many of those first toys came by postal home deliveries. Sasha's "grandmas," both living over a thousand miles away, would not meet the new grandpup until later that year. Until then, packages addressed to "Princess Sasha" graced our doorstep periodically, usually for the occasional holiday. In timely convenience, the first posted puppy gifts arrived for Saint Valentine's Day.

Opening each box paralleled Christmas morning. Those magical packages were always filled with special surprises: cute furry toys that squeaked under pressure, delightful mini-morsels that tasted deliciously different from the normal dinnertime nibbles, and wrapping paper! Sasha became so accustomed to unwrapping the contents, she assumed every delivery or gift was for her. She never missed the opportunity to unpack every box that came into the house. When packages were not for her, she seemed disappointed toys or treats were not inside. Nevertheless, she relished the revealing ritual.

Discovering what lay within extended to anything that might contain hidden treasures. From unpacking suitcases to opening Christmas presents, Sasha was always the first to help. The precursor to opening the container was sitting on top of it. From the first box addressed to our petite princess when she was no more than ten weeks old, to the large tuff-storage plastic bins I used for packing percussion hardware, she never failed to check out the view from on top.

As a tiny pup, she challenged herself to hop up on top of anything barely big enough to hold her. Small boxes, a tower of telephone books (it didn't take many Dallas and Fort Worth phone books to make a sizeable stack), her pet carrier kennel, and the bottom shelves of bookcases were all plateaus to conquer, allowing her to sit a bit taller.

Attaining new heights took many forms, including family fitness. Carol soon found out she had a worthy workout proponent during her daily step aerobics. The real exercise became a competitive challenge to reach the step in regular rhythm before Sasha claimed it for her dancing-to-the-oldies platform.

As Sasha continued to grow, so did her elevated destinations. It wouldn't be long before she could make the leap to the bed and living room furniture. Until that time, we never hesitated to lift her to these temporarily out-of-reach areas, accompanying her to sit and watch television, or to go to bed.

A decade earlier, just before my grandfather's passing, he and my mother had a La-Z-Boy-style recliner delivered to us as a holiday gift. It became my favorite living room chair (while Carol claimed the length of the couch) and as our collection of DVD movies began to grow, we often spent many a night sunken into comfy cushions in a dark and deafening living room theater experience. Sasha had little choice but to join us during our regular cinematic excursions from reality.

With popcorn popped, lights dimmed, and the rumble of 5.1 surround sound beginning to rattle our senses, Sasha would stretch out squarely on my chest while I reclined in comfort to enjoy the motion picture. Ear-popping explosions or hard rockin' soundtracks never bothered her. She slept comfortably through until the final credits, only ready to move on to the real bed when we did.

WHEN SASHA first came home with us, she was no larger than my hand and barely weighed two pounds. Maltese pups are very tiny. As an adult, most Maltese are less than ten pounds—Sasha only topped that weight for a brief time. But as an eight-week-old puppy, she was only a handful—literally.

Her size did not diminish her courage to think big, however. From scaling new heights to bold vocal warnings, Sasha remained fearless from the start. Her chirp-like puppy barks dominated the chimes of the doorbell, real or televised. (She soon recognized the difference, ignoring the TV fake-outs.) Eventually her pitch lowered perhaps an octave, but her tenacity persevered. At any sign of unsettling emergency, she'd release blasts of barks, blaring in rapid-fire fanfare. Her explosion of staccato shots in succession elevated her range to tones and decibels that tested the tensile strength of our stemware.

Sasha was not afraid to use her voice, but did so only in warning, not for attention.

HER EARLY BRAVE demeanor extended to our vehicles. Sasha enthusiastically looked forward to going for a spin. It never mattered whether the destination might entail an undesirable vet exam. The chances were much better that the fantastic voyage would lead to an incredible adventure in new places or to meeting new people.

When she became big enough to stand steady during a ride, her choice seat usually meant my lap, the easiest spot to view the outside world from our minivan. The view was a bit higher, but also a bit bumpier, when riding in my truck.

Although our roots are in Michigan, our rhizomes spread and grew deep in the heart of Texas. We have blossomed under the Lone Star longer than anywhere else. While the ways of the Wild West have stirred our spirit, I've never taken to cowboy boots and hats. I'd more likely be lassoed in jeans, sneakers, and a Hawaiian shirt. But I gladly yielded to one Texas tradition: the pickup truck. While plainly not the urban cowboy, I nevertheless found my preferred metro travel in a Dodge Ram. Our business needs regularly required moving equipment from here to there and back. I wouldn't have managed well without a truck no matter where we lived.

Sasha was equally at home in the truck. Just like any Labrador Retriever or Rottweiler. Dogs and trucks go paw in hand.

I'm sure it was an amusing sight to behold, whenever someone pulled up next to my macho manly pickup and glimpsed our petite sweet girl happily panting in the window, her fountain of white hair tied up with a pink bow.

And there was proud papa incognito beneath dark shades and a baseball cap.

(Actually, that was my typical driving attire.)

It was great to see such enthusiasm for a simple trip around town.

"That's my girl!"

I loved it—because I loved her.

Sasha was born ready for the rocky road.

THE SPONTANEITY of her adoption meant we hadn't properly prepared for our new housemate and so had little choice but to let Sasha sleep in our bed that first night. Because of her size, we did consider—for about a millisecond—putting her in the new dog kennel on subsequent nights, but it became clear she would have nothing of the sort.

If that tall, soft giant mattress is where Mama and Daddy sleep, then that's where Sasha will sleep, too.

No question about it.

It doesn't matter if it's way too high to jump up on or jump off of, just put me up there and I'll take care of the rest.

And that she did.

Lucky girl.

Yoda and Açúcar were never allowed to sleep on our bed. There were plenty of good reasons. They were too big; there was not enough room; and they shed their fur as if they thought we needed an extra blanket. Beyond that, the only bed compact enough to pack for our cross-country move had been a waterbed. Add two fifty-pound dogs with toenails, each ready to hang twenty over that surf, and there was just no way we were going to ride those waves and risk waking to a waterbed wipeout.

A tiny pup that did not shed, and faded memories of the abandoned waterbed, flipped our dog-on-the-bed rule one-eighty. Without hesitation or discussion, we welcomed Sasha to meander over our majestic mattress.

Actually, luck had nothing to do with it.

She belonged there.

(On one—and only one—early occasion, Sasha made a tremendous effort to convert our majestic mattress into a waterbed when we obviously missed her cue to run to the backyard. After that, she made sure we never missed another high tide warning.)

She confidently cuddled next to our warm bodies night

after night without a threat of injury—except once.

Sasha liked to sleep between us, in the middle of the bed. On rare occasions, she would snuggle up to me on the outside edge, so I encouraged her to stay close. Considering all the chances of being smashed and squashed in an unconscious rollover—especially as an itsy, bitsy pup—Sasha always managed to avoid such hazards.

However, one time when she nestled close near the edge of the bed, I did the unconscionable act of turning away from her without thinking. Guess where Sasha went?

With a teeny thump on the carpet, and most likely a bounce or two, I gasped in horror, "Oh no! Sasha just rolled off the bed!"

I reached for our baby Bumble before she knew what hit her. Resilient and no worse for wear, she began to prance between us while I frantically checked all her angles and movements to make sure she wasn't hurt in any way.

No worries—just another night and another adventure for our precious pup.

BEDTIME ALWAYS SET the stage for our aspiring dancer. Evolving into choreographed routines, Sasha had various rituals that became the expected norm before we all drifted into sweet dreams. She was obliged to perform a head-to-toe walk over us and back, precariously balancing and walking a tightrope, but without a net or a concern. She had the most fun jumping from one of us to the other. It was a game she devised, avoiding touching the bed for as long as possible.

When she tired of her quicksand-evading maneuvers, she'd plop down across Carol's chest, from shoulder to shoulder as she grew older, with legs outstretched and delicate waves of snow-white hair softly caressing Carol's neck. This habit—her respite from dance that caused her to resemble an ascot—inspired a new nickname, essentially a title: The Living Scarf.

Sasha's bedtime performances inspired many nicknames or titles, often selected from popular song titles of the '70s and '80s: "Dancing Queen," "Private Dancer," and most fittingly, "Tiny Dancer."

She was always the star of the show.

Her greatest dance, though, would come many months later. It became her signature move, her own inspiration based on her attachment to a simple plush toy she discovered at Grandma's house. This soon-to-be-revealed, holiday-themed toy quickly became her favorite and had to come home with us. She always kept it near. I don't believe she thought of it as a toy. It was a security blanket, a proud possession, a cherished keepsake, and a symbol of extreme happiness and welcome pleasure.

It was her holy grail.

But months before this unexpected, sacred discovery, and even prior to her tiny dances over our bodies and in our hearts, a different sort of quest was taking place that would undoubtedly include Sasha—the search for her soon-to-be best buddy and puppy playmate.

After just a few weeks having Mama and Daddy all to herself, she was going to have to share the spotlight.

It was time to bring home her little brother.

♪♫

Sweet Girl

chapter four

siblings

Sweet Girl

Siblings

FREEZING RAIN and icy highways put a hold on our first attempt to adopt our Aussie boy pup in mid-February. The road trip to Houston had to wait for a change in the weather. In Texas, the wait is not long and in a few days, the minivan was packed for a day trip down (and back) Interstate 45. It was light packing: a cooler with drinks, sandwiches and other snacks, a pillow and blanket, towels, two pet carriers with dog bowls, collars, and leashes—and our new tiny traveler—Sasha. She was comfortable riding in the car (mainly on Carol's lap), but a six-hour round-trip drive would be a true test of passenger patience and endurance. We set off early one morning, three weeks after Sasha "came home."

TWO YEARS EARLIER, in May of 2001—during the "empty kennel" period of our lives—we traveled to New York City to attend the James Beard Awards presentation. *Cookin' with Carol* had been nominated for "Best Local Cooking Show." (We did not win.) During the few days of our trip, we hastened to see six Broadway shows, including the brand new Mel Brooks musical, *The Producers*, starring Nathan Lane and Matthew Broderick. The show later went on to win a record twelve Tony Awards, and for good reason; it was inventive, entertaining, and hilarious—the funniest stage production we had ever seen.

We loved our first New York experience—the food, the shows, the sightseeing, the hustle and bustle of Times Square. Our golden delicious trip to The Big Apple had us biting hard, so we planned more tours throughout the next year. A rendezvous with our parents took place just one month before the horrific tragedy of 9/11. Six months later, we never hesitated—rather, we felt more resilient and empowered—to go back and share the marvel of Manhattan with our friends. Each visit was saturated with the sights and sounds of Broadway.

We were not strangers to Broadway tunes, though only a random song here and there ever received much consideration. We always listened to an eclectic variety of styles and artists. From pop to rock to country to classical, every genre had its own appeal. But witnessing one musical after another on the Broadway stage focused our attention and had us hooked on show tunes. We collected cast recordings and listened often, many times in the car. During one of our subsequent trips to New York, we attended the musical *Chicago*. When written and filmed as a motion picture the following year, we were ready to trip the light fantastic on opening day. Of course, we had to have the soundtrack, a rousing recent album acquisition to entertain us on our February commute to Houston.

WE NEVER HIT THE ROAD without a compact disc wallet full of music to drive by. We were still reeling from our two-year Broadway high, so the hours of our trip across Texas were highlighted by back-to-back show tunes. *The Producers*, *Phantom of the Opera*, and *Mamma Mia!* were the intended mix, but the newly released *Chicago* soundtrack took priority in loop mode. For our cute car pool companion, the songs did not go unnoticed.

While Sasha pounced and pranced around the floor of the minivan and then slept comfortably on Carol's lap, the melodies of "All That Jazz" and "Razzle Dazzle" were seeping indelibly into her tiny impressionable brain. We must have played that CD dozens of times over the next few months. When we watched the movie on DVD six months later, the muted "wah-wah" notes from the solo trumpet and opening refrain of the overture grabbed Sasha's attention. She suddenly had visuals to go along with the peculiarly familiar music. And this began her lifelong love-hate relationship with that giant magic box with moving pictures and memorable jingles.

Sasha watched television.

She was forever interested in animals on the tube. People, not so much, but other creatures seized her undivided attention, causing her to charge the screen. She would notice without a nudge any dog or cat that dared to make an unwelcome entrance into our house through that menacing monitor.

Her favorite TV to keep in check stood impudently on a pedestal in the living room. The forty-six-inch rear projection widescreen was bigger and more steadfast than most animals it dared to portray, but that did not deter Sasha. Any sign of a canine invasion warranted a sudden growl and forcible lunge with her front feet against the TV cabinet. The televisions in the kitchen and bedroom were not within her reach and thus were protected from her spontaneous springing. But she watched those as well. If a kitten caught her eye in the kitchen, Sasha ran to the living room to see it there. She knew where those annoying animals could show up in any room. If the TV was off in the living room, or set to a different channel, it caught her off guard.

She would throw me a look as if to say, *Hey, turn this thing on—there's a cat I need to chase!*

Sasha seemed more concerned than entertained, but she enjoyed every opportunity to watch those invulnerable animals. She recognized recurring pet store and pet food commercials with familiar jingles, sounds, and images. The Super Bowl halftime break introduced her to an overwhelmingly fascinating, yet aggravating experience the first time the *Puppy Bowl* took the field on Animal Planet.

Wow! Look at all of those puppies! Let me at 'em!

Her all-time favorite TV moments occurred every weeknight at the end of *The Late Late Show with Craig Ferguson*. It became such a regular event over the years, I began to prompt her with, "Here comes the kitty," before the show returned from ads to this familiar melodic tease: "What did we learn on the show tonight, Craig?"

An animated photo of a kitten always appeared on the screen with the proper kitty response, "Meeooww!"

Sasha listened for that musical tagline and loved to watch for the kitty, whether prompted to or not.

She could get really worked up about these animals invading her home. When she wasn't lunging at the living room television, she'd strut around the room huffing and puffing about it.

I'd usually let her know, "It's all right; all gone."

Her expression confirmed her concern: *Are you sure? Where did they go? I need to chase those critters away from here!*

She grasped the concept of animals appearing and moving on the screen, and that they could magically transport from one screen to another, even to another room, but that they were untouchable, trapped in a flat world, and did not respond was just a bit beyond her understanding. (Sometimes, by coincidence or precisely timed reaction, it seemed to her that they did respond.)

Nevertheless, she never grew tired of attempting a cautionary dialogue with any television intruder.

When we pulled into the circular driveway of a ranch-style home in the suburbs of Houston, a quick glance at the large fenced-in backyard and unmistakable yard ornaments indicated we had arrived at the House of Bear. Our Silky breeder of choice required new owners to follow one rule when registering one of her puppies with the American Kennel Club (AKC): the dog's name had to include her kennel name, "Amron," and in some form, the word "bear."

This would designate and identify the extensive lineal heritage of dogs bred at her kennel.

It did not take long for us to determine a full name to register with the AKC. The name came before we met our new pup. Relishing several recent voyages Down Under—and our pup was an *Australian* Silky Terrier—we had to make a clear Aussie connection.

Inside the breeder's home, we promptly made the acquaintance of an attentive little black-and-tan pup with perky ears and a fuzzy goatee. Our soon-to-be family member—and Sasha's new sibling—instantly touched our hearts. He would be registered "Amron Sydney Blue Bearamundi," but commonly, he was Sydney boy, our little man.

(For his AKC name, we concocted a pun on the Aboriginal word "barramundi," an Australian river fish. Along with black, silver, and tan, "blue" would be the description of Sydney's adult coat—and, fittingly, brought to mind the vibrant blue Australian seawater in Carol's favorite panoramic view of Sydney Harbour.)

Our other bundle of joy waited briefly and ever so patiently in a pet carrier, with only the slightest of whimpers, while we spent a few moments fawning over Sydney. He was a relaxed, yet curious little guy, showing no apprehension in response to our attention, as mother dog and a few other Silkies dashed around the house in nervous excitement. We introduced Sasha to Sydney, nose-to-nose, and for an odd awkward moment, she was calm and unsure how to react. Sydney could not have been more excited to welcome a warm nose that did not belong to a familiar Silky Terrier into his world.

This first meeting was brief and the pups found temporary residence in separate pet carriers under my watchful eye while Carol finished with the AKC and breeder's paperwork and discussed the possibilities of showing Sydney as a dog show competitor. It seemed we would be on the road to raising a Silky Terrier champion hopeful.

Successfully attaining a title was a long and winding road, to say the least, and much longer than most dog show professionals would choose to endure, I imagine. Carol wanted to get back in the show ring for fun, and teaching Sydney the ropes to run with the big dogs would be a nice occasional weekend adventure in and around Texas. There was no hurry.

Good thing.

Our boy from Oz never found—let alone followed—the road paved with yellow bricks.

Sydney would eventually become a "finished champion," his AKC name designated with a "Ch." prefix; granted, this was achieved literally by a hop, skip, and a jump.

His tendency to become giddy in the show ring caused him to skip like a little girl playing hopscotch in the schoolyard. Judges could not award points for such flagrant "defects," so Sydney had an uphill battle to amass the points and major wins needed to secure a championship.

Through Carol's assiduous training sessions, cautious show ring handling efforts, and perhaps a judge's wandering eye at critical moments, Sydney passed his "Champion of Record" requirements and celebrated his retirement from the conformation show ring two weeks short of his third birthday.

Westminster would not be privy to the one-and-only Ch. Amron Sydney Blue Bearamundi, our happy-go-lucky, adorable, skipping Silky.

Sasha could not be a show dog. She did not meet the physical standards required by the AKC to qualify as a champion competitor.

She surely had the spirit.

And she had the pedigree.

Her sire and dam were AKC-registered Maltese dogs, and Sasha would be registered as well: "Shirazldazl Apricot Sasha Su."

(I went a little crazy with her AKC name, taking many hints from naming Sydney, and maximizing the character limit. My inspiration came from her sparkling theatrical personality, puppy ear color, nickname, and even an Aussie wine reference—Shiraz—because it sounded cool.)

But, dismayingly, she could not follow in her brother's paw prints into the show ring, save for one fleeting event in her early life when she and Sydney shared a winning blue-ribbon moment.

A SMALL LOCAL DOG SHOW was just a few weeks away, and with many encouraging words from the breeder, we headed home from Houston with hours of discussion about diving headfirst into dog show mania, while Sasha cuddled in Carol's arms and our newly adopted Sydney rode comfortably in the backseat pet carrier.

"There's a dog show coming up next month in Bryan, Texas," Carol informed me.

"They have a puppy class scheduled."

"A training class for puppies?" I inquired.

"No, a conformation class—a dog show event. You know, a competition, but for puppies. It would be a good introduction to dog shows for Sydney."

Dogs are not eligible to compete until they are six months old; however, many times a dog show will host a fun event for underage puppies to be shown in the ring, and prizes will be presented.

"Bryan is over halfway to Houston," I retorted. "And there are entry fees."

From the beginning, I hadn't been too excited about the dog show scene for Sydney. He was to be our pet, Sasha's brother and member of our family, and not a trophy on display, traveling from city to city, and living out of a crate for months on end.

But I was receptive to an occasional dog show if it didn't mean separation from his new family. This would have to be a family venture with Sydney remaining under Carol's supervision, care, and guidance the entire time.

"We could enter Sasha, too. She would be great in the show ring," Carol added.

Well I couldn't argue that fact. Sasha may not have been a show dog, but she clearly was a *show-off* dog, always commanding attention.

"When is this dog show? Is that a weekend? When is the deadline to register?" I asked, weighing the details against all the reasons I could think of not to participate.

A few weeks later, when Sydney *and* Sasha became registrants in their first official dog show—yet *unofficial* competition—plans for another Texas road trip commenced. We headed out on the wet, blustery spring day of the show, arriving three hours later at a large open-air, yet covered, dirt floor exhibition ring on the county fairgrounds. The show was indeed small, but that did not deter our excitement to participate, and that carried through to the pups.

Decked out in their everyday collars with leashes (not the formal and expensive braided leather leads commonly used to show dogs), their coats freshly combed, Sydney and Sasha blissfully entered the show ring with Mama and Daddy (and a handful of training treats) in tow.

We didn't have a clue what we were supposed to do. But the pups behaved and remained close while we followed suit with the few other participants. A couple quick trots in a circle and a stop at the presentation table for a judge examination led the way to first-place ribbons for Sydney and Sasha.

I could say that we all were in top form and did remarkably well, considering this was a first for us all. But truth be told, amid the handful of cute pup competitors, Sydney was the only Silky Terrier and Sasha, the only Maltese.

They won their breed categories by default.

REGARDLESS OF THE OUTCOME at a dog show, we knew from the moment of adoption that our family had grown to include two winning pups. They playfully competed for Top Dog as they became best buddies, but that title was incontestably Sasha's from the start. Although our home had only been hers for a few weeks, Sasha took full pleasure in welcoming Sydney to *her* house. She was only nine days older than Sydney, but she had seniority in our household and she did not let that sense of rank go unnoticed. Add that she was a Maltese and female—undeniable qualifications to support *her* dominance—so poor Syd never had a chance to challenge *that* status, even with his male-domineering and sprightly Terrier personality.

Behaving badly was never a problem, despite Sasha's occasionally lunging with ferocious fangs to keep Sydney in line. He seldom did anything to warrant such behavior, but she was the boss and any out-of-line eye contact easily set off an attempted psychological tough-love session. One early photograph caught her Hyde in mid-air leap toward Sydney, teeth bared and with painful intent in her eyes. In that instant, Top Dog became "Devil Dog!" A moment later, our dainty Jekyll returned while Sydney shrugged it off, none the worse for wear.

The first few months of life with our new family were fraught with dog walks, vet exams, new toys, playtime, mealtime, potty training, puppy kindergarten, and more traveling. I spent all my waking hours, day after day, looking after their needs and being there for them while they learned and played. We planned our schedules such that when I could not be home with the pups, Carol would be. Of course, occasionally, Sasha and Sydney had to stay home alone.

They did surprisingly well, adjusting to our random work schedules and household activities. They shared a dog cage, obeying our command to "Kennel up!" whenever we prepared to leave the house, and burst out with exhilaration when we returned home to open the door. The bed-lined kennel was a safe haven; they were comfortable and together whenever Mama and Daddy were away. They were always together, to cuddle, commiserate, compete, and celebrate all our family events, as they continued to grow out of puppyhood.

When they were nearing six months of age, it was time to think about Sasha's trip to the vet for spaying. Sydney was conveniently excused from his male-altering procedure while standing at stud, working on his championship, gleefully skipping around dog show rings. Neither had shown serious interest in a "romantic relationship" at that point. Sasha would not have let that happen. On the contrary, she was hopping on top of Sydney to reinforce her canine dominance in the household. Coming into heat would have changed that attitude instinctively, I imagine. We didn't want to find out, so we scheduled her operation to coincide with a rather spontaneous flight of fancy.

IN APRIL OF 2003, the pups shared their kennel while we went to the movie theater to see the newest release from director/actor Christopher Guest. His comedic "mockumentaries" include the riotous *Best in Show*, a hilarious look—and not far from the truth—into the world of dog shows. His new movie, *A Mighty Wind*, spoofed folk musicians, although it was rife with great music. Like his earlier works, we thoroughly enjoyed the movie and in typical fashion with musical entertainment, we purchased the motion picture soundtrack.

As we became obsessed with the songs over the next few weeks, I often surfed the Internet for information about the movie and the music. One incidental search led to a surprising announcement about an upcoming live performance by the three faux music acts from the movie.

The event was one day only, with strictly limited seating, at the Getty Center in Los Angeles—and it was free!

They were accepting online reservations, so in my utter bewilderment, I artlessly put in an impulsive request for two tickets.

Bingo!

I instantly had two reservations for us to see A Mighty Wind in concert—in less than a month—and in California.

With two new pups in the house, learning to find their way in this world and looking to us for leadership, I committed to be there for them every day. I felt that responsibility more deeply than I had ever before, with a strong conviction against traveling without them during that impressionable time of their lives. This commitment weighed heavily on my mind as I contemplated the exciting concert news and how I would tell Carol.

My thoughts bounced back and forth between neglecting the pups and jet-setting in La La Land, the former only possible if we chose the la-la latter.

If we did go, how would we get there?

Or stay there? (So to think.)

We did not have the resources to make those kinds of spontaneous travel arrangements, although we could be resourceful with attentive planning. The wheels were turning in maximum overdrive.

The concert is perhaps a once-in-a-lifetime opportunity.

So is every day spent with our pups.

We've got the tickets, though.

Hmmmm. What to do?

With impassioned thought and consideration, I devised an itinerary that offered the best of both worlds. It was time to break the wondrous news to Carol. She loved to travel, she loved the movie and the music, she'd certainly love my choice of hotel, restaurants, and other activities I'd found to fill our time in the City of Angels. And my solution to puppy care was clever and convenient. The announcement would surely be welcomed as a terrific weekend getaway.

"How would you like to see A Mighty Wind in concert?" I asked Carol maladroitly, still not confident my idea was sound.

"What do you mean?"

"All the music acts from the movie—The Folksmen, The New Main Street Singers, Mitch & Mickey—the actors are going to do a live concert next month at the Getty Center," I began to explain.

"Where is the Getty Center?"

"Los Angeles."

"What? How can we go to Los Angeles next month?" she questioned expectantly.

I explained to her how I came across the announcement for this show, how I had requested and received the tickets, where and what the Getty Center was all about, how I had determined we had enough airline miles to cover the trip, and on top of all that, how I could score tickets to see our favorite musical, *The Producers*, concurrently opening in L.A., starring Martin Short and Jason Alexander.

I continued to present my case, "We could stay at The Beverly Hilton and enjoy a dinner downstairs at Trader Vic's," knowing the mention of that iconic restaurant would draw her undeviating attention.

And then came the much-anticipated question …

"What about Sasha and Sydney?"

Here's where the timing was critical, not only in the schedule of events, but also in the deliberation of the plan ...

"Sasha needs to be spayed soon. That requires an overnight stay and recovery at the vet clinic. They can board Sydney as well, and that would be a perfect opportunity for us to get away for two days," I began to clarify.

"The concert is on the Friday before Memorial Day. We can travel early Thursday, check into the hotel, have dinner, and see *The Producers* on Thursday night, go to the Getty Center on Friday for lunch, do a museum and garden tour and the concert, and catch the red-eye back to Dallas on Friday night. We'd be back Saturday morning to pick up the pups before noon," I continued, barely containing my excitement.

I felt this was impeccable timing and a fantastic plan to seize the opportunity and occupy our time with illustrious entertainment during the mandatory vet stay Sasha would require for her spaying procedure. Much to my surprise, Carol didn't see it quite the same way.

There was no doubt that Carol had instantly become a caring, loving mother to the pups, and our family was now unmistakably defined by their inclusion. Her immediate embrace of our new family unit was a far cry from the protracted and gradual willingness to welcome the step-dogs, Yoda and Açúcar, into our world over a decade earlier.

In younger days, our selfish impulses always took precedence over the dogs—we moved to Texas without them—but in our prime, the story had changed dramatically. Sasha and Sydney were our babies. Sasha would be anesthetized. She would be under the knife.

How could we possibly go anywhere—let alone two time zones away—while our precious sweet girl was in surgery?

But the vet clinic would require her to stay overnight.
But what if there were complications?
But the veterinarian would take care of her and make sure everything was all right ... right?

Entertaining these thoughts challenged my deepest desire to do the right thing—a valid feeling I knew well. It tugged at my conscience.

Carol obviously shared similar concerns, only focusing on our pups, and had a much different reaction than I had expected. This was another one of those life moments, when I thought I had everything figured out, but quickly realized there was a lot I hadn't begun to understand; it was an eye-opening turning-point, and a time to pause and ponder.

Many issues throughout our relationship seemed superficial, skimming the surface to placate each other. I could honestly share and sincerely appreciate the heartfelt devotion and cogent concern that became the root of this family matter, emotions that had been absent from many earlier considerations. From that point forward, our primary responsibility became making decisions in the best interest of our family, a family that included two loving, yet unquestionably dependent puppies that required our undivided attention.

In the end, after discussing the details with the veterinarian who insisted that we rest assured, and placing more consideration into this decision than any decision we had ever made when buying a car, we had our whirlwind Hollywood getaway with little worry, while Sydney kept a recovering Sasha company under the vigilant care of the vet clinic staff.

DURING THE SIX YEARS between pets, we had become comfortable traveling, many times for business, but often to visit family. Travel by plane became the norm. When researching dogs to consider for pets, the Maltese and Silky Terrier breeds were at the top of the list for many reasons, including temperament, no shedding, and their size with regard to travel. They were airline-friendly, able to ride in a carrier under the seat. This option would have fit our style perfectly, but as it turned out, we took to the road for our family travels and the pups looked forward to each journey. The treks through Texas introduced them to long rides, but none would compare to the cross-country marathons we'd soon be driving.

Their first long-distance drive was a mere thirteen hours to the foothills of the Rocky Mountains, just outside Denver. We were visiting Carol's cousin, Debby, and a gathering of relatives for a summer family reunion. A road trip meant traveling music and this adventure would begin a listening trend for every subsequent extended family outing. *A Mighty Wind* was always the first album on our playlist and it became the soundtrack for our travelin' pups. Sasha promptly absorbed this music into her ever-expanding playlist memory, forever recognizing and associating these melodies with exciting minivan adventures.

One tune, "Never Did No Wanderin'," was teasingly designated Sydney's song due to lyrics that parodied folk traveling songs. Although never refusing to go, Sydney—our soon-to-be seasoned dog show traveler—ironically did not take to the road as Sasha did. He would require a light sedative to prevent car sickness and he'd always prefer to ride in his kennel or a big comfy dog bed.

Sasha loved to ride in the car—the longer the trip, the better. She had to start each journey in the front seat, on my lap or Carol's, to see where we were going. Eventually, she would end up in the back with Sydney, usually riding on a high perch atop safely secured packages or luggage, settling down for a cozy nap while we blew down the highway like a mighty wind.

For puppies not even a year old yet, they loved to travel. It was not so much the ride, but rather the destination that piqued their interest and demanded their patience. The long road always paid off with sensational spectacle. In Colorado, hikes in the brisk mountain air and log cabin living opened the world to doe-eyed pups. In Michigan, having graduated to an eighteen-hour driving adventure, walks in the park and the introduction to snow heightened their imagination. Overnight stops along the way revealed the concept of hotel rooms and breakfast buffet treats. Above all, the throngs of new people and doggies to meet became the underlying motivation for enthusiastic anticipation.

Our tiny tourists were becoming social butterflies as they crossed state borders and counted the sights, racking up the frequent-traveler mileage rewards.

WE WANTED THE PUPS to become used to our recurrent travels, including the people they would meet, for a sense of comfort and security to recall later that year. Earlier in the year, when we were considering their adoptions, we knew that one huge issue would need to be addressed. We were planning a month-long trip to Australia during October. This would be our fourth visit since 1997 to attend a biennial food conference, Tasting Australia. Over the years, we had made friends in Adelaide, and we would be visiting and sightseeing with them during our stay.

A month would be a long time away from our pups. That notion tested our conscience. Two days in L.A. was nothing compared to this, but we had commitments to fulfill during this trip. There was only one viable solution. With our mid-summer introduction to my family in Michigan, it became clear that a month with Grandma would be our saving grace.

Mom had two dogs, Sophie (the Maltese) and Hannah, a Shetland Sheepdog, and they kindly welcomed Sasha and Sydney into their world. Our little guys enjoyed staying at Grandma's house from the start, so we had high hopes they'd adjust for the month we would be overseas.

When we made our way back to Michigan in October, it was not easy to continue on to South Australia without our pups. After a few days to allow Sasha and Sydney to become reacquainted with life at Grandma's, we had to pack for the airport without looking back.

Once settled Down Under, our email correspondence back home confirmed that our little girl was grief-stricken for at least a week. Distraught and whimpering, she often went upstairs to the vacant guest bedroom where we were supposed to be staying. Living in the comforts of Grandma's home, with loving attention and plenty of distractions, wasn't enough to keep Sasha's hopeful mind off our eventual return.

Sydney adjusted a little more easily. He took a liking to Hannah, looking to her for matriarchal comfort; she was a gentle and patient mother dog figure to follow for guidance and friendship.

As much as we treasured our trips to Oz, on this

occasion, the days began to wear tired and long. I caught the flu and did not feel well for the better part of a week. We longed for updates about our anxious, adorable pups. We wished that they could understand we would be returning soon.

When our long voyage home led to my mom's front door, we incited the greatest surprise and feeling of thankful liberation in our pups' young lives. And we were on the receiving end of the most enduring body-hopping, face-licking, story-barking reception we had ever known.

Mama and Daddy had returned!

As Sasha and Sydney grew to be mature dogs and truly the best of friends, to each other and to us, we were astounded by the amazing abilities, tantalizing traits, and idiosyncratic personalities that were developing on a daily basis. They continued to be highly trainable and social, always looking forward to weekly puppy kindergarten classes in the vet clinic's exercise yard, neighborhood walks through springtime Texas bluebonnets, navigating a labyrinth of doggie treasures at pet stores, and all other happy, people-meeting opportunities.

Our good friends, Becky and Tracy—the first visitors to meet our new pups—were instantly decreed "Aunt" and "Uncle" to Sasha and Sydney. A mere mention of "Aunt Becky" would beget a tilt of the head and a quizzical look, sending Sasha running to the door, or in some instances, to the TV. Becky was a local TV meteorologist and Sasha readily recognized her weather forecasts. This was the single exception to all the random animal appearances that attracted

Sasha's attention to the television.

Sasha always had to be the center of attention, much to Sydney's dismay. (Our attention was equally shared.) Her ebullience was omnipresent; however, her personality seemed to shine when we were with family and friends. Her many unique traits were revealed during our first trip to Michigan.

The layout of the guest bedroom at my mom's house presented Sasha with a direct view of a busy-body white puppy, playfully pouncing all over the bed. She discovered the strange properties of her own reflection in a dresser mirror. Similar to her relationship with TVs, mirrors became objects of her great affection, and occasionally, frustration.

Our floor-standing mirror at home always attracted Sasha's loving attention. My suggestion to "Kiss the puppy!" was all it took for her to come face-to-face with herself, passionately licking the mirror in a sweet doggie embrace. I could sense her delight every time that white puppy in the looking glass reciprocated with a cold, wet kiss.

The dog toys at Grandma's house were always of interest as well; so different—and so much better!—than all the ones at home. A small squeaky plush mouse became the object of Sasha's obsession. Sydney preferred a rope tug-of-war, but Sasha cherished her baby, the mouse. That's how we began to affectionately address the toys she desired immensely. Later, plush ball-shaped toys became the compelling "ballie," but this first affinity was her "baby." She would hover over the charlatan house mouse, fixated on it until I tried to grab it. She was quicker, moving away with her prized catch, only to return moments later to repeat this act—over and over again.

Sasha loved her baby. But it was to be another special toy—her pinnacle possession and cherished keepsake—that she could not live without.

SASHA'S HOLY GRAIL was a candy cane. A plain, plush, stuffed dog toy, shaped like a jumbo iconic holiday treat became her symbol of reception.

From the moment of discovery, she devised a unique method to pick it up and carry it. Her signature move was unlike anything I've ever witnessed by any pets. This revelation occurred during her first Michigan family visit and became a lifelong attribute, defining Sasha's welcome to guests, and her crowning happy dance between Mama and Daddy at bedtime.

Whether we were returning home (from work or errands), or guests were arriving, or if I was ending a telephone call, Sasha would rush to grab her candy cane and trot around in circling sashays expelling her excitement. Bearing witness to this routine was a special treat for any lucky recipient; her specific manner became phenomenal to behold.

She only held the candy cane upside down, from the end of the hook with the stick shooting directly up and backward past her head, a metaphorical crest.

She wore the candy cane as if ready to snorkel the Great Barrier Reef.

She never once picked it up any other way.

It was her security blanket.

It was her badge of honor.

It was her trademark.

It was her snorkel.

The candy cane dance was an astounding performance she repeated consistently, on her terms, in her own way, and it was distinctly Sasha.

SHE WASN'T ALWAYS as sweet as her candy cane, though. She could be a tough little cookie at times.

A real brat.

But never to us.

The target of her wrath was her loving brother.

Sasha and Sydney were always inseparable, but occasionally insufferable when Sasha's dominatrix attitude surfaced. Her happy, sweet demeanor could flip in a flash. She'd start cracking the whip if Sydney became overbearing, but just for an instant to set him straight. She'd snap right back to our sweet girl, letting us know everything was under control.

Sometimes she liked to tease him. Sasha taunted Sydney with toys, slowly approaching while squeaking a stuffed animal. When within inches, she would start to shake the toy violently in an attempt to intimidate him. I was concerned that she'd smack her head on a table or chair during her rapid-fire gyrations.

"Sasha, stop! You're going to shake your brain right out of your ears," I'd humorously holler.

By then, Sydney would be crouched in front of her, his stubby docked tail in flutter overdrive, and barking at her exhibition of dominance, bouncing back and forth as she continued to creep forward. Eventually, he'd snatch the toy and they would be off on a room-to-room chase until she relented.

Sydney, always ready for a dash around the house, returned to continue the game. But it was game over. Sasha was already on to something more important, like sitting with Daddy or kissing Mama's face.

Often, her apparent rage was justified.

In the midst of a happy candy cane dance, Sydney, not to be outdone, would try to grab the opposite end of the toy from behind, pulling Sasha backward in the process. Her cheerful, tail-wagging waltz twirled instantaneously into a growling, teeth-baring tango. Our sweet girl became a ferocious defender when it came to her most cherished emblem.

Sasha lived by the Texas motto, "Friendship," but when infringed upon, she took the Texas anti-litter slogan to heart, adapting it for her own, *Don't mess with Sasha's snorkel!*

Sydney was oblivious to her potentially explosive fury, so we had to encourage him with other toy distractions. His favorite rope chew toy became the key to his symbolic greeting. When clenched in the center, with knotted, frayed ends hanging on either side of his mouth, we teased that he resembled a legendary Chinese dragon.

"Sydney, where's the Mighty Dragon?"

We'd lightheartedly encourage him as he'd scamper to seize the rope.

"Who's the Mighty Dragon?" we'd continue prompting him, to boost confidence and fire up mythic folly.

"Sydney's the Mighty Dragon!" we'd proclaim, bestowing the regal title as I'd playfully try to grab the rope from him in a tug-of-war.

And Sasha continued her perky peppermint twist.

FOR TWO-AND-A-HALF YEARS, we grew accustomed to our two-dog digs, a routine lifestyle the pups also came to expect. We never anticipated a change in our canine status quo. However, in 2005, a summer solstice surprise sent a stork to our doorstep.

I was loading the minivan with Carol's cooking equipment that sunny morning when she shouted out, "There's a puppy behind you!"

I turned to look, "What? A puppy? Where is it?"

"It was just there, behind you," she said as she walked outside to take a closer look.

At that moment, a little white dog with four prominent black spots and a black head with large pointed ears darted out from behind the car in a spastic dance. I knelt down with my hand extended and the dodgy doggie came right over to me. I noticed it was a girl as I gently petted her, picking her up to keep her from running away, and out into the street.

"Hi, Sweetie. Where did you come from?" I spoke softly to her.

"It's a little girl Chihuahua," I said as I carried her over to Carol.

Ironically, she wore a masculine spike-studded leather collar with no tags. She was thin and lively, yet calm in my arms—almost relieved to have found someone to notice her. She appeared to be full grown, but less than a year old, and not surprisingly, in heat. That likely explained her escape from who-knows-where and her running astray.

"She belongs to someone. We'll need to find her owner," I said as I contemplated what to do with her.

Sasha and Sydney were in the house, corralled behind the kitchen gate, but they sensed the unusual commotion outside.

They clamored to learn what we had discovered.

I brought the puppy in for a drink of water. Our pups were instantly engulfed in curiosity. I introduced the puppy through the gate and their excitement grew exponentially. The skinny Chihuahua did not seem fazed. Her attention was directly drawn to the small bowl of kibble I set out for her. She devoured the food in seconds.

She waited in a pet carrier while I set out to ask the neighbors if they knew who she belonged to. No one had seen her before. I took her to our vet to scan for a microchip. No luck there either.

As the day wore into weeks, I checked surrounding neighborhoods, vet clinics, and local pet shelters for posted notices of lost puppies. No one seemed to be missing her; however, Sydney hoped to claim her during promiscuous advances.

After nearly a month of foster care, trying to find her rightful owner, and keeping Sydney at bay, we decided the spry small Chihuahua would officially become a spayed sibling to Sasha and Syd. And by then, she was affectionately known as our little Millie. We were thrilled she would be staying for good.

Our complacent two-dog days had cheerfully changed into three-dog nights.

EVER SINCE THE MONTH-IN-OZ heartbreak with separation anxiety, I silently vowed never to leave the dogs again. Any travel away from home would have to include them. Occasionally, Carol would be required to travel on her own for business, including another trip to Australia. I would remain home to take care of the pups. The decision was never difficult. Our family had grown to include Millie, and while they all were best buddies and enjoyed each other's company, they individually grappled for *our* attention. I felt an unwavering responsibility and wholehearted desire to be with them daily—to care, nurture, and love them.

We traveled to see family and enjoyed local excursions with the pups. They stayed home without issue when our schedules kept us away for upwards of ten hours at a time. But that was the maximum extent of my time ever away from them. Our interests remained the same as always, just more home-based. Our choices in entertainment became less far-fetched than before, but just as satisfying.

Movies began to stockpile on DVDs.

Bookshelves spilt over.

Music tracks flourished.

Computer correspondence entered into overload.

We no longer sought the neon lights on Broadway—we would tailgate shows on tour at Dallas Summer Musicals. Our frequent visits to the theatre continued to influence life with our pups.

The lead character in *Thoroughly Modern Millie* (wearing a flashy black-and-white flapper costume) had inspired our newest monochromatic pup's name, although, "thoroughly old-fashioned" would better describe our Millie.

Her initial instincts were stereotypical Chihuahua—apprehensive and defensive toward strangers, and occasionally, yappy. But Sasha and Sydney would be highly influential in nurturing Millie's personality. She soon competed to welcome friends and family, holding her tongue when the others wouldn't.

She was happy to be the third wheel on a bicycle built for two, a refreshing new design for our family.

The dynamic duo had become the terrific trio and Millie was right at home as the baby sister. As usual, Sasha reinforced her queen bee position, while Sydney was satisfied with any good-natured attention. Millie, or Mil (as we tended to call her), was never as agile as the other pups, even with her two-year age advantage. She loved to prance around and play with the others, but took little time transforming from that playful pup into a sluggish senior.

She never refused a good meal—she never refused any meal for that matter!—and started packing on the pounds. Food was her friend. Sleep was her pastime. As long as Millie had her dinner plate and cozy bed, she was happy and comfortable, and it didn't matter what the other dogs thought about that.

That's not to say she couldn't be coaxed to participate in more rigorous or entertaining activities. The slightest jingle of dog tags had Millie racing Sasha to be the first for a dog walk. While Sasha would mischievously bite at her own collar and leash, Millie impatiently bounced up and down for her chance to jump in line and strap up. She was as ready to run as the next pup. It didn't matter that she needed to be carried home after about two blocks. Walks meant a change of scenery and an opportunity for much-needed exercise.

When Mil was still a skinny girl, Carol found a puppy purse to carry her around. The designer arm candy was all for fun and not intended as socialite bling. It became the exclusive mode of transport to the pickup truck when we all piled in for a pizza pickup run. When Millie heard the attached jingle bell ring, she beamed into the bag in less than a blink. She knew that producing the purse meant a ride to refreshments, so she continued to wedge in, while the pounds were packing on.

Our puppy purse popover.

After a while, I'm not sure Millie's feet touched the bottom when her muffin top rolled over the rim.

Blame it on the pizza.

For every meager bite of pizza crust indulgence, the dogs savored a better fresh treat: baby carrots. Sasha and Sydney enjoyed this root vegetable delicacy long before we tempted Millie with a taste of crudité. She was quick to jump onboard. All three raced like rabbits to munch happily on crunchy, cool carrots.

Activity in the kitchen drew a captive audience. Carol could always count on her trusty taste testers to be awkwardly underfoot. Millie was the most difficult to avoid—she was the most difficult to see. Naturally camouflaged, cloaked in kitchen floor colors, she disappeared into the design. Never fear. When it came to food, Millie was near. With a vociferous voice, she would not let us forget she needed a nibble.

When the kitchen was closed, a warm bed was always waiting for our pot-bellied piggy. Millie preferred a comfy cushion for her siesta, while Sydney found a spot on the floor and Sasha stretched out on a bookcase shelf (we had to leave bottom shelves empty for her). The computer desk served as a central haven, encircled by many good places for the pups to nap. I spent many hours typing to surround-sound snoring (that would have been Millie) and dynamic dreams. With muted barks and lashing limbs, Sasha undoubtedly chased lots of kitties during her catnaps, and for Sydney, I'm sure it was squirrels. (*Squirrel? Where?... Did you say "squirrel"?*)

Naps are nice, but bedtime is better.

Every night when we shut down the house, a call to the pups for "Last time to tinkle!" would bring Sasha and Sydney running to the back door. Millie, often already comfortable in bed, needed a nudge to budge. I could always count on Sasha to urge Mil to move.

"Go get Millie. Tell her it's the last time to tinkle tonight," I'd say to Sasha.

Sasha would run to find Millie and kiss her ear. She'd back away for a second, watching and waiting for Mil to react. A few more kisses, then Millie would stretch her front legs and yawn widely. Sasha's nose to Mil's mouth verified sobriety so they could get down to backyard business and get back to bed.

After all, the highly-anticipated bedtime cookies were waiting in the wings—a unique selection of dog biscuits reserved only for the midnight special.

The final treat of the night always set the scene for a doggie lineup. Sydney, Millie, and Sasha—always in a row on the edge of the bed—were never offenders, just eager pups waiting for a delicious late-night ransom.

To witness this bedtime ritual was my just reward for having lived another day, sharing in their unconditional love and devoted companionship. These qualities would stand out most clearly in Sasha when I slipped into a mid-life struggle with my own health, happiness, and well-being.

♪♫

chapter five

companionship

Sweet Girl

Companionship

DARKNESS DRIFTS WESTWARD *as a soft pink glow appears on the eastern horizon. Stars dissolve in the sky as jet fades into blue. The morning is warm as an innocent sun slowly rises, teasing with tenderness before igniting another blistering summer day.*

Sounds like a dream, but that's the reality I've come to expect in Texas—a sardonic sunrise painting the pure illusion of a perfect day. Briefly ideal, until daybreak pastels become awash in superfluous splendor, like crayon drawings that melt away in the midday heat. When I am witness to this sensational scene, it usually means I'm a little late to bed. Just as the solar inferno sears staunchly from dawn to dusk, I have always burned the midnight oil. The lifestyle of a musician. My internal clock is eternally adjusted to sleep by day and stay up all night. Everyday life is constantly upside down in my world.

Is it a coincidence that I have been drawn to Australia time and again?

Honestly, I find quiet, cooler, peaceful overnight hours conducive to working at a computer or behind a mixing board without interruption. Hence, I am not a morning person.

When my divergent schedule calls for activities before noon, those days are preceded by short sleepless nights. That's a recipe for disaster. When a short night came without warning in 2006, it was clearly catastrophic.

LATE AT NIGHT, in late July, I was designing a website until six in the morning. The dogs had no trouble sleeping; they were used to my nocturnal schedule. They would all find a spot to sleep within a few steps of my computer desk. Every now and then, I'd have a visit from Sasha or Sydney to check on my progress. Millie was down for the count, unless we collectively decided to break for the backyard. We'd return inside for a cookie treat, then the dogs would head back to bed and I'd be back to work. At the time, Carol was on a week-long business trip. Everything at home had been running like clockwork. She would be returning the next day. When I finally went to bed, I expected to sleep until noon or beyond.

I awoke abruptly at nine o'clock in a panic.

Actually, it felt more like stress, but it caused me to panic. I was not a stranger to stress. My business interests—music performance and television production—have always been a source of uncertainty and extreme stress, mentally, physically, and emotionally. I was used to it. I had had decades of experience. But this time the feeling was different. The stress was overwhelmingly physical. My neck was tight, my cheeks tingling with numbness. My heart was racing and I was finding it increasingly difficult to catch my breath.

Was I having a stroke?

Was I having a heart attack?

The panic was overwhelming.

I got out of bed, the dogs on my heels. They sensed something was wrong right away. I drank water and walked around the house, laboring to breathe deeply, trying to relieve the sensations and stifle the panic. The symptoms just continued to get worse. My sinuses were congested and I was afraid my throat would close. I found it difficult to swallow. My face continued to tighten. I began to worry that I might become incapacitated and possibly pass out. I was home alone. No, the dogs were with me, anxiously trying to find out why I was becoming frantic. They were attentive to my every move.

Then for the first time in my life, a terrifying thought became the central issue stirring my battle within: an inevitable fear of dying alone. The fear was not for me, but rather for the dogs.

If something happened to me while Carol was traveling, the dogs would be helpless.

The onset of this thought—plus the ongoing inner clash of stress, anxiety, and now fear—began to consume me.

I would recover from this event and begin visits to the doctor, never diagnosed with anything beyond slightly elevated blood pressure and cholesterol levels. These issues were hereditary, so I needed to consider a medicine regimen, along with better attention to my diet (including an efficacious daily-bowl-of-oatmeal remedy).

While my lifeblood issues were effectively reduced, my lifestyle became increasingly difficult.

Threats of anxiety and the fear of my recurring symptoms prompted several visits to Spence's home, including an overnight stay, when Carol traveled out of town. The dogs were always welcomed as well, remaining close by as I tried to relax and recover in a hospitable habitat without encumbering my friend's family and schedule. My friends were incredibly kind and accommodating, but I just couldn't fully recuperate.

Panic attacks, for lack of a better description, began sporadic assaults on my body and mind throughout the rest of the year with little warning. I could not ignore the fact that the random invasions were not without cause.

By 2006, the increasing economic issues of the nation had seriously affected our business. Most of our work provided education for home cooks through cooking classes and local television, but patronizing these resources was more of a luxury than a necessity for many people. When my first panic attack hit, we were desperately trying to keep afloat. We were in a downward spiral from there, sucked into a whirlpool of lost opportunities. We worked for months to pitch several potential business ventures that never came to fruition.

And my symptoms continued to get worse.

IN JANUARY 2007, Carol was in San Francisco when I had the worst heart-pounding scare to date. She returned home to find me in the ER for every imaginable cardiac-related test. Ravaged by fear I couldn't shake, my pulse had accelerated out of control without brakes. My body was evidently *breaking*, though. Chaos had consumed me.

Two days later I was released from the hospital with a normal pulse and no apparent heart issues, although I had instructions for follow-up cardiac care. Juggling unstable financial issues with erratic health concerns had set the scene for a high-anxiety circus.

Unpredictability became the predictable course for daily issues and activities, dotted with regular visits to health specialists ranging from a cardiologist to a psychologist to a hypnotherapist. I had become consistently sick, tired, and depressed, and everything always pointed to stress. I did my own research and mind-body exercises to control the panic attacks, productively reducing the occurrences to zero; however, my subliminal mind continued to control my nerves at random, setting off internal spasms and irritable bowels. I frequently endured bouts of lightheadedness and, oddly enough, hot flashes. I was ensnared in a tremendous struggle of mind, body, and spirit. Throughout my misery, I could not ignore the steadfast attempts at consolation from the companions circling my feet.

Dogs are a barometer of health and emotion. They can detect the slightest variation from the norm and will respond accordingly. When my signals went awry, the dogs' anxiety became evident to me. Much of my recovery effort was in response to their concern, but always in vain. They gradually began to accept my unconventional levels of stress. I continued to be plagued by an unmitigated fear of a scenario in which the dogs would be left alone and helpless. This perpetuated my symptoms and I found myself spending many random days in bed, sick and depressed. The irony of this vicious circle gave rise to the resolution of my condition. I had an obligation to shatter this sphere of fear and illness, to be healthy for the pups and our family. Fortunately, they were strong and healthy for me.

Sasha tried to keep my spirits high. She rarely left my side when I was bedridden. She kissed my hands and face until her tongue was dry. She brought toys to toss, did candy cane dances, and cuddled close. She urged me out of bed to carry on with necessary regular dog routines, like dinnertime and bathroom breaks.

She wanted me to feel better.

She wanted me to *be* better.

Sasha was strong when I was weak.

It was a trying time, not just for me, but for Carol and the dogs. They wanted to help, but it was up to me to climb out of this chasm. Summer was approaching and nothing would have buried my spirit deeper than several months of excruciatingly hot Texas weather. We needed a fresh outlook and it was not going to happen at home. We once again took to the north road for an extended stay with family in Michigan. The pups were raring and ready to go. It would be a highly effective break for us all—a chance to reevaluate our prospects for the future.

Whenever we packed for our road trips, Sasha was there to lead the way. She inspected the contents of every suitcase, usually from within. As mountains of bags, boxes, and pet carriers formed near the door, she insisted on scaling every stack. The view was much better from the top, plus there wouldn't be a chance we'd forget her. No dog left behind. She always monitored the loading and packing process until it was time for her to hop in the car and assume her first-class, front row seat on Mama's lap.

Unpacking was equally appealing. Carol's return from a business trip usually meant a special doggie treat waited inside the luggage. The anticipation was like Christmas for Sasha. While Sydney and Millie waited nearby with curiosity, Sasha had her head in the bag, scanning the contents. Any box, bag, or case that entered the house required Sasha's thorough inspection, our personal homeland security. If it remained closed, she would find her way to the top of it. No climbing adventure was off limits to our miniature mountaineer.

The dogs became ecstatic with anticipation, knowing a trip to Grandma's house was forthcoming. Packing the minivan floor-to-ceiling was the first clue. After a few hours on the road, crossing the Red River and continuing along pine tree-lined highways in Arkansas, it became clear we were heading "over the river and through the woods." They could all settle comfortably for the long ride, only checking our progress during stretch and bathroom breaks at gas stations.

Sasha was always notified when we were about to cross the Mississippi River at Cairo, Illinois, the ceremonial halfway point of our trip. With sights set squarely on visions of Emerald City rapidly approaching our windshield, Sasha rushed to stand on my lap, front paws and toenails gripping the steering wheel. Curiosity and awe captured her imagination for nearly a mile while we drove within a massive, sea green framework of steel, cleverly hovering like a hot air balloon over the Mighty Miss, but guilelessly masquerading as a spectacular through arch bridge joining our nation's East and West.

After nearly a full day on the road, a celebration was always in order. Reaching our destination sent the dogs scurrying through the house to jubilantly announce our arrival. They knew Grandma's house (and the occupants) very well. It was their home away from home. After all, Sasha and Sydney had spent a month there as puppies, and we had returned for the holidays nearly every year since. Even Millie knew what to expect.

But what they didn't know was that they would meet a fuzzy new friend when we arrived for our summer stay.

Abby, a bouncy brindled Pomeranian puppy, was the newest addition to my mom's pet family. It was the summer of six: Sophie, Hannah, Abby, Sasha, Millie, and Sydney—in his harem heaven.

But poor Syd, the most animal attention he usually could muster was a good chase or rope tug-of-war with Abby, the new pup. Hannah, older and heavyset, knowing it was much too difficult to participate, would cheer them on with intrepid barking. Sasha chose to ignore their nonsense. Sophie, oldest of the group and having health issues, stayed clear of the action, as did Millie, usually occupying one of the countless dog beds scattered throughout the house. The sextet got along well, enjoying a change from the regular routine.

Our trip began in early June as a month-long summer vacation. My mom's home is the house in which she grew up (my grandparents' house), in the same neighborhood where I grew up. We conveniently had the entire second floor to ourselves, a renovated garret with bedroom, living room area, and office to set up shop. I had packed files and equipment—with Sasha's eager assistance—to work remotely on assorted activities. Through our correspondences, a few interesting and unexpected opportunities altered our original travel schedule.

Ultimately, the dogs and I remained for seven months while Carol began presenting culinary events for the Taste of Home Cooking School tour. She traveled often between Michigan and Texas, and random cities across the nation.

Surrounded by family and loving pups, I was on the road to regaining my health, facing my frustrations, forcing away the depression, and sorting out the issues that brought about this chaos in our lives. I was settling into a comfort zone far and away from the fear that had driven me to the edge of insanity.

The attic isolation wasn't lost on me.

I spent most of my time taking full advantage of the disconnection with my world that had turned upside down back home. I tried to forget about the lost business opportunities and thought about moving forward in a new direction. I had a safety net of family living downstairs, while I often remained upstairs, focused on projects that had been eluding me for months, if not years. I also had a trusty companion dedicated day after day to seeing me through this radical recovery. I could have been living on the moon and that wouldn't have kept Sasha away. She wanted to be with me, not always by my side, but within range of her finely attuned senses. She tracked my every move, always knowing where I'd be or where I'd be going as we carved out this half-year retreat in my hometown.

The opportunity for me to spend lots of quality time with the pups wasn't lost on Sasha.

She cherished every moment.

TWO BLOCKS from my childhood home—and from where we were staying—was a spacious city park that had always been a favorite playground. It remained well-kept and well-suited for child's play, team sports, family picnics, and dog walks. The park was sparsely stippled with stately oaks, sturdy maples, and pristine pines and the trees outlined a paved walking path around the perimeter of vast grassland.

I spent many days of my youth in that park. Plenty of open space provided a canvas for neighborhood kids to draw upon. It yearned for year-round activities and youthful imagination. As grasses and wildflowers began sprouting in spring, my sister and I had learned to fly kites and toss Frisbees. When older kids occupied the "real" ball field, my friends and I used blocks of wood to mark improvised baseball diamonds for summertime softball. As trees of forest green burst into flaming reds and burnt orange, leaves soon began to drop like confetti as we ran touchdowns through the fall. Two tennis courts, usually in desperate need of repair, begged for love most of the year, but the winter winds froze their surfaces solid when they were flooded for ice skating and hockey.

At the south end of the meadow, a hill gently rose from the path to the busy avenue above. A large boulder marked the top of the hill, the pinnacle destination for kids to gather and rest before running back down into the peaceful grassy expanse below. In the deep freeze of winter, kids dotted the snow-covered hillside with Flexible Fliers and toboggans in a patchwork palette of snowsuits and caps. Lynne and I spent many frigid days in a slip-sliding, snow-climbing, sledding loop, continuing until frostbitten fingers and toes began to tingle and sting in burning delusion. It was arctic Arcadia, a kid's frozen fantasyland.

The first activity to schedule when we arrived at Mom's house that summer was the daily dog walk. The temperatures in Michigan were ideal for strolls in the park and the dogs could not wait to check out every tree. Well, that was mainly Sydney—leash taut, nearly choking his way to the park in unbridled excitement—but all the pups fervently pined for every path. (Sydney insisted on running during dog walks, hardly honoring his show dog past. So much for puppy kindergarten training, too, I guess.)

Sasha had a pleasantly paced stride. I enjoyed watching her evenly stepped motion just ahead of me, a steadfast trot, keeping metronomic tempo along the edge of the sidewalk.

Many times, walking the dogs was a family affair. Occasionally my mom and stepdad, and sometimes our nieces, Lauren and Sarah, with Lauren's infant in a baby stroller, joined Carol and me as we leashed as many excited pups as we all could handle. Sometimes it was a rotation of two or three dogs at a time; sometimes it was all six at once: Sydney, Sasha, and Abby led the way, Sophie was riding comfortably in the base of the stroller, and Hannah and Millie slowly took up the rear.

It was quite a parade of pups.

On one occasion, we lingered at the base of the winter snow hill, now plush with viridian summer grasses. While the others waited or slowly moved on, I jogged up the hillside with Sydney and Sasha leading the way, hopping along through the thick turf. The fragrance of fresh-cut grass was becoming stronger as each footstep disturbed the innocent, opulent growth.

When we reached the iconic rock at the top (the summit for ten-pound pups), I paused to survey the history of years past in the park below us. I remembered dizzying spins and slides on the playground equipment, broken kites and lost toys, a class picnic celebration to end another year of elementary school, baseball games until the street lights came on, tennis volleys with more chasing than hitting, snowmen and snowballs and sleds (oh, *sigh*), and a scary spill off my bike at the bottom of the hill when I shouldn't have been riding *ad lib* on the knoll in the first place.

And now, add to those memories, many cherished dog walks.

With a lump in my throat, knowing these days in the park had become just as important to Sasha and Sydney as they were at one time to me, we raced down the hill without tripping and tumbling.

We resumed our place in the parade of pups and marched our way home, with plenty of hope to repeat the pace in the park tomorrow.

And weather permitting, repeat *ad infinitum.*

BACK AT THE HOUSE, Sasha remained close while I was at the computer, at the dinner table, in front of the TV, and on the screened porch enjoying a cool breeze as the wind chimes sang softly while we dozed on the couch. When it was time to run errands in the car, she was ready to ride, joining me on quick trips around town. While the other dogs found comfort in areas downstairs, Sasha remained upstairs as I worked into the night. At bedtime, she nestled between pillow and headboard, a favorite spot within my reach.

Before settling down to a good night's sleep, sometimes the bed could spin Sasha into an urgent frenzy of sorts. A comforter, a pillow, a large cushion, or a giant dog bed spontaneously became a construction zone for our furious digger. Mesmerized on one spot, her rear feet spread slightly and set in stone, she spun her front legs and paws wildly, like the front wheel of an exercise bike. She was going nowhere fast. Not satisfied until hitting her imaginary pay dirt, she could excavate forever—or at least until we snapped her out of the hypnotic trance. It must be a "Maltese thing," because

Sophie did the same. Their ancestors likely prepared the foundations for the pyramids in record time with this dedicated hard-labor work ethic.

When she wasn't digging at the bed, Sasha liked to tumble all over the bed. I'd sit down next to her and she'd go right for the candy cane, always kept close and ready for action. With snorkel firmly clenched, she'd jump on my lap and stand with her front paws against me until I fell backward on the bed.

"You're gonna knock Daddy right over," I'd tell her as she tackled me under the power of her delightful dance.

"You knocked Daddy right over!"

She was proud of her feat and continued her candy cane cha-cha, bouncing back and forth and over me.

If she had the bed to herself, she liked to roll. The belly-up pup squirmed on her back, then from side to side. She'd cheerfully grunt and growl while trying to sink deeper and deeper into the bedspread.

"Look who's rollin'," I'd start to encourage her.

"Sasha girl is rollin'. Keep that doggie rollin'!"

This wasn't a cattle drive, though; no dogies here. Just a silly pup rustling frolic and fun from the bedtime trail.

When it was time to play, a dog toy was always near for a long toss. Sasha would run at top speed to retrieve it, squeaking it all the way back to me. She'd drop the toy at my feet, but declared a competition to grab it. She was too quick and on one occasion, grabbed my thumb before retreating with the toy.

"Ouch! Sasha, you bit Daddy!"

She was unimpressed with an expression that said, *Move quicker next time*, as my thumb began to bleed. This was a first for me. I'd experienced plenty of bloody cat scratches, but never a dog bite that drew blood. Luckily, this chomp was barely a nick.

Sasha did not mean to bite me and she was not ashamed. She would never know a guilty feeling. A firm "No!" plainly set any limits the pups happened to test, with follow-up praise for all their good deeds. There was never cause for her to understand shame, perhaps only displeasure. Sasha remedied any wrongdoing through unyielding love and companionship.

Always near, following my whereabouts and activities religiously, I could count on her presence and readiness to adjust to my every move. The confines of my crisis reinforced our bond as the year wound down and better health returned.

Sasha was a great friend and a loyal companion.

THE RETURN TO NORMALCY, if I can call it that, was not strictly a story of me and my dog.

I wandered away from "life as a hermit" every now and then. I enjoyed the company of family and hometown friends often. Our extended families lived within miles of each other, so we shared many meals and familial activities during this reclusive chapter of my life. The dogs also enjoyed visits with familiar faces and those they hadn't yet met.

No one was ever a stranger to Sasha.

She was ready to be a friend and did not hesitate to make it known. A candy cane dance around the feet, or bouncing from lap to face, she would always welcome friends and family with a wide-waving tail and cheerful radiance.

Companionship

Many of Sasha's new acquaintances were friends I had known long before we moved to Texas. Several calls led to an unexpected reunion of old friends; bandmates from my first country music group. We met on several occasions with instruments, jamming through set lists of decades past, inspiring a real gig for a holiday party in December. Between tour dates of pots and pans, Carol joined us to sing several songs, evoking many music performance memories. I began to think that maybe this was the direction I should take once again.

It was nearing the end of the year and we still had not set a date to return home. Carol's tour would be ending soon and the holidays were upon us. We would decide something after the first of the New Year. It was time to celebrate and Sasha was ready to share the Christmas spirit.

The first sign of presents put the pups in gift-opening anticipation. Christmas was the quintessential occasion for Sasha's packing, stacking, and unpacking mania. She loved everything about the gift-giving holiday, but mainly, she loved tearing into her packages. She knew which gifts belonged to her. I made it easy and they all understood—the dog toys were always wrapped in tissue paper.

At home, Sasha, Sydney, and Millie waited impatiently behind the kitchen gate, like the start of a horse race—jumping, tapping feet, and whining—until they were free to run like kids to the Christmas tree, sorting through gifts, looking for the tissue paper to shred, and discovering treasures within. (This was never good for the *person* receiving a gift wrapped in tissue paper.) It was always a similar sort of happy-frenzy, whether at home, or that Christmas at Mom's, and we'd repeat it once again in

Michigan the following year.

That was a long time away, though. First, we had to return home and move our lives forward. The decision came abruptly and in a manner I'm much ashamed to admit. An overload of emotions erupted when Carol and I began to discuss our departure to Texas.

"How long are you planning to stay here?" she insisted. "We have to return to *our* home. We have to decide what we're going to do."

Feeling healthier after this seven-month sabbatical, but still feeling lost without work opportunities on the horizon, I said, "I don't know what to do. I feel like I have nothing. I feel like I have nowhere to go. We have no business. Do we start over? Do we pursue new interests?"

Carol was afraid I would decide not to go home at all. I wasn't so sure myself, but I knew I had to face the fear that had sent us packing to Michigan in the first place. As our private discussion became heated and known to the household, Carol was in tears when I finally exclaimed, "We're leaving! We've got to get out of here. We'll pack our stuff and head home by the weekend."

A final explosion of agony for all to witness was not the way I ever intended to end our extended stay. But that's what it took to kick my butt out of woe and complacency and to start approaching the problems that had gotten us there in the first place.

We were forever grateful to have caring families, willing to be there for us, share their time and homes with us, and support us in our time of need. With many thanks—and apologies—we packed for our journey home.

Companionship

WE WERE BACK on the road just days after New Year's 2008, to a house I had not seen since June (Carol had been there a few times during her travels), with a positive outlook and a fire inside me to fight recurrent health concerns. The dogs were glad to be going home. Those seven months had been a fun time in their lives, but even they knew our family needed to be home.

Once we settled back into an acceptable routine in Texas, I could not ignore my recently inspired interest in music. I unpacked drums and musical gear that I hadn't seen in decades. I began searching online for local bands looking for drummers. After a few auditions, I stayed with a group that booked a few gigs throughout the year. It required many rehearsals and eventually began to wear on most of its members. I contacted other musicians I had not seen since our early music days in Dallas, and through a gathering of recent and former bandmates, another new band was formed.

Another year of rehearsals and hit-and-miss gigs reinvigorated my musical chops. Plus, the physicality of drumming provided much-needed tension relief in my fight against years of accumulated stress and aggravation. The advent of music performance at this time in my life proved to be a powerful healing process on all levels and revelatory for my self-awareness. I began to understand the truly important matters in my life, separating the day-to-day small stuff (and releasing unwarranted credences) from life's bigger panorama.

I searched deep in the mirror and unveiled virtue and veneration stared back.

I welcomed the fruitful fragrance of every sunbeam rose, while respectfully dismissing every bloodlusting thorn.

I banged on my drums in an anthem of celebration.

I found my awakening in a more defined existence, something I'd fallen far away from, having slipped into a seemingly inconsequential "life coma" for many years. Taking hints from Sasha, I began to appreciate the simple things, without worries.

I would continue along a musical path as other cooking opportunities continued for Carol. Everything seemed to be getting better and back on track. And the pups were catching up with us in dog years.

This new schedule of music gear coming-and-going became a point of interest for Sasha. Much of my drum equipment was packed and carried in large storage containers and portmanteaus, often stacked near the door for the next rehearsal. Guess who had to hop atop every case? It wasn't a proper nap unless Sasha could sleep on a heap of drums.

On one occasion, the drums were removed from the cases and Sasha stood by as they were assembled for practice. We were holding rehearsal at home—with guitar amps, speakers, and microphone stands scattered around the floor—and a houseful of people for her to welcome and navigate, as well. When the music started, Sasha took a front row seat on the back of our couch, taking in every minute of music-making excitement these people brought to her house to enjoy. If there was a party, she wasn't going to miss any of it.

Sasha was a real rock-and-roller.

CAROL'S SCHEDULE had changed as well. She accepted a position with a local gourmet grocery store as their cooking school manager. Working away *from* home gave rise to the daily return *to* home. This became a much-touted rite for the pups to anticipate. When Carol arrived in the driveway, the pups would jump frantically at the door.

When I held Sasha, I'd tell her that Mama was home. She'd look out the door and begin little nervous howls—she could hardly contain herself. I'd open the door to let Carol in and the pups would head out to greet her, quickly turning back and dashing into the house to grab the nearest toy. For Sasha, it was her candy cane and she did everything to keep Sydney from grabbing it from her. This usually meant bouncing from chair to chair until Carol would sit on the floor within body-leaping reach. By then, the candy cane dance was over—Mama was covered in Sasha kisses as Millie was hopping around with her own favorite kangaroo toy, and Sydney stood by barking in protest, until we could urge him to once again become the Mighty Dragon.

My returns home set the stage for a much different scenario. The dogs stayed behind the kitchen gate while we were out, so I would always come home to the same scene. Sasha sat on her dog bed and had the optimal viewing location to see who was coming in the door. Millie was in the middle and Sydney to the left, barking and hopping straight up and down like a pogo stick. When I'd remove the gate, Sydney ran around my feet, giving me an exultant welcome home. Millie stood out of the way, wagging her tail as her body shimmied out-of-sync, waiting for a quick pat on the head. And Sasha headed straight across the room to the pet kennel, turning around inside to watch from within. Her hiding habit was the funniest thing—strange and humorous. She usually let me catch a quick pet along her back as she retreated undercover. She was happy I was home, but maybe a bit embarrassed, until the excitement settled down. She'd come out when I called for all the pups to go outside to pee.

All other times, Sasha was my best buddy. She always came to sit with me when watching TV, snuggled between my leg and the arm of the chair, or on the ottoman near my feet. She seldom moved unless I moved first. Extended hours at the computer might find Sasha napping on the desk, in my lap, or under the chair.

She continued to treat our pillows as the premier bedtime spot. Many nights, she slept above Carol's pillow, so I'd reach over to stroke her back every time I'd settle into bed. Occasionally she would nestle down between us, but that might entail an unfriendly encounter with Millie, always first to the warmest place in bed. Sasha only left my side to share equal time with Carol. She was always near—never more than a moment away—and a true friend.

SASHA DISPLAYED uncontested courage at home. She defended her house and family at the front door, in the backyard, and when confronting the TV. But her weakness appeared against the face of technology. It invariably occurred as we all dozed dreamily in darkness.

Cheep!

A single squawk disturbed the peace, then nothing at all.

I slowly regained consciousness. Did I hear something? Was I dreaming? I started to doze again.

Cheep!

Then consciousness came quickly as I caught a glint in the eyes of our furry eight-pound child-having-nightmares, suddenly seated center on my chest.

"What's wrong, girl?" I asked, just as another bird call cheeped faintly, but annoyingly, outside the bedroom.

"Oh no ... not now!" I exclaimed as I realized my dreamtime songbird woke up Sasha for real.

It always frightened her. Sydney, too.

They would become nervous wrecks when anything beeped out of the ordinary. They knew something was amiss. These potential emergencies—power outages that set off computer battery backup warning signals, a falsely triggered home alarm siren, and in this instance, the middle-of-the-night bird calls, randomly scattered around the house ceilings—really scared them.

Although hardwired to electricity, when batteries croaked, our smoke detectors "cheeped" systematically as a spiteful warning to restore the backup power.

More like insomniac birds giving me the bird.

I wanted to rip the offending plastic disc off the ceiling and skeet-shoot that buzzard once and for all.

But as a responsible homeowner—and a good dad *and companion* to my concerned and terrified pups—it only meant immediate, late-night ladder teetering, tangling with lifesaving technology in midair, surely designed for nearly impossible 9-volt replacement, so all could rest in stressless relief.

Meanwhile, Carol and Millie slept through it all.

ANTICIPATED BEEPS—alarm clocks, appliance timers, telephone calls, and the home security panel—were not a concern. I don't know how they knew the difference, but the dogs could discern the lesser significance. They tolerated "normal" warnings without anxiety for dozens of seconds while we made way to stop the recurring tones.

On one occasion when we returned home to our patient pups in a dark house, I approached the squealing keypad to disarm the security system. A surprise was in store, altogether unrelated to the alarm.

A surprise of this sort was rare. Only on this occasion was it discovered in a less-than-ideal manner. With the keypad in sight, I took one step closer. My foot hit the floor with more cushion and glide than I had expected.

"Shit!"

Carol knew right away that my one explicit word expressed more meaning than just expletive. It conveniently described my darkroom discovery.

At that moment, it was no laughing matter—at least for me—but we did have a history of bathroom humor when arriving home.

Before we were married, when Carol was becoming familiar with the ways of Yoda and Açúcar in my Michigan home, I cautioned her about the occasional land mine mishap when the dogs were left alone.

On one opportune occasion (happily with no unattended accident to avoid), I pulled a priceless *Caddyshack* swimming pool prank. When Carol approached, I stood from leaning over, paper towel-wrapped candy bar in hand.

"It's no big deal," I recited Bill Murray's line and took a bite.

Carol never knew what to expect after that.

The smirks and snickers have all been hers (while conveniently leaving the Nature's Miracle duty to me) ever since.

Companionship

I'm glad our pups have rarely favored us with a Baby Ruth surprise. When it's unavoidable, I perform miracles with paper towel and spray bottle in hand.

And without reason to giggle.

WHEN SASHA AND SYDNEY were only a year old, I resumed efforts to work on our backyard. The spring project was a major landscaping endeavor, a winding design of boardwalk decking, geometric herb gardens, and fertile young fruit trees outlining a small oval lawn (reserved for good doggie bathroom duties). I always had my sweet puppy apprentice standing by to make sure every flagstone fit perfectly.

While Sydney commonly stood guard along the fence as our dedicated border patrol, Sasha sat near to measure twice, cut once. A dry fit was all it took for her to confirm my progress was on track. Cautiously sidestepping building materials, she checked every board before it was fastened. She made sure every garden bed was ready for mulch, tiptoeing and teetering through perennials and dirt, her predominant concern being to keep her feet clean. On a safe and less muddy track, she'd follow the rosewood brick path along a raised flower bed for a geological survey of our yard under construction.

Finding a comfortable spot seemed Sasha's best option to keep watch, an excuse to soak up the sun while I sweltered on the job. More often, her surveillance was from a shady patio.

I'd interrupt her symbolic coffee break, "Does that look all right?"

She'd leisurely stroll over toward the direction of my

attention, and then stick her nose in a newly planted rosemary, basil, or lemon verbena, hop up on a new bench, scan the span of a split-rail fence, confirm the placement of a Texas-shaped patio stone, test the tread of a new deck, or inventory our newest denizen of the deep as variegated shades of gold glimmered just below light ripples in the lily pond.

She kept tabs on the impulsively fluid blueprint. When each task met her approval, I could proceed with improvements. And she could return to Margaritaville under the palm tree.

Sasha was a great supervisor.

Moreover, she was the best companion.

DAILY STRIDES FORWARD during our transformation out back gave Sasha plenty to notice, but the pond consistently generated the most curiosity. Sasha retired belly flops after her first leap into the deep—she was always a quick study when learning her lessons—so she chose to sit warily near the edge of our backyard biology project to observe life below the surface. Goldfish aside, we never knew what reptile or amphibian might emerge from the teeming ebb and flow.

Green frogs, water snakes, geckos and lizards, and one humongous bullfrog, took up residence in our tiny wildlife watering hole from time to time, but often, the focus of Sasha's unwavering interest randomly hopped around the perimeter. Her obsessive toy "baby" came to life in the great outdoors whenever "toadie" stopped by for a visit.

Once Sasha spotted a toad, she had to follow it

everywhere. She never tried to pick it up; she never tried to cause harm. She just wanted another friend.

Can we keep it? Can we keep it!?
She bubbled with excitement.

"Toadie has to stay out here. We'll come out and look for toadie again later," I'd try to reassure her as she cocked her head and stared at me, absorbing every word.

She reluctantly returned to the house with the rest of her canine crew, waiting patiently for the next opportunity to find her new friend. Hours later, when we'd return to the yard, Sasha raced to the toad's last-known station. But our backyard hobo had hopped aboard the last train out.

Feeling a bit despondent, Sasha moved on to bathroom necessities, remembering that tomorrow could bring another train of toadies to town. She could rest assured of a good night's sleep, sure to dream of backyard buddies she yearned to meet.

Life is curious, life brings surprise. With loving curiosity for all strange creatures living in her yard, Sasha never failed to surprise us.

She defined and demonstrated companionship beyond the human connection, proving time and again that it is indiscriminatory and all-encompassing.

Music has always defined moments in my life, a companion of a different sort, always ready to entertain the mind and soothe the soul. Coupled with our sweet girl, music redefined companionship for us—it came with a soundtrack.

From the early beats on my toy drum to the pulsing thud kick drum keeping tempo in my band, a rhythm track makes up my musical timeline, with many greatest hits along the way. Carol added a colorful chorale for every measure of our verses. Sasha and her siblings formed new chords for the repeating chorus. The songs continue to expand and multiply.

Old songs, new songs, original songs, true songs; there were always songs. Songs to share, songs to write, songs to keep, songs that light every moment of our lives; there is always a song to sing.

A radio hit or a favorite album, a band rehearsal or a drum solo, or a simple special song sung sweetly by Mama, the music played on when Sasha was near.

When the dogs stayed home alone, the radio provided ambient comfort. When working around the house, we were rockin' and Sasha was rollin'. When I recorded tracks for the band, Sasha had a front row seat at the mixing board. And whenever Carol was mixing in the kitchen, she always had an original song to sing.

"Mama loves her pups, yes she does, yes she does. Ma‑ma loves her little puppies."

Sasha would hop to her feet in an urgent search for her candy-striped baton. Soon, her sweet dance was splendidly choreographed to Mama's tail-twirling tune.

Sydney and Millie were never excluded from household musical refrains; they equally welcomed the melodies. Carol often had theme songs for each pup, but many times a popular song fit the bill for spontaneous singing. The lyrics seemed to benefit our sweet girl the most.

We called her "sweet girl" often.

Many more times simply "girl."

Sasha soon began to recognize songs when we'd playfully sing her favorite moniker in the chorus's melodies:

"Girl" by The Beatles, "Oh Girl" by The Chi-Lites, "My Girl" by The Temptations, "Just A Girl" by No Doubt, and "Sweet Girl" by Fleetwood Mac.

The songs, the singing, the soundtracks, the traveling music, my band, the drums, the cadence of her stride, and the candy cane dances—it all became the rhythm of her life. She loved to share the phenomenon of our music. It was her music as well, no doubt.

Sasha loved all music and she was the sweetest melody of our lives.

♪♫

Sweet Girl

chapter six

health

Sweet Girl

Health

SASHA HAD JUST TURNED SEVEN. She was in the prime of her life. She was the picture of good health. At least that's how it appeared, considering that she never missed her annual health exams, received up-to-date vaccinations, took her heartworm meds regularly, and had never suffered a serious illness. Not to mention her healthy appetite and regular moderate exercise. She led an active lifestyle. She routinely tested her agility with circus-like feats of balance and flexibility, bouncing from chair to couch to chair to floor and back again. She could turn on a dime. In her excitement, she would run across the room, then whip-turn in a playful check as if to say, *I'm ready to play!*

These playful ways were contagious. And it didn't always start with Sasha. A lively urge could hit any one of the dogs and the other two would most often join in a circuitous chase. Over the furniture and through the house, around the rooms they went. The hot-on-your-tail dog race detoured to the backyard where deck paths became the stopgap racetrack for a lap or two. Sydney, a bit larger and built for speed, usually kept a length ahead, but Sasha could hold the pace.

These brief sprints usually ended with a barbed, yet amiable exchange. As if she were saying, *Yes, we're playing, but I'm still your big sister. I'm Top Dog here. I will keep up with you!*

For little dogs, a few minutes of raucous running is always a lap-up-the-water-worthy workout, and these small challenges never failed to exhibit Sasha's tremendous physical fitness.

FORTUNATELY, with all the bouncing up and down and all around the house over the years, Sasha never broke any bones or, more unbelievably, never seriously crashed headfirst into walls, doors, or furniture. I worried about an underestimated leap, a misjudged spin-around, or an unbalanced topple from the back of the couch, ever since the treacherous tumble off the bed when she was only a couple of months old. I vowed never to let that happen again and we made efforts to eliminate potential puppy playhouse disasters. But accident prevention is limited with unforgiving pieces of furniture and a determined-to-be-an-acrobat, fearless Maltese.

Usually, simple living room layout adjustments could avert a misplaced step. We often positioned the couch against a wall, since Sasha never hesitated to jump to the top for a better view. She truly had the spirit and, seemingly, the balance of a cat. Chairs, couch, and ottoman were easy and expected targets to tread. Living room tables and lower shelves of bookcases also stayed on her radar. She loved to lie on hard surfaces, so office desks and end tables became favorite areas to nap while we worked or watched television. Consideration would be needed when placing tables near chairs. Sasha wanted to be close by and a table usually fit the bill. There was no fighting it, just accommodating it. And that was never a problem. But we did draw the line at the dining room table. Not that she would have refused a seat as the centerpiece, if invited.

She knew she wasn't supposed to get on the dining room table, but that didn't stop her from trying if we held her on our laps. If there was food on a plate, she was keen to check it out. An unoccupied chair within reach of the table was an open invitation Sasha happily waited for. Carol made this mistake a few too many times, much to Sasha's delight.

"Sasha, get down!" was the typical response to front paws on the table.

The reaction elevated to a gasp and a horrifying "Sasha!" when Carol noticed Miss Manners enjoying an entire chicken breast snatched from her dinner plate.

Sasha was not the only pup to notice these oversights. Carol was also the dining room victim when a young, peppy Millie stole a few quick slurps of spicy Cajun gumbo. Within seconds, reprimand unnecessary, our brazen hot tamale made a mad dash to the water bowl for an extended tongue soaking.

It wouldn't be long after that incident when a dinner plate was safe from Mil. Her accumulated doggie dinnertime indulgences soon prevented her from indulging anywhere above the floor.

Yet attempts to purloin food were not common. The bigger issue was keeping your place at the dinner table. Sasha always felt she deserved a seat, and she often got one. Leaving the table for only a moment could guarantee a return to our little four-legged seat warmer with an expression that said, *I've got mine, how you doin'?* We'd pull out an adjacent chair and she'd graciously hop over to her own temporary seat for a closer view of the dining action. She would sit there patiently, nose and eyes barely above the table, hoping for a tiny nibble of anything, having a front row advantage over her buddies below. Most of the time, her tactics won the anticipated prize—just not the whole enchilada—and we never worried about cold seats.

Above all, Sasha just wanted to participate. She loved a

nibble from the table, but more importantly, she wanted to take part in the family dining experience. If we were sitting at the table, she assumed that she should be there as well. If a seat was not available, she would decide to eat a few bites of her own dry dog food, bringing one kibble at a time to eat it next to us.

If we happened to offer an unexpected treat while her mouth was full, she would drop the nugget promptly as if her jaw had gone slack, popping the morsel out like a Maltese Pez dispenser. Anything we had to offer from the dinner table was certainly better than a disgusting chunk of dry dog food. It was worth offering a treat from the table just to see Sasha's silly spit take.

Dining room chairs and living room furniture were not much of a leap for Sasha. Placement was always the biggest concern. But as a danger zone of hazardous height and perilous perimeter, our bed required the most radical modification. The combined elevation of mattress and box spring was a mighty leap for an aging toy breed pup. It became increasingly difficult for the dogs to hop up on the bed, especially without concentrated effort and a running jump. We set makeshift steps (inverted laundry baskets covered with bath towels) on both sides of the bed. We placed large throw pillows on the floor. These small changes helped and the dogs appreciated the adjustments. Though never seriously hurt, Sasha was not exempt from the occasional mishap. A spontaneous leap to track a misguided tossed ball triggered a body slam into the side of the mattress. Missing her mark did not happen often, but it was a concern. Jumping off the bed could potentially cause injury as well, so something needed to change. Soon.

Although padded cushions dotted the bedside, Sasha didn't always feel the need to hit those spots when hastily disembarking from the bed. She did eventually discover an ingenious exit strategy that was less stressful on her front legs, neck, and shoulders. She often leapt from the bed horizontally, perfectly parallel to the floor, a skydiver in training, landing lightly and evenly on all fours. She'd purposely jump in front of our floor-stand mirror so she could watch herself soar off the bed. She solved her own less-than-ideal bed height predicament, and she entertained herself in the process. All she needed was the parachute.

Although her free-fall jumps were entertaining, we needed a better bedstead arrangement. We agreed that our box spring was unnecessary, so after some shuffling of the mattress, pillows, and plywood, the top of the bed was a good ten inches closer to the floor. The doggie steps and floor pillows remained, only to buffer continued bounds from the bed. But lowering the bed was the minor change that allowed us to rest assured that chances of injury were majorly lowered. An ounce of adjustment for us was a pound of prevention for the pups.

Unfortunately, taking every feasible step to prevent injury is only part of the health picture. Having avoided any serious injuries for seven years is a terrific track record for a compact canine companion known to playfully thrash around the house and daringly dash underfoot. And, considering all the factors beyond our control that can cause sickness, it was also amazing that in those seven years, Sasha never got sick.

The closest incident to becoming ill occurred when she was young and inquisitive in the backyard. And it scared us to death. Only Sasha knew exactly what had happened, but the evidence suggested that her nose came too close to a fire ant mound. When she came running to the house, shaking her head and pawing at her face, I noticed immediately—fortunately—no more than a half dozen ants crawling on her. No sooner had I brushed away all the terrorist ants, than Sasha's face began to swell like a balloon.

Even more fortunate, we had previously discussed dog allergies with the vet and made sure we always had Benadryl on hand. The doctor had recommended small doses should the dogs ever develop minor allergy symptoms. Whether the affliction of a few fire ant bites qualified as minor did not make much difference at that point.

In terror, I raced to grab the antihistamine as Carol held Sasha and prepared to administer the magic medicine. With no time to spare, Sasha swallowed the potion, and, within minutes, the swelling began to subside. I then shifted my focus to fire ant eradication.

After that, Sasha was a sadder but wiser girl. She learned to keep her nose at a safe distance from anything in the yard. She also remained much more healthy. And we became much more vigilant.

Like injuries, becoming ill, developing allergies, or simply aging can take their tolls quickly. Symptoms, mild or serious, can appear without warning or apparent reason. Or there may be no symptoms at all—just a subtle change in behavior or routine.

A few days after Christmas in 2009 (Sasha's favorite day of the year—a day to exemplify her great health—full of excitement and vigor), she experienced an incident unlike any we had seen before.

Sasha lost control of her bladder while she slept.

SASHA LOVED EVERYTHING about Christmas, from the presents to the decorations. Whether she understood why we had such a celebration once a year didn't matter. She just loved the drama of moving things around, unpacking boxes and crates, and decorating the house with trees, lights, and strange items that only emerged from closets for a few short weeks when the outdoor temperature began to drop. This annual ritual was always an indoor project.

That year was different, though. Strings of LED lights were becoming a hot holiday item, having only been introduced to consumers a few years earlier. With affordable prices, combined with low energy costs, we decided to upgrade our holiday illuminations. Why stop with the Christmas tree? Our pine trees in the backyard would also look great trimmed with these new, blindingly colorful light-emitting diodes.

One strand of LED lights led to another, which then led to large outdoor ornaments and lighted candy canes and snowmen. Before long, our backyard would become a scene saturated with sparkling swag—a tangled web of extension cords and wires, with festoons of lights and dangling ornaments littering our landscape.

Most people proudly flaunt such holiday assaults of light and sound out front for everyone driving by to witness. My thoughts were a bit different. I wanted to enjoy the decorations where not only we had a better vantage point from indoors, but where the dogs could enjoy them as well. Our backyard was well suited to a display of this nature with several trees to decorate and many paths to outline with lights. So for the first time, and with the help of all three dogs, on a sunny Texas day in December, our backyard was gradually transformed into an unlikely winter wonderland. It truly lived up to that title when we welcomed a few rare snowstorms that winter, the twinkling lights shining brightly, bouncing between dancing snowflakes, reflecting like sparkling mirrors in the mounting snow.

Like Snoopy and his contest-winning decorated doghouse, the dogs loved their shimmering snow-covered playground. Sasha especially liked to stroll leisurely along one stretch of deck lined with illuminated candy canes and a cheery grapevine snowman. For that Christmas, this was Sasha's Candy Cane Lane. And it was worth sharing, so we invited friends over throughout the season to see the dazzling new display.

On the occasion of Sasha's first known health "incident," some friends had come over to see the backyard lights, share a nice post-holiday dinner, and stay to watch the recently released DVD foodie movie *Julie & Julia*. While we were immersed in the stories and recipes of Julia Child, I noticed Sasha suddenly jump up out of a sound sleep on the end table next to my chair. The lamplight reflected in a puddle where she had been lying, and her hindquarters were damp. At first, I thought perhaps she had bumped my wine glass, but I quickly realized that this was no spill. Sasha had inadvertently wet the table, and she was embarrassed and more surprised about it than we were.

As alarming as this random "symptom" seemed, we thought it was nothing more than an accident during her sleep. Although she was potty trained at an early age, Sasha was known to dribble a bit when she was excited. That only occurred during her first few years when she'd greet us upon returning home. Lack of bladder control was no longer an issue when she was a mature dog in her prime. The Christmastime incident seemed isolated and unrelated to anything else, so we didn't think much more about it.

Several months passed with nothing unusual to note, although, when Sasha chose to rest on tables, I'd check to see if the same sort of accident had occurred. I wasn't concerned that this was a health issue, rather a clean-up issue. Sporadically, she did have a few more mishaps. With her history of excitement leaks, I didn't find it unusual and wrote off the few occasions to an unconscious response to bladder pressure from lying on the hard surfaces.

SIX MONTHS AFTER this noticeable change in her health—although I didn't define it as such at the time—the first symptom of concern arrived stealthily like a masked bandit. Summer had officially just begun, although in Texas, summertime temperatures start to become agonizing as early as April. By the time the summer solstice arrives, the afternoon heat is usually intolerable. Air conditioning is the only saving grace, and with AC units in round-the-clock operation, a prayer now and then to keep the cool air flowing throughout the hot weather months is usually warranted.

A good haircut helps, too. We often liked to let Sasha's hair grow out, but although fine textured, it was just too much to tolerate once the heat set in. Her trip to the groomer usually coincided with the arrival of summer heat, but that year the heat came first.

Seemingly out of the blue, Sasha began to pant regularly. We probably would not have noticed, except that she panted at night, when she normally would have slept quietly. She began to move around more as well, trying to find a comfortable position on or off the bed.

After we had her groomed, she was able to sleep more comfortably and the panting stopped—at least for a while. This "symptom"—Sasha's plundered comfort—seemed an unfortunate coincidence with the summer heat, her long hair, and perhaps her stress from tolerating that combination. We convinced ourselves that everything was back to normal.

It wasn't. It was just the beginning.

The next random symptom raised a red flag and gave us reason to pursue medical advice.

INDEPENDENCE DAY was another fun holiday for our dogs. We would pile the pups in the minivan and head out to the nearest shopping center parking lot to watch one of many fireworks displays scattered across the cityscape vistas of the Dallas–Fort Worth Metroplex. Sasha loved to perch upon the car door, peering out the open window at the rockets' red glare, rainbow bursts in the air. Once home, the snaps, crackles, and pops of neighborhood firecrackers usually continued into the night. Without hesitation, the dogs ran to the backyard to let their voices of disapproval be heard.

It was always an exciting night.

That year would be no different from previous years. It was a sizzling Fourth-of-July evening—sudden thunderous blasts echoing across a concrete landscape, a dark Texas sky painted in fancy colors raining down to earth, and Sasha's snapshot of good health to enjoy it all.

Two days later would paint a much different picture.

An unnoticed attack could have gone seriously wrong. It

was a stroke of good luck, however, that I happened to see Sasha gripped by what seemed to be a mild seizure. She often liked to lie along the top of the couch. Our latest living room layout had the couch away from walls, so when I saw Sasha sitting on the narrow ledge and suddenly lifting her left front leg stiffly toward her head, I quickly ran to her side. She began to lean sideways and I grabbed her in that instant. Had I not been at her side, she would have fallen to the floor. As I steadied her, her eyes appeared glazed and I feared the worst.

She's having a stroke!

I ran to the bedroom, holding her close and speaking her name, trying to comfort her, setting her on the bed in hopes of her regaining her composure. I had never experienced anything like this with my previous pets. However, I immediately recalled the heartbreaking last few moments of Sophie's life (Mom's then twelve-year-old Maltese), lovingly cradled in my mom's arms. It was a brief, agonizing scene in the predawn hours of Christmas Eve 2007, awakening an unexpected and sudden pathos during our Michigan residency at that time.

Seeing Sasha suddenly having this eerily similar attack of unknown origin was terrifying. My heart was racing and my thoughts were instantly focused on getting her to the vet clinic as soon as possible.

As Murphy's Law would suggest, pet emergencies only happen when the vet clinic is closed. At ten o'clock in the evening, the only medical option was a twenty-four-hour emergency animal hospital, ten miles away and presumably hundreds of dollars beyond our budget. Sasha was conscious, sitting steadily on the bed, but she seemed disoriented. I told her, "Stay," while I was gathering the belongings I would need to dash out the door with her.

In that instant, Carol arrived home from teaching a cooking class, and, much to my surprise, Sasha flew headlong off the bed, out of the bedroom, and along to the front door. She welcomed Mama home with the usual excitement and enthusiasm, apparently a return to normal, as if nothing had happened at all.

A sigh of relief and close attention for the next few hours confirmed that Sasha was not suffering ill effects and this isolated incident seemed, once again, insignificant.

But not forgotten.

I called our vet the next day and had her promptly scheduled for her annual examination as an opportunity to discuss this latest heart-pounding episode. We were thankful and relieved when she passed all the health tests and exams with flying colors. As a precaution, we went home with a prescription for Valium—for Sasha (though it just as well could have been for us!)—in the event that her panting continued or if she seemed to have bouts of anxiety. She only required a few doses over the next few weeks before we discovered there might be more to these random symptoms than simply heat-of-the-summer stress.

IN AN EFFORT to put these episodes of anxiety behind us, I thought that dog walks would be good for her. When Sasha and Sydney were puppies, we kept to a schedule with regular walks through our neighborhood. By the time Millie moved in, our dog walking at home had all but been lost to less strenuous backyard recreation. Our Michigan walks in the park had been exciting times for the dogs, but upon returning home, that type of exercise had become just a pleasant memory. Now more than ever, Sasha needed to revisit the occasional dog walk. (Sydney and Millie would not object to that idea for themselves, either.) Dusting off the leash was once again a clear signal to dash for the door.

With Sasha first in line to pound the pavement, we could not get to the end of the driveway before she stopped in her tracks and started to cough. She always walked just ahead of me at the end of a relaxed leash, which only became taut as we set out on a sidewalk sally. I thought perhaps she was a bit too eager to mark her stride and her collar had pulled too tightly against her throat.

When the slightest tension caused her to stop on several occasions, I knew that the collar was going to be a problem. Though unusual for Sasha—it was a rare occurrence we had seen with Sydney as he dragged us down the street—she had become subject to choking when leashed by her collar.

On her next dog walk, we tried a new spandex harness that fit snugly around her chest. That was the solution. No more coughing or choking. With that problem solved, stress relief again became the purpose of adventure.

Anxiety begone! We were exercising again.

Surely that would help.

ALTHOUGH WE WERE feeling good about helping Sasha feel better—praying that whatever was making her suffer at random with strange symptoms would go away—the fixes were temporary at best. She started to have restless, rough nights where no position and no location seemed comfortable. I woke up several nights to see her sitting underneath a table or off in a corner, panting and anxious, often staring blankly as if dazed. She would dig at, crawl on top of, or try to get under anything stacked on the floor, such as books or paperwork, clothes or shoes.

When the anxiety became too much to bear, Sasha would wake me, sit on my chest, stare at me, or crawl deep under the covers—anything to warn me of her trouble, looking for answers to escape the distress.

I'd try to provide comfort and reassurance, taking her to sit with me in the living room in front of the television, or holding her close and walking in figure eights around the kitchen island and dining room table.

"It's okay, girl. Just take it easy. Relax. I'm here. Daddy's got you. Everything's gonna be all right."

I'd speak quietly to her as we slowly followed a meandering path. Our nighttime kitchen lap count sometimes reached triple digits.

Her anxiety could last for hours at a time.

Eventually, we would return to bed where she'd settle into a sound sleep, and I'd hope to do the same. The next day, she would be fine. However, when a second seizure came six weeks after the first, we began regular visits to, and a frequent dialogue with, the veterinary clinic.

(On this second occasion, I heard her cry out from another room. In trying to get to me, she fell over in the doorway and Sydney ran to her to see what had happened. When I got to her, she was wobbling on her feet. But within seconds, she was back to normal, albeit a bit disheveled.)

During this same time frame, Sasha needed to have her teeth cleaned. We were concerned about her sudden random health issues, and equally concerned about subjecting her to the procedures required for cleaning her teeth—specifically anesthesiology. The vet clinic required blood tests prior to this procedure to determine whether her organs were functioning normally.

Sasha's blood test results were normal. This was great news; however, her liver enzymes were elevated, which raised more concerns. Her results mandated another test to determine the specific condition of her liver and kidneys. Once again, these results were good, offering confident relief that she was healthy enough to undergo anesthetics. Her teeth cleaning could go forward.

Although Sasha's test results were promising, I remained solicitous and began to research her random symptoms online, trying to connect the dots. While loss of bladder control, heavy panting, anxiousness, and increased liver enzymes could be attributed to many issues, I thought that seizures might narrow the field. Much of the information I gathered pointed to issues with the pituitary gland at the base of the brain. This led to more research about one specific disease.

Years earlier, Sophie had been diagnosed with Cushing's disease, so I was familiar with the troubles it could cause and how it took its toll on hapless victims. Many of Sophie's symptoms had been different from those Sasha was experiencing, although my research into Sasha's symptoms continued to point to Cushing's.

The seizures, although those only happened a few times, were my biggest concern. The primary cause of Cushing's, often seen in small breeds, is a microscopic benign tumor in the pituitary gland. The tumor can cause seizures. It also throws the adrenal gland out of control, resulting in overproduction of the hormone cortisol.

This could easily explain the excessive panting and anxiety Sasha had been having. It could also have contributed to the elevated liver enzyme levels. My beliefs were validated when our vet discussed this possibility during the tests leading up to Sasha's teeth cleaning.

When she was cleared to go ahead with the cleaning, we opted to postpone tests for Cushing's disease. The teeth cleaning went well, and for seven months (opportunely during the 2010 holiday season, passing her eighth birthday, and into the 2011 spring season), the random symptoms seemed to be gone.

We were thankful and hopeful that maybe she had somehow beaten this disease, whatever was bringing her down, or sent it into remission.

Out of sight, out of mind.

I tried to convince myself that maybe the cleaning had fixed it all. After all, everything did seem much better after her teeth were professionally cleaned.

In hindsight, I probably shouldn't have been so sanguine.

But we had no reason to believe that the few instances she was indisposed warranted change. The good days far exceeded the bad. While for a year and a half, the variables in Sasha's constitution (good and not-so-good) presented a picture of unstable health, conversely, as her blood test results revealed, all seemed to be fine. But with the inevitable return of night anxiety and occasional incontinence symptoms, I knew a change was needed. I resumed my own research to see what we could do at home to make things better for her.

An apparent breakthrough came when I decided to

change her diet.

The dogs were raised on what we were advised and what we determined to be a high-quality-brand, lamb-and-rice dry dog food diet. Three small bowls of kibbles, about three-fourths-cup each, were ready day and night for the pups to nibble on. At dinnertime, I'd embellish each bowl with a few small bites of cooked chicken and a few tablespoons of broth. This offered an incentive to dig into the dry food, something special for them to look forward to each day.

I always believed dogs should eat dog food, so I intended to find the best quality dog food we could afford. I studied the package we chose, comparing ingredients and noticing the content and proportions were much better than that of other brands. But dog foods are processed foods. When Sasha once again started to exhibit random symptoms and we could not find a specific problem, my first thought was to change her diet.

Eliminate the processed foods.

Still trying to address the possibility that Sasha might have Cushing's disease, and following good reviews, I purchased an herbal supplement, a liquid mixture of herbs specifically blended to benefit the adrenal glands of dogs. I started giving this to Sasha daily and then tackled the diet.

To my astonishment (although it shouldn't have seemed remarkable because I had suspected it), a few weeks into the herbal remedy and as soon as I changed to wheat-free treats and a homemade diet, I could see a discernible difference. Not only were the dogs thrilled to dine on fresh, warm, home-cooked meals, but more noticeably, Sasha seemed in healthier spirits and the anxiety symptoms were rapidly diminishing.

I continued to keep a small bowl of dry food ready for an occasional nibble, but the primary entrée for dinner was an original recipe I devised, consisting of healthful brown rice, oatmeal, chicken, and vegetables:

Sasha's Chicken, Rice, and Veggie Dinner

2 cups cooked brown rice
1 cup cooked oatmeal
1 cup diced or shredded cooked chicken
1 cup diced carrots, cooked
1 cup diced broccoli (stems and florets), cooked
1 cup diced cauliflower (stems and florets), cooked
½ cup diced red potatoes, cooked
½ cup sliced green beans, cooked
½ cup diced sweet potato, cooked

Mix all ingredients in a large bowl; keep refrigerated.

Depending on the accuracy of measurements and portion sizes, this mixture would last up to a week at a time. Occasionally, I'd make bigger batches and freeze some of it. Once-a-week preparations made daily dinnertime prep quick and simple. Once a day, I'd scoop out one-half cup of the mixture for each dog, warming it briefly in the microwave to remove the chill from the refrigerator.

A few drops of fish oil topped the dinner plate for added health benefits. Although the mixture seemed bland without seasonings, it was undoubtedly delicious and nutritious for the dogs. And the ingredients were fresh.

No processed foods.

When I first found out Sasha's liver enzymes were a little high, my research pointed to another natural herbal supplement to help liver function. I began adding a few drops of milk thistle liquid extract (alcohol free and vegetable glycerin-based) to the dinner plate each night. Every subsequent blood test result showed liver enzyme improvement.

I knew we were on to something. The herbal supplements seemed to improve her health and the homemade diet seemed to maintain it.

Feed the dogs better food and they'll be in better health.

Seems obvious, but unless something's wrong, it's convenient to remain oblivious. Sasha's health issues became my wake-up call to take notice of potential causes and to change—and I hoped we weren't beyond the point of no return.

With each adjustment, I wanted to believe we had gained a foothold in maintaining her health. But it just wasn't so. Sasha's condition was a gradual decline in progress, difficult to detect unless symptoms became severe and recurring.

And that they did.

Her anxiety and threats of seizures were always within my ken, but her ailments often varied in function and form. When she was not feeling well, but the slight troubles slipped past my acumen, Sasha took measures of her own to remedy her symptoms. She often found that grazing on long blades of grass temporarily settled her suffering. And in these instances, she was discreetly indicating to me that something was still not right.

Not knowing what was happening to her was the most frustrating part. Her fill of ills were on a scale of mild to great intensity. I had a dinner plate full of cures to fight those ills. But we still did not have a diagnosis.

We were treating symptoms and not a disease.

BY THAT TIME, mid-2011, more opportunities had arisen for our business and I continued to do freelance work with video projects. This arrangement provided the needed flexibility to work from home and spend as much time as possible watching over and caring for Sasha. She always waited patiently with Sydney and Millie while we were away, but the chance that a life-threatening issue might arise when we were not there to help her was always on my mind. I was afraid of what I might find upon returning home. I thanked God every time I opened the door to see her happy face and wagging tail, eager to once again share her sweet candy cane welcome.

It had been nearly a year since a seizure-type episode had taken place. I hoped we'd seen the end of those. The first hint that this distressing symptom was once again rearing its ugly head happened just as she was awaking from a solid night's sleep. Still on the bed and lying on her side, Sasha woke up coughing and choking. She started arching her neck, tilting her head backward, and it gave me the impression of another seizure. I quickly picked her up and she seemed fine.

The next day, as I ended a phone call, Sasha was excited as usual and danced around my feet with her candy cane. Suddenly, her exhilaration ceased. She dropped her toy and began to cough as she had the day before. I patted her back and she stopped choking. I thought she was all right, so I started to turn away, but I noticed her stagger to the bedroom doorway where she fell over sideways on the carpet. I scooped her up and set her on the bed where she regained her composure.

She was not having seizures. Sasha was fainting.

Over the next five months, there were at least half a

dozen similar incidents, each unique and of varied intensity. Usually prompted by excitement—someone coming to the door, playing with and chasing toys too vigorously, Carol arriving home—the patterns became familiar. It started with a cough, and then she could not catch her breath and consequently would pass out.

Miraculously, I was usually within reach whenever these episodes occurred and, at the first sign of trouble, I'd pick her up and run to the door to get outside for fresh air, blowing in her mouth as we ran. I was able to stop the attack on most occasions and she would resume breathing normally. The worst times, she'd severely throw her head backward, start crying out loudly in desperation, and briefly lose consciousness. Thankfully, these episodes only lasted a few seconds; then she'd snap out of it and be back to normal.

In several instances, she lost control of her bladder upon fainting, a couple of times down the front of me. I always tried to get to her quickly, to hold her close and steady her head, while trying to get air into her lungs. I soon began to anticipate unavoidable occasions of overwhelming excitement, and attempted to curtail breathing or fainting episodes before they began. Trying to keep Sasha settled when she wanted to burst with enthusiasm was a near impossible task. Either we had to avoid the situation altogether, or find a good distraction.

The focus of my continued research moved from seizures to fainting. Something was causing a loss of air to her lungs and a loss of blood flow to her brain and, as a result, her fainting spells.

The brief coughing that was often a prelude to these spells reminded me of the choking issues she had experienced when we attempted a new dog-walking schedule over a year earlier. At that time, I had not considered that a few coughs at the end of a taut leash could be a symptom of impaired health. But now, that memory seemed to support the idea that her throat would be a good place to look for potential problems.

A common health issue with small breed dogs is a collapsing trachea. The narrow, oval-shaped windpipe can become weak in some dogs and flatten briefly, shutting off the flow of air to the lungs. This issue seemed to be a plausible cause for the recent symptoms. Yet it was disconcerting if true.

I discussed the possibility with Sasha's vet. The verdict: It wasn't ruled out, but it was highly unlikely. If she did have a collapsing trachea, other than risky, expensive, somewhat experimental surgery, there would not be much we could do to prevent it. The best solution: Continue everything we'd been doing.

Keep her calm and comfortable.

One day at a time.

EARLIER IN THE YEAR, we had received exciting news that Carol's uncle and her cousin, Debby, wanted to visit during Thanksgiving. As the date drew near, and we were dealing with Sasha's increasingly difficult health issues, we felt a little apprehensive about hosting guests that by their mere presence could involuntarily instigate perilous episodes. For the sake of spending priceless holiday time with family, it was a risk we had to take.

As fate would have it, Carol was not home and Sasha fell

into a coughing episode the moment our holiday guests arrived. Juggling a choking dog on the verge of fainting in one arm while opening the door to greet family we hadn't seen in several years made for an awkward welcome, but I quickly dismissed myself and Sasha to the backyard. Keeping her close and calm, I was able to rejoin our guests and the long weekend moved forward. It didn't move smoothly, however.

The day before Thanksgiving, not even twenty-four hours after our house guests had arrived, Sasha had already fainted five times. A last-minute call to see if our veterinarian could squeeze us in before the holiday proved lucky; the fully booked schedule had just opened up with an appointment cancellation. I promptly took Sasha for an exam, in hopes of a remedy to calm her choking sensations.

The thrill of the car ride, combined with nervous anticipation wondering where we might be going, gave Sasha the distraction she needed to keep her mind and body from relapsing into any significant symptom for the doctor to witness. A thorough physical examination once again provided little relief. There was simply no determinable diagnosis.

I inquired again about issues we had discussed during prior exams: Cushing's disease, heart disease, trachea collapse, and anxiety. None of these seemed to be the problem. The best determination was perhaps that Sasha was having neurological issues and we could look into having her tested at a later date.

I returned home with Sasha hoping she would somehow feel better and make it through the long holiday weekend. Miraculously, her symptoms waned throughout the family visit and, for the first part of the following week, Sasha was feeling better again.

Whenever Sasha was back on track and her normal self for a few days, we remained optimistic that the worst of her symptoms were over, and that she was in full recovery mode and would return to the chronically lively, happy pet of years past.

Sadly, our optimism couldn't stop this runaway roller coaster. An ascent to well-being surely guaranteed a rapid, terrifying plunge into near-death dramatics, only to be repeated time and time again. This latest promising convalescence reached its apex a week after Thanksgiving, only to plummet without warning, deceitfully disguised as a fun-loving romp-and-roll in a soft, new blanket on the bed.

Sasha was rolling around as she did often, with little grunts and happy barks escaping during playful back massage exercises. Suddenly, sensing an attack coming on, she hopped from the blanket to sit on my lap, gasping three times before violently writhing her neck backward and letting out a cry of anguish.

"It's all right, it's all right girl … breathe easy."

These words were becoming more and more common.

As I supported and cradled her close, carrying her around for a few minutes, I couldn't tell whether or not she had fainted. We went outside to the patio where she seemed slightly disoriented, but once again, returned to normal, if we could even call it that anymore.

We were back to another valley of brief treacherous assaults on body, mind, and spirit. But then, thankfully, we'd be off to the top of the happy hill where the symptoms abated.

This was no thrill ride, however.

It was literally a death race we distraughtly wanted Sasha to win—alive and well. We were in desperate need of a winning strategy to beat this health predator.

It had come to the point where her change of condition appeared and disappeared rapidly—and unexpectedly—a twisted magic act of grotesque mind-and-body pranks, for Sasha to perform and for us to endure. We had little time to react, but always needed to act quickly. Every vexatious episode tested my own fragile nerves, by the severe instant distress it was causing us all, and by the lack of understanding as to why this was happening randomly over and over again.

Just as I had suffered unpredictable health symptoms of unknown origin month after month for several years, Sasha's health seemed to be mirroring a similar pattern. Her mid-life crisis, like mine, kept us confused and incessantly searching for relief.

Nearly two years had passed since her first incontinence issue, a year and a half since her first near-fainting episode, and countless menacing moments and speculation along the way.

Frustratingly, we still did not know what kind of indomitable monster we were up against.

♪♫

chapter seven

heartbeats

Sweet Girl

OUR HOPES FOR LASTING RECOVERY were persistently dashed. The symptoms were becoming relentless; they were always familiar, yet slight variations on the theme. I frantically continued to examine these pieces, trying to fit them together into a cohesive whole.

We sought solutions from books, websites, friends, family, and pet health professionals.

We tried prescription meds, herbal remedies, changes in diet and activities, and the introduction of distractions. We gleaned much information. We lived through constant trial and error.

There were good days.

There were bad days.

There were great days.

There were excruciatingly horrible days.

It just could not go on like this.

We needed an answer. We wanted desperately to see the big picture, but we were missing a crucial piece of the puzzle. We wanted to understand what was causing Sasha such unpredictable agony—and we wanted to fix it!

We had to have a diagnosis.

ON SUNDAY, a week after the Thanksgiving holiday weekend, I just couldn't stand to see Sasha continue to suffer. Her choking, breathing, and fainting episodes had begun to threaten every potentially heart-racing waking moment. Her fragile condition allowed normal activity, but she balanced on the precipice of terrifying collapse. Anything that could possibly evoke stressful attention (and put her over the edge) was avoided, but impossible to dismiss.

The day started out as an average day for Sasha—typical of what we had come to expect—with no adverse health symptoms. But as the day wore on, and without any apparent reason, the balance shifted.

And it was all downhill from there.

Carol was teaching an afternoon class at a local gourmet kitchen store while I attentively monitored Sasha's decline minute-by-minute. It soon became evident that she could no longer rest comfortably without a breathing issue or a choking moment. Although she avoided fainting, living normally for more than a few minutes at a time had become next to impossible.

I phoned Carol when I assumed the class was over to tell her that we could not wait any longer; Sasha had to go to the hospital. Carol quickly packed her pans and came home straightaway.

Typically, being Sunday, our regular vet clinic was closed; however, another animal hospital with weekend hours was not much farther away. It had become clear that this was where we should take Sasha, not only because they were open, but also because it was time for another professional's point of view.

We rushed to the vet, Sasha panting anxiously, riding on

Carol's lap while I drove. Upon arrival, we were promptly assigned to an examination room for yet another round of poking and prodding to see what a different veterinarian had to offer.

Unexpectedly, with no time to lose and through this second opinion, we found an answer.

ARLINGTON, our city of residence ever since we moved to Texas, is a large community. Nearly one hundred square miles and with a population of over 375 thousand, the city ranks third largest in the DFW Metroplex, just behind Dallas and Fort Worth. It is geographically situated smack-dab in the middle of the Metroplex, "The dash between Dallas and Fort Worth." Recently proclaimed as "The American Dream City," Arlington is the entertainment capital of North Texas—home to Six Flags Over Texas amusement park, the Texas Rangers major league baseball team, and, since 2009, the Dallas Cowboys football stadium.

Plus, there's the University of Texas at Arlington, General Motors, The Parks at Arlington mall, and countless shopping centers, stores, and restaurants. Arrays of geometric subdivisions and congested highways leave little room to breathe. A community of this size would support and require many health care options as well, including those for pets. There are dozens of veterinarians in Arlington proper, not to mention hundreds of others throughout the surrounding DFW Metroplex communities.

When Sasha and Sydney were puppies, we were fortunate to select a wonderful vet clinic as their primary health care provider. As many might do, we conveniently chose the location nearest our home. The reasoning was simple. In case of emergency, we could get quickly to the closest pet hospital.

We could not have picked a better-qualified, more trustworthy, more gentle, and more caring veterinarian if we had tried. Determining whether to take our pups anywhere else—in the event this office was closed—was always difficult.

Three years before we faced this decision with Sasha, it also happened to be a Sunday (isn't it always?) when Sydney was running ferociously in our backyard. He'd get into a back-and-forth chase with the neighbor's Jack Russell Terrier, although they were separated by our six-foot stockade fence. Our landscaping was like an agility course, so Sydney darted in, around, and over mulched shrubs, scattered trees, wood plank decks, and stacks of patio stones.

Resistance was futile.

Our only hope of stopping this behavior—his gut instinct to dominate and conquer his competitor (and an accident waiting to happen)—was direct intervention, removing him from the competition. These "races" took place periodically (more often than I'd like to admit) and, on that occasion, after a few firm requests for him to stop, Sydney came limping back to the house.

When he would not leave my side and I could not keep from tripping over him, I knew he must be in great pain. Upon further examination, I noticed a toe on his front foot was bleeding. It required more than ice and a bandage.

This was the first occasion on which we had contacted a local animal hospital that promoted weekend hours, but not at emergency room prices. Normal fees, extended hours, every day, year round. They were well established in the community (had been there for over thirty years) and were not far from our home.

We rushed Sydney to this clinic where he was examined by a kind, older gentleman, the head veterinarian and owner of the facility. A brief exam with diagnosis suggested quick surgery for a severely broken toenail. Hours later, Sydney was home in recovery mode.

We took Sasha to this hospital to pursue whatever remedy we could find on that late Sunday afternoon, a day before her ninth birthday, in early December 2011.

We had been thoroughly pleased dealing with the clinic's owner during Sydney's ordeal. We realized, however, there were several veterinarians on duty at any one time. We didn't know who would open the examination room door to meet Sasha for the first time. We could only hope the vet might find something to explain her condition that, up until then, no one else had been able to do.

Enter the doctor.

IN THE DEPTHS OF DESPAIR, waiting with Sasha trembling in my arms and prognosis unknown, we couldn't have been more pleasantly surprised and relieved when a courteous younger woman with long brown hair, stylish blue-rimmed eyeglasses, and doctor's attire entered the examination room and introduced herself.

"Hi, I'm Doctor Nowlan."

"Who do we have here?" she asked.

"This is Sasha. She's been having a very rough time lately," I explained.

I went on to introduce ourselves and run down a meticulous synopsis of Sasha's recent health issues. Dr. Nowlan proceeded to give Sasha a thorough examination, checking her mouth, eyes, ears, temperature, and physical condition from head to tail. Putting a stethoscope to her chest for a listen to her heart and lungs was most revealing and put an end to ambivalence.

"She's got a heart murmur," Dr. Nowlan stated confidently.

My heart suddenly skipped a few beats, too.

"There may be fluid in her lungs as well."

A chill ran through the already cold, sterile room.

After dealing with Sasha's random symptoms for nearly two years, I was glad to finally hear about a definite infirmity to address. But I still felt skeptical about the doctor's immediate certainty.

She went on to explain the possible condition of Sasha's heart.

"When the heart has difficulty pushing blood in the proper manner, congestion within the system can occur. A heart murmur is the sound heard reflecting turbulent blood flow within the heart. We use an intensity scale system to evaluate the sound—from one, very faint and difficult to hear, to six, loud with palpable vibration and can be heard at multiple areas, even without the stethoscope making contact with the chest wall. Sasha's heart murmur is prominent and perceptible at more than one location, a grade three to four."

Carol's eyes began to well with tears, while my mind raced through a myriad of thoughts, including the unanticipated severity of Sasha's health issues, the potential urgency to treat her condition and save her life, and shamefully (but necessarily), the unknown financial burden we were likely unprepared to bear. And we were trying to comprehend exactly what Dr. Nowlan was expounding.

"This scale doesn't necessarily indicate the gravity of the disease process, though. Further testing would be necessary to help make that determination. Since her breathing is also a bit more forceful and her lungs sound more harsh than normal, I would recommend that we take X-rays and do blood tests."

Within five minutes of our meet-and-greet, I began to have great confidence in Dr. Nowlan. Without hesitation, we surrendered Sasha to the good doctor to proceed with her recommendations.

Dr. Nowlan knew from an early age she wanted to be surrounded by animals her whole life. As a young girl in Canada, starting with stray cats, she began to understand responsible pet ownership. Her goal to love, care for, and keep them as happy and healthy as possible translated perfectly to "veterinarian." As a graduate of the Atlantic Veterinary College in Prince Edward Island, she went on to practice small animal medicine in Massachusetts, before moving to Texas.

Forever fascinated with medicine and all that could be done to help animals, Dr. Nowlan was always drawn to the bigger picture: the patient's well-being. Diagnostic results, data, and understanding the variables of each situation and how to use that information contribute to a patient's success, but the patient is most important. "Always look at the patient" and "treat every patient as an individual" became her challenging, yet ultimately rewarding methodologies and goals.

As we waited briefly in the examination room while Sasha was posing for her internal snapshots, the reality of what we might soon learn began to sink in. My thoughts turned to denial. By all appearances, Sasha was an active, happy, usually healthy, still fairly young, *normal* dog.

How could she possibly have an ailing heart?

Moments later, as a relieved-to-be-done Sasha was returned to my arms, Dr. Nowlan let the image on the computer screen speak thousands of words. Sasha's full body radiograph was the missing piece of the puzzle. It gave us the picture—literally and figuratively—we'd been trying to see for close to two years.

It just wasn't the picture we had hoped to see.

The X-rays revealed the silhouette of an enlarged heart, as large as her rib cage could hold. It had become so large, it was pressing against her trachea, causing her breathing problems. Her liver was larger than normal as well, and there was fluid in her lungs. The reason behind the symptoms she'd been struggling with became painstakingly clear. The panting, incontinence, restlessness, breathing, choking, coughing, fainting, mild seizures, and visibly pulsating heartbeats were all troubling effects of an overworked heart.

When Sasha was able to sleep soundly (something she did often, considering her increasingly difficult health issues), it became evident her body was not resting as it should have been.

For comparison, I'd watch the other dogs sleep, taking a breath every couple of seconds, then I'd look at Sasha sleeping—her breathing much faster and her chest pounding. Her mind was at rest, but her body was running a marathon. It was difficult to watch, knowing we'd been doing everything we knew how to do to help keep her comfortable, while still not knowing what was causing her bodily distress.

But we finally had an answer.

Sasha was suffering from heart disease, also known as congestive heart failure (CHF).

Unlike with human heart disease, dogs seldom have heart attacks. A different problem occurs. The heart valves start to malfunction and blood begins to pool rather than circulate as it should. The heart works harder to keep the blood circulating to compensate for the damaged valves, and, in the process, grows in size. Fluids tend to accumulate in and around the organs, and they start to suffer as well.

It's a gradual death sentence.

And there is no cure.

WE ALWAYS KNEW Sasha had a bigger heart than her body could hold, figuratively speaking. She was always bursting at the seams. She could not contain her affection and enthusiasm, and she wore it proudly as a badge of her love for living. It was her greatest trait and a joy to behold.

When we saw how big her heart muscle appeared, it was startling and distressing. How ironic! Sasha had such a huge heart for life when her physically huge heart was undeniably stealing that life away.

Dr. Nowlan was able to gather pertinent information during this initial exam. She also recommended other tools—an echocardiogram, an EKG, routine blood pressure evaluations, and advanced diagnostic imaging (CT scan and MRI)—based on specialists' exams if we decided to pursue that path of diagnostics. These tests would help to clarify or diagnose the inciting cause of Sasha's CHF and presumed seizure activity.

"Is there anything we can do right now to help her feel better?" I asked before committing to further tests and procedures.

"We can treat presenting symptoms with medications and monitor her closely, making adjustments as needed along the way," Dr. Nowlan suggested.

"The goal of the treatment for congestive heart failure, even without a distinct diagnosis, is to try to balance a system that has become unbalanced. Physical exams, with the addition of routine diagnostics such as blood work and radiographs, help me make judgments on the efficacy of the treatment plan."

If we had not ascertained the cause of her suffering, Sasha would most likely not have lived another week. The disease and accompanying symptoms had become insufferable. Dr. Nowlan's willingness to work closely with us based on all considerations—the urgency of Sasha's health issues, the priority of suggested tests and exams, and the continued financial cost—guided us to determine the best course of action for managing Sasha's condition. With immediate medical attention, we were able to start a treatment program that brought relief and normality back to our lives.

Dr. Nowlan prescribed three important medicines to stabilize Sasha's condition: an ACE inhibitor to control blood pressure, a diuretic to eliminate excess fluid from her lungs and other organs, and an antibiotic to treat or prevent infections. Circulatory problems can present conditions more prone to infections. Sasha may already have been suffering from a mild infection, making her symptoms worse. It was best to attack these issues before they started or worsened. Although for a few days she did show occasional signs of recurring symptoms, Sasha was once again feeling better.

TWO WEEKS LATER, we returned to see Dr. Nowlan for a follow-up visit. A new prescription was added to Sasha's daily medicine regimen: pimobendan, a wonder drug designed specifically to dilate the arteries and veins of dogs with CHF and help their hearts work more effectively. Studies have shown that dogs on this medicine, in combination with the traditional heart meds, survived longer and had a better quality of life than those on the heart meds alone.

In a matter of days, Sasha began to resume the normal activities she had always enjoyed without the interruption of life-threatening symptoms. Her new daily schedule of pill-popping was just the ticket for survival that she urgently needed.

The medicines helped to control her heart activity, essentially eliminating the disturbing symptoms we had been seeing with increasing frequency. This was the best possible scenario we could hope for, although the new meds brought a new set of issues that would require our attention.

The diuretic effectively reduced fluid around her organs, but also made Sasha very thirsty, which in turn created an incontinence issue once again. Until her body became accustomed to the continual water flow, Sasha had to wear a baby's diaper (with hole cut for her tail) during the night. She was able to go outside often throughout the day, so there was seldom a problem with daytime accidents. After a few days, she was able to control this issue and we could forgo the diapers.

Whenever changes were made to the prescription, we'd need to revert to the diaper strategy temporarily. Although she growled under her breath whenever I'd suit her up, Sasha was willing to tolerate these precautions. I do think she understood why she needed to wear the diaper. Whenever she did accidentally leak in the diaper, there was no mistake—it was saturated and heavy. I know she felt better not having that happen all over herself. (And I felt better not having to clean that up!) The good news was that she adapted quickly to changes in her prescriptions and did not need the diapers for long.

Taking a minimum of three medications required a regular routine. Juggling the dosages and daily intervals was my responsibility. Coordination with the daily dinner schedule, coupled with the continued herbal remedies, gave good reason to create a computer spreadsheet to track the daily intake of meds Sasha was receiving. The routine eventually leveled out to three doses a day, eight hours apart, but different requirements in each dose.

The pimobendan was the easiest to administer; it was an edible pill with a flavor Sasha enjoyed. She never refused to chew and swallow those right away. The others, however, were pills for people and given in small doses. The best method for Sasha to take those turned out to be wrapping them in cheese.

Of course, Syd and Mil wanted their share, so three times a day, all the pups got their tiny balls of cheese treats. And Sasha conveniently took her pills.

Like clockwork.

Sasha never lost her appetite. She looked forward to every dinner no matter what problems she had to face with her illness. She began to be finicky, though, taking her time and carefully selecting ingredients to eat first. When Sydney was done inhaling his plate full of goodness, I had to stand guard to keep him from helping her finish. Without looking up, her fierce growl would let him know if he got too close. He would stand back and watch, waiting until she was done so he could lick the plate clean. (There was always a chance she might miss a grain of rice!) But Sasha polished off every plate of homemade chicken, rice, and veggies night after night. It was always good to see.

Sadly, although her tummy stayed full, her muscle mass did not. Her heart worked tirelessly. It essentially drained every other muscle in her tiny body. It was not crippling her—she was still able to move freely and continued to run and jump around as she always had. But any rigorous activity was potentially harmful to her health (and could easily arouse portentous symptoms). It was difficult at best—and felt like the worst thing to do—to curb her enthusiasm. So, much to our chagrin, we would occasionally—although unintentionally—fail to protect her from overexertion.

As she gradually began to look like skin-and-bones, we had to step up our efforts to restrain her instinctive behavior. Curtailing actions that she always expressed with alacrity required hands-on attention. Calm did not come easily. She often had no choice but to calm down, though, when, ultimately, her body could not keep up.

Slowly but surely, her body was beginning to fail her ready-and-willing mind and youthful spirit.

Sasha's muscle loss was most evident on her back and around her ribs. When she'd sit on my lap for a shoulder and neck massage—something she enjoyed regularly for years—I could count her ribs and feel every vertebrae along her spine. It didn't matter how much nutritious food she was eating, her heart disease was melting her muscle mass. Every visit to the vet clinic confirmed that her weight was dropping a few ounces each time. This was just more evidence that no matter how well she seemed to be coping with CHF, it was stealing away her life force little by little.

Nevertheless, she yearned to live and we were undeniably optimistic with her. The truth was clear, but hope remained.

A few breathing issues continued to cloud the weeks following her diagnosis, but they were minor in comparison with what she had been experiencing prior to that. A few times, the problem breathing led to near fainting, but I was always close to grab her and get her outside for fresh air and a distraction.

These symptoms were always caused by excitement. Her heart would begin to beat faster. It would press against her trachea and cause her to lose her breath, which in turn could cause her to faint. Having learned what was happening, our goal was to stifle the excitement and keep the airflow coming into her lungs. This was usually accomplished by a quick change of scenery (for instance, taking her outdoors).

In the midst of finally understanding and making a concerted effort to accommodate Sasha's condition, we were about to make another huge decision.

Should we grow our family?
How could we even consider that at this crucial time?
Would a change like this hurt or help Sasha?

We were positively hoping that it would help her when we decided a week before Christmas to adopt a kitten.

IT WAS MID-SEPTEMBER when we first heard that our neighbor's cat had had a litter of kittens. There had been several occasions throughout our married years when similar news had tempted us to inquire further about cat adoptions. But we always resisted.

I had always been interested in getting a cat again one day, but as the years went on, that notion faded to fancy. It had been silently understood, due to allergic tendencies with Carol's family, that adopting a cat would not be an inviting idea. Above any other consideration, this concern had been paramount, precluding any capricious cat talk, stopping it in its tracks. This time, however, there were several conditions in alignment and too many tempting tracks to halt.

As the kittens were becoming independent of their mother, we learned that two were calico. Twin females, their black, white, and gold markings were nearly identical.

If we were ever to get a cat, I'd insist on a female.

Check. (Some males have that annoying spraying tendency I'd rather avoid altogether.)

She would need to be used to living with dogs.

Check. (The kittens were born into a home with five Pomeranians. So, yes, I think these kitties were used to doggies.)

I'd also want to adopt a young kitten, with little or no memory of influences except ours, in its new home.

Check. (These kittens would be twelve weeks old in mid-December.)

The prerequisites for cat adoption satisfied my impromptu checklist. But what about our family's cat allergies?

That consideration wasn't nearly as pressing this time when we contemplated the other facts weighing heavily on our household.

Sasha's diagnosis was terribly distressing. We needed something uplifting in our lives. We believed the kitten adoption would help us all—including Sasha—feel better. Sasha always seemed fascinated and entertained by kitties, whether on television, or as temporary guests in our house.

How would she react to living with a cat?

It was a risk that we hoped would have a positive outcome. A kitten would be a huge distraction—for Sasha and for us. We wouldn't be obsessed with Sasha's illness. The kitten would help keep our minds off the inevitable. It might be good for Sasha, perhaps? We didn't know. The only way to find out … invite the kitties over for a get-acquainted day.

It was two weeks after Sasha's diagnosis and a week before Christmas. That's when the twin calicos came to visit and won our hearts, including Sasha's, whose holiday spirit trumped her ailing heart. As the dogs tailed the kittens throughout the house, it quickly became clear that one was more interested in ditching the dogs, while the other settled comfortably into a quiet position with Carol in the living room chair. While Millie and Sydney kept pace with a kitty chase, Sasha came to see the cozy kitten. When she started gently kissing the kitty's ear, and wanted to stay close, we knew she had made a choice.

How could we deny Sasha a cute new companion?

Even if (from the cat's perspective perhaps) she were a reluctant distraction.

The stars must have been aligned.

The kitties went back to the neighbor's house with instructions to return Sasha's kitty later that evening, after I had had time to pick up the necessary kitten accoutrements. She would at least need food, a cat bowl, and a litter box.

She would also need something I couldn't get at the store—a name. I had a name in mind; it was something left over of thoughts from years past. I always liked jasmine—as a name and as a fresh floral fragrance in a sweet summer breeze. It just seemed pleasant and uplifting, perfect for a sweet, playful kitten.

For our newest family member, just one musical modification though—the name would be Jazmine, with a "z"—Jazz, or Jazzy, for short.

Sasha was thrilled when her kitten returned. And Jazmine quickly settled into her new home with fewer dogs and cats than she had been living with. She seemed pleasantly pleased to be independent and the lone kitty amid the crazy pups. Jazzy felt right at home with the dogs' schedule and activities. She instantly became "one of the guys."

We were amused to see her line up, taking a place next to the dogs when bedtime cookies were handed out. As the dogs found sleeping spots on the bed, so did Jazz. She assumed her place in the family from the start, never felt intimidated, and always simply belonged with us. And she kept Sasha busy and entertained for months to come.

It was a love-hate relationship. Sasha loved the kitty when she could be in control during a playful romp. But when Jazmine refused to play by the rules and challenged

Sasha's authority, a quick lunge with a growling snap expressed Sasha's displeasure. It was most aggravating when Jazz could escape to the top of her five-foot cat tree, a private perch primarily procured for kitty dinner service, well above the dogs' reach.

There were many fun times, notably Christmas Day, a week after Jazzy became a member of our family. Sasha warmly welcomed Jazmine to our gift exchange ritual where all enjoyed playful chases through piles of wrapping paper and ribbon, in and around boxes and bags, and circling the Christmas tree.

Considering the recent rough weeks she had been having before her diagnosis, and her sudden adjustments to new prescriptions and life with a new kitty, it was truly a Christmas miracle that Sasha enjoyed not only a fun-filled, gift-unwrapping holiday, but unaffectedly the best day—without incident—in a long time. It seemed that we had our normal, healthy, sweet girl back, and we could not have been happier.

WE WERE ABLE to put aside health concerns for that day; however, the unfortunate truth is that heart disease is unforgiving. It was my task to keep it tamed, and Sasha's to suffer through it. She grew accustomed to the daily pill regimen and learned to anticipate oncoming symptoms. She was adapting to accommodate the disease.

And she did astoundingly well.

She was such a fighter.

However, there were always fights to lose. Sneaky little jabs that took her down, but she wasn't out. A near fainting spell here, some choking issues there, and diapers on and off as meds were adjusted through several follow-up visits with Dr. Nowlan.

"Congestive heart failure is challenging to treat," Dr. Nowlan reminded us.

"It's a balancing act. There are many clues along the way pertaining to what should be done. If you're able to truly acknowledge these subtleties and act accordingly, you are doing all that is possible to balance or maintain quality of life for as long as possible."

Dr. Nowlan consistently offered kind and encouraging words, but the facts continued to tear at our hearts, bleeding our optimism for a miraculous full recovery. We could no longer deny that there was no turning back—Sasha was living with heart disease—but the emphasis was always on "living."

"With you and Sasha, I have an incredible amount of knowledge on what is happening to her, on the inside," Dr. Nowlan reassured us.

"You are so in tune with her and how she responds to medications. You decide what works best for her, based on subtle changes. It is a precise schedule and I know it is perfect for her. Your contribution and devotion are outstanding. I feel I know her so well and know what to do because you give me in-depth insight—she could not receive better care."

There were days in a row, sometimes weeks, when she didn't show symptoms of bad health. Sasha lived every day as if she were perfectly healthy. There were many times I'm sure she thought she was once again perfectly healthy. And just when we felt good about how good she seemed to be feeling, the ugly truth set in and a terrible episode would remind us of reality.

The reality we had longed to know for so long.

The reality we had finally come to know and hoped to understand.

The reality we hated, but learned to live with, making the most of every day.

The reality with a name: congestive heart failure.

CHF.

CHF sounds less intimidating.

For Sasha, CHF could only mean "can have fun."

IT WAS SIX MONTHS into this new reality and Sasha was indeed having fun once again. Nothing more than a few coughing spells over several months caused serious concern. When the slightest sign of trouble started to appear, an immediate distraction would do wonders. Along with consistent doses of heart meds, anything to keep her mind off imminent health danger seemed to be the best mode of defense.

As a kitten, Jazmine provided a much needed shift-of-attention for many months, but as she became fully grown (taller and almost larger than Sasha), Sasha was not as interested in the daily antics of the kitty. I think she began to despise the cat, eventually ignoring her altogether. If Jazz came within lunging distance, with a small growl and quick snap, Sasha let her know it was too close and she had better mind her own business. Menacingly, she was reminding Jazzy who was boss.

Other familiar distractions never failed to catch her

attention. A glimpse of animals on TV, a special toy, or games with toys could draw Sasha away from all other activities. For her favorite game, she would often single out a plush ball toy—from a selection of various sizes, shapes, and colors—to chase, retrieve, and guard. Her choice would become "ballie." (Everything eventually ends with "ie" when you live with doggies—or if you speak Aussie slang!)

Her newest squeaky toys were shaped to resemble Christmas tree ornaments, about the size of tennis balls. She loved to bring one of these to me, drop it at my feet, and begin an intense stare down with the plush faux decor until I would try to pick it up.

"Are you gonna let Daddy get ballie?" I'd ask, as I watched every muscle in her tiny frame quickly tense.

Her feet were planted firmly, the point of convergence in her unwavering sight, waiting for me to make the first move.

C'mon, I dare ya! she taunted silently as she stood her ground.

Sydney wanted to join the game, but usually steered clear. He'd voice his challenge from the sideline. It was a double dog dare.

"Let Daddy get ballie," I'd tease back, as I began to slowly reach for the toy, testing her true grit.

Sydney's sideline chants were also of no consequence. She was unflinchingly poised.

I'd make my move to steal the ball, but she would quickly grab it and turn away, out of reach. This routine would continue over and over. Occasionally, I'd snatch the toy, beating her to it by milliseconds. Disappointed for allowing me to grab it first, and somewhat bewildered, she'd reestablish her foothold, never losing focus on the crown jewel orb in my hand. I'd toss it just a few feet away, knowing that a longer run might cause overexertion. She'd grab it before Sydney could and start the mind meld with ballie all over again.

Sasha loved playing this game, but only if I participated. My participation rarely meant grabbing or throwing the toy, though. She enjoyed mocking me, if only to demonstrate her quick wit and spry reflexes. If I did not pay attention for a few minutes, she would lie down until I moved to grab the toy. Then it was game on again.

I'd grow impatient with this game long before she would, but I always indulged her desire to play since it kept her mind and body active and off her health issues. And I couldn't help but be entertained, watching her sharp concentration and dedication to this simple, yet distorted game of "fetch" with ballie.

ANOTHER ROUTINE became a nightly ritual, sometimes occurring several times each evening depending on the need to distract. When Sasha first began having coughing, choking, and breathing issues, I turned to quick exits to the backyard for fresh air. These dashes to the door usually proved helpful, alleviating further serious symptoms.

It was often more convenient to go out the front door, and that would become the focus of our newest, and always effective, distraction. A trip to the front yard meant we were on a quest.

"Do you want to go look?" I'd ask her.

She'd jump up at once and stand with her front feet against my leg, begging to be held.

I'm ready. Let's go! were the thoughts her actions conveyed.

I'd lift her with my left hand supporting her chest, but more importantly, my right hand was under her rear legs to support her weight. This kept pressure off her chest. As we walked down the driveway, she'd adjust her body in my arms to alleviate stress, sometimes sitting upright, sometimes lying down across my folded arms. By the time she was comfortable, we were usually in position at the edge of our property to draw attention to the purpose of our nightly quest.

We were on a bunny hunt.

Our neighbor's large yard was dotted with evergreen, ornamental, and fruit trees. Shrubs and hedges bordered the house. A towering bush of pampas grass grew boldly at the base of the property line, near our prime viewing spot. A host of nocturnal woodland creatures visited this grazing sanctuary.

More times than not, we could count on nightly sightings of busybodies foraging through the yard. We often saw opossums and cats, but rabbits got our full attention.

Sasha loved to look for bunnies.

Occasionally, we'd see two or three scampering about. Sasha perked up, barely able to contain her deepest desire to leap from my arms into a hare-raising chase. She knew better, though, forcing herself to be content with the sighting, her attention firmly focused until the bunnies disappeared under a bush or behind the house.

At the rear of our property, a small forest of sorts was home to assorted wildlife. Sightings over the years have ranged from squirrels, snakes, and a variety of birds (including wild turkeys, hawks, owls, and a roadrunner), to raccoons, bobcats, and coyotes.

Our stockade fence kept most predators at bay, and sightings were rare at best. It was usually a random stray dog outside the fence that set our pups off on a midnight barking tirade at the mysterious trespasser lurking beyond.

The most interesting late-night visitor came around later in the summer and it always piqued our curiosity. Sasha would start to salivate when we could sneak up on a busy little armadillo digging up the neighbor's yard at two o'clock in the morning, hunting for grubs. Often so intent on dinner, armadillos can become oblivious to their surroundings.

On one occasion, though, when a little guy noticed that we were merely a step in front of him, he jumped straight up, a foot in the air, and trotted away to a safer distance. His jack-in-the-box maneuver startled us as well, and I nearly fell over as we promptly backed away.

I'm not sure Sasha knew what we were looking at during those late night searches for unusual little creatures, but she sure didn't want to miss a single one. The few minutes we spent with each other every night was precious time we could not wait to share and experience.

EARLY IN JUNE, Sasha was leading an active day, jumping up and down off the couch, running at the TV, chasing Jazmine, antagonizing Sydney over toys, and just acting as normal as could be expected. Another good day—until a reminder of CHF hit hard once again.

Sasha had taken her evening dose of meds when, seconds later, she started to faint, just like the spells she used to have when excited. She was sitting in the kitchen and started to lean her head to the right, then backward, crying out in agony. I steadied her head and body, holding her as she quickly regained composure. She was winded and out-of-breath for an hour or so, until she went to sleep. I sat with her in bed for a while to keep her comfortable and calm. She slept well through the night. The next morning she was back to "normal" once again with no new signs of fainting.

During these distressing fainting spells, I was quick to come to her aid, although Sydney was quicker. Every time Sasha fell under attack and began to struggle, Sydney was at her side forthwith to attend to her condition. He had a valiant intent to ease and assist her symptoms. It pained him to see her in pain. If Sasha fainted when the dogs were home alone, I could confidently assume Sydney was always near to comfort her and see to her recovery. For better or for worse, Sydney loved his big sister.

The rest of the summer saw two similar episodes, but they were negligible compared to the prevailing good days she was having at that point. A few follow-up exams with Dr. Nowlan confirmed good blood test results, and, except gradual weight loss, essentially little change in her condition.

Occasional adjustments to meds kept her feeling well through October. By that time, special holiday plans were taking shape and I determined that a new approach to Sasha's health would be implemented. It was a daily behavior modification. Not Sasha's, but my own.

I began to pray often.

And especial circumstances required special prayers for Sasha.

♪♫

Sweet Girl

communion

chapter eight

Sweet Girl

DAILY PRAYERS were not something new to me. Prayers for family and friends to remain safe and in good health have been important throughout my life. My pets have always been in my prayers as well.

As Sasha began to have symptoms of an unknown illness, my prayers were modified to help heal her condition. When we discovered her illness was heart disease, my prayers continued to change.

Throughout the year, as she bravely fought CHF and upcoming events were planned, the timing and specifics of my prayers would become significant to Sasha's continued endurance. I would not realize the full scope of my prayers' significance until much later. Yet throughout her illness, my faith never required proof to prompt prayer.

SOME PEOPLE are animal magnets. Personality traits and their love for animals undoubtedly influence and enhance the attraction, but there is something much deeper in play. Domestic animals sense a strong magnetism and closely connect with people who radiate it. I seem to exude this magnetism since I've been a pied piper for dogs throughout my life.

This is not true for every person, but many do possess this attribute, some to a greater extent than others. In my family, my mom, sister, and nieces seem to have this attraction with animals—dogs in particular—to a strong degree. My niece, Sarah, exhibits this quality to a far greater extent than the rest of us. If we're animal magnets, she's an electromagnet.

Ever since she was a toddler, my family's dogs have befriended and protected Sarah like no one else. My mom's Sheltie, Hannah, was forever devoted to my mom, yet had a strong affection for Sarah, never leaving her side during family visits. My sister's dogs shared a similar attraction to Sarah throughout her formative years. They were sad when she went off to college, but welcome relief and great excitement returned during her semester breaks.

Our dogs always enjoyed visits with relatives in Michigan, but Sarah consistently received the most attention. Sasha loved Sarah. She knew her by name. I'd say, "Sarah's coming to see you," and Sasha would hop to her feet and run around, often toward the door, whining lightly in thrilled anticipation. Sarah's unsolicited, yet welcoming hold on pets' psyches is an extraordinary example of an incomprehensible force at work.

Or maybe it's just that she loves animals?

I think it's really both, but what do I know?
It doesn't matter, the animals know.

WHEN SARAH GRADUATED from WMU (also my alma mater) in 2012, Carol and I invited her to visit us for a graduation celebration holiday later in the year. In mid-July, I finalized a flight schedule for her week-and-a-half visit to coincide with the Thanksgiving holiday. Sasha was in the midst of a long streak of decent health, having adjusted to the daily medicine routine and fought off most CHF-related symptoms. My daily prayers for her to remain in good health continued faithfully. With Sarah's travel plans firmly in place, my prayers for Sasha were uniquely amended to accommodate this new timeline.

We had last visited family in Michigan during the 2008 holiday season, a year before Sasha showed any signs of health problems. It was vital that she remain well through Sarah's visit. I wanted this to be a happy, memorable time for Sarah *and* Sasha, as it might be their last time together. It wasn't easy to think of things in those terms, but due to untimely and urgent circumstances, that was the situation. In facing that reality, and having a cherished occasion to plan and anticipate, I turned to praying for Sasha's continued good health throughout a specific time frame.

I routinely prayed in bed before falling asleep. As I modified my prayers for Sasha, my place of prayer also began to change. Every night, as I'd accompany the dogs outside for their "last time to tinkle," I'd stand on the deck, scanning the stars in the midnight sky and pray quietly to myself, yet loudly to God in heaven above:

"Dear Lord, Creator of Heaven and Earth, please hear my prayer. Please be with us, guide us, protect us, and watch over us. Keep us healthy and safe. Please be with Sasha and send a guardian angel to watch over her. Heal her ailing heart and keep her in good health. Please do not take her from us. Keep her here with us through Thanksgiving and Sarah's visit, through her birthday and Christmas, and into the New Year …"

My prayers for Sasha to the stars above continued every day—during times of good health and in times when she took a turn for the worse, primarily in early November when a congestion issue prompted a return to Dr. Nowlan for antibiotics once again. A few more fainting episodes—one particularly traumatic day with mild seizures and three fainting spells—and adjustments to the daily meds occurred just a couple of weeks before Thanksgiving.

I continued to pray that Sasha would be strong and stay healthy through the fast-approaching holiday season—and most importantly, through Sarah's impending visit.

My prayers seemed to be working.

The week leading up to Thanksgiving proved to be better days, and Sasha was in much better health when Sarah arrived on Thanksgiving Day.

Carol's uncle and Debby once again joined us for Thanksgiving, and we invited friends over for the big feast, so along with Sarah's arrival, we were entertaining several guests at home. We remained concerned for Sasha's ability to withstand all the excitement. I relied on faith and my prayers for strength to make it through. And she did—we all did.

Sasha had a fantastic week.

It had been over ten years since Sarah's prior visit to

Texas. There would be places to go, people to see, things to do, and lots of catching up during our much-anticipated celebration. We planned a busy schedule that included restaurants, shopping, and holiday shows. We also planned many activities at home and Sasha was forever grateful. Although her enthusiasm was not as animated anymore, Sasha was nevertheless excited to spend every possible moment with Sarah during her visit.

When Sarah first arrived and knelt to say hi to her, Sasha crawled into Sarah's lap straightaway and sat comfortably, as if to say, *It's good to see you. I've missed you. I'm so glad you're here.*

Throughout the week, as dozens of photos would attest, Sasha was the center of attention as often as possible, much to our collective delight.

Sasha was able to maintain her energy without suffering severe CHF symptoms. Unfortunately, though, her declining health was becoming more evident with muscle-related activities. She could no longer jump as she wanted to. It would require all her strength to hop onto a chair. We would discourage and halt her attempts if we could catch her in time. Sometimes she'd make it, sometimes she wouldn't.

A SPONTANEOUS INVITATION for Sasha to join us for an evening ride to the burger drive-in marked another moment of clarity, exposing her true condition. Unexpectedly, I became full of angst as we prepared to leave.

When Sasha knew a car ride was imminent, her favorite maneuver was a dash-and-leap into the minivan. I'd press the remote key to open the sliding side door and she would run and hop into our Caravan parked in the driveway. The jumping distance was no more than a foot in height; however, it had been a few months since she had attempted the jump. I should have given it more thought, but I didn't.

I opened the door for Sasha. She ran to the car as usual, but by the time she got there, she didn't have the strength to jump in. She tried, though, and didn't make it, falling backward onto the ground. She picked herself up as I quickly ran to her. I then placed her in the car.

"Are you all right, girl? Oh, Sasha, I'm so sorry!"

I felt horrible. It was like getting hit in the stomach, except it was higher, where the painful truth resonates deeply. I hoped she hadn't hurt herself, but I felt worse that I had let her attempt the jump in the first place. I let my overconfident belief that she was "back to normal" supplant the fact that she unquestionably was not. There was always a thin line that separated living with hopeful optimism from blind denial. Either way, we believed Sasha was going to beat that debilitating disease.

Sasha believed she was going to beat that debilitating disease. But, no matter how much we wanted our healthy girl back, it was not going to happen.

Reality check. I was sad and upset.

A happy run and simple jump into the car was no longer happy or simple. This was another eye-opening confirmation that CHF was stealing our little girl from us one activity at a time.

Whenever *my* heart began to crack, I had to patch it up quickly and get back to the happy. Sasha wasn't going to let a little spill get her down.

Suck it up Dad, and let's go get a burger!

Communion

FOR MOST OF SASHA'S LIFE, the holiday baking season officially began with an invitation to Becky's gingerbread house building and decorating bash. It was usually a small gathering of family and friends, with a welcome extended to our impassioned pups. Regardless of the reason, the dogs could not wait to visit their Aunt Becky and Uncle Tracy. Plenty of surprises were often in store—a savory snack from Tracy's grill, Becky's healthful homemade dog biscuits, or a long and winding walk with our friends and their sagacious Border Collie and loyal, sweet Shelties.

For Sasha, going with us and visiting friends were the only reasons that really mattered. Everything else was just icing on the spice cookie house. That's not to imply that she ever denied the extra fun, though.

During our festive gingerbread get-togethers, Sasha always claimed a front row seat for the bedazzling, bungalow-building action. She'd find the prime place, trading seats across many laps and chairs, to witness daubs of albescent icing and a kaleidoscope of candies bedizening fragrant ginger-spice flats.

As marshmallow snowdrifts and candy cane lanes crisscrossed our workspace, a hamlet of scrumptious chalets, garishly decked with ornaments of gem-like confections, teased our taste buds. Sasha had no interest in tasting the sugary tidbits (of course, it always tempted Millie's tongue), but she continued to count every colorful gumdrop and tallied every truffle.

Only minutes after arriving on turkey day, Sarah joined our busy kitchen crew. She gladly helped Carol and Debby with Thanksgiving feast preparations, brandishing the blowtorch over delectable pumpkin crème brûlée desserts.

With ardent kitchen confidence, she never shied away from her Aunt Carol's culinary challenges, even with the potential peril of a holiday smoke alarm drill.

As an avid home chef and diligent baker, Sarah specialized in copious cookie delights. In anticipation of our upcoming annual candied-cottage construction party, conveniently coinciding with her stay, Carol promptly assigned Sarah the task of baking the gingerbread. She was soon up to her elbows in edible tract houses and cute cookie creatures.

We were thrilled to share a fun-filled gingerbread development in candy land with Sarah, but sadly, Sasha had to sit this session out. We did not want to risk making her fragile condition worse with the excitement that inevitably accompanied these bustling holiday occasions. We reserved her participation for sweet indulgences to be held safely at home.

Far from finished in the kitchen during her vacation celebration, Sarah joined Carol again, creating seasonal snacks and mixing snickerdoodles while Sasha sat by to see every step-by-step procedure. She watched as the cookies were formed on a sheet, then put into the oven, and taken out—a taste treat.

Sadly, Sasha had to miss the gingerbread-decorating extravaganza with Becky, but she did not miss the joy of cooking and baking with Mama and Sarah in the comfort of her own home.

The dogs were all terrific taste-testers, but Sasha was always Carol's sensational sous chef.

SASHA TOOK GREAT DELIGHT and longed to participate in every activity during Sarah's stay. Her curious nose peeked patiently at the edge of the table during board games. Movies at home were optimal opportunities to snuggle close. And with the promise of rock and roll, Sasha joined Carol and Sarah for fanatic rock chick preps.

We bewildered Sarah with tickets to see Rush, on tour in Dallas. She had no idea who that was, nor had she anticipated attending a rock concert with her aunt and uncle. Upon learning about the iconic band, its music, new album, and our longtime dedication to the power rock trio, Sarah welcomed the idea and joined Carol behind the makeup mirror for pre-concert primping.

But they weren't alone.

Sasha equally wanted to be a rock-and-roll princess, so she sat near, observing the clockwork adaptations of hair, makeup, and wardrobe that transformed the musician-turned-cook and our unsuspecting niece into progressive rock angels. To further feel the spirit of the approaching evening, Carol revealed a long-lost relic—her bass guitar—to capture the moment with Sasha.

With guitar in hand and magic music on the mind, Carol assumed a former identity for moving pictures on the deck. Sasha shared the spirit and posed for every glamour shot. Never one to sit idly backstage, she wanted to rock front and center, in the limelight, in the camera eye.

Sasha loved the attention, but above all, our interests were her interests. She wanted to experience life as we did. Nothing seemed too strange, too difficult, or too crazy. Nothing seemed boring and everything always full of promise for once-in-a-lifetime opportunities. Her life in this world was undeniably on a stage.

Sasha was *our* iconic superstar.

Always.

WITH ONE FULL DAY remaining of Sarah's visit, we went out for brunch and shopping. Sasha had been enjoying good health without serious symptoms for two weeks, but when we returned home that day, the excitement was just too overwhelming and she passed out on the deck. As rehearsed for every previous fainting spell, I quickly held her and she regained consciousness immediately, just a little shaken.

By that point, Sasha had fainted more than a dozen times during the year, so we knew what to expect and how to handle it, but that never made it any easier. We were always deeply shaken. I never knew if the next time would be the last; and by "the last," meaning she might not recover from it. That notion consumed my thoughts during these daunting attacks and it haunted me.

The next morning Sasha and Sarah shared their goodbyes—warm embraces at a breakfast seat—as we prepared to leave for the airport. I sighed in relief that the week had gone so well for Sasha and was especially glad that Sarah had seen her in good spirits with little evidence of CHF.

My prayers had been answered.

We made it through the Thanksgiving holiday and Sarah's visit—not just in black and white, but in flying colors. However, there had been more to my prayers and I continued to pray for Sasha to remain healthy through her birthday, Christmas, and into the New Year.

THE NEXT DAY was December 3, one day shy of the one-year anniversary of Sasha's CHF diagnosis and two days before her tenth birthday. We took her to see Dr. Nowlan for a follow-up exam. Due to the occasional coughing and choking issues, Sasha was back on antibiotics for the rest of the month. We celebrated her birthday with a "pup-cake" cookie treat and lots of hugs and kisses. My prayers continued with a joyful Christmas in our sights.

Anticipation of the approaching holiday kept Sasha's spirits high. As I dug through boxes and bins looking for decorations, I stumbled upon dog toys from Christmases past. These road-worn toys were chased and chewed until the stuffing was missing and the fabric was shredded. They were never discarded, simply stored away for moments like this.

Years of Sasha's favorites were there. Generations of ballies that had burst at the seams. An eclectic team of talkies—puppy, kitten, bunny, duck, and monkey—all sadly succumbed to dastardly dissection. Her candy cane was her comfort zone, but her absolute favorite toy obsession was a plush Mr. Bill. The disquieting cries of "Oh, Nooooooooooo!" had to be locked away to avoid mesmerizing Sasha into a crazed frenzy of desire to dominate and destroy.

Poor Mr. Bill.

As these toys came to life for a few playful chases, an old friend sat patiently, buried in the pile of memories, waiting to be revealed. Toys were shuffled left and right as I continued to dig deeper into the past.

And suddenly, there it was.

The big orange dog with floppy brown ears—Sasha's first toy—the toy she dragged around the house nearly a decade earlier, when she was our tiny white pup with apricot ears and her favorite play pal was nearly twice her size.

The big orange dog was a lot smaller than we remembered. But a huge find.

Her humble old rag dog had lost some stuffing over the years, but like the other misfit toys, Sasha needed to play with her good buddy again.

One more time.

That evening, a week or so before Christmas, was a reunion of sorts; it was a walk down memory lane with a history of toys to recall and revisit.

While previously forgotten toys were being chased throughout the house, holiday decorations were sprouting once again. With every box came a curious nose—or two. Sasha always needed to know what was going to be unpacked next. Sydney and Millie were never as interested at this stage, but Jazzy shared Sasha's interest, especially when it was time to hang the ornaments and light the tree. Just try to keep a cat away from dangling ornaments and a string of lights dragging across the floor and around the Christmas tree. Holidays and decorating are not just for people. This has been the joyful truth my entire life.

My prayers continued, toward the cool winter skies, and Sasha enjoyed symptom-free health through another paper-ripping, toy-unwrapping holiday with her siblings. Another Christmas and another New Year's Eve had come and gone, and Sasha held her ground against that terrible disease, but it inevitably continued to drain her strength and spirit. My prayers had been answered, though.

Thank you, God!

We wanted her to be strong. Another day to celebrate was just around the corner. February 3 would mark an important milestone.

"Please, God, keep Sasha in good health and with us through her tenth anniversary and beyond," I amended my prayers. Sasha continued on antibiotics through mid-January and seemed to be doing well.

ANOTHER UNUSUAL SYMPTOM had appeared out of nowhere earlier in the fall, and it continued to bother us, but did not seem to bother her. Sasha would often sit on my lap, facing away as I'd rub her back and shoulders. Sometimes I'd run my fingers down along her front legs.

Back in early November, I had had a notion to grab hold of her front legs and perform a thorough exam. To my surprise, her right forearm had a bump on it. It was solid and felt like a marble. I continued to feel both legs to compare and confirm this finding.

Perhaps she bumped her leg and it was a large bruise?

She wasn't bothered by my thorough exam and did not show any sensations of pain.

What could this be?

It didn't seem to be a life-threatening issue, so we didn't rush to the vet; however, we did draw attention to it at her next visit. The swelling seemed a bit perplexing for the doctor as well. Sasha's X-rays didn't indicate a change in bone structure. The mass was beneath the skin, but it wasn't affecting her joints and she wasn't limping or in pain, so we just kept an eye on it to note any changes.

By mid-January, the bump was virtually unchanged. It hadn't caused pain and she all but ignored it. That still didn't make it right, so we remained observant and concerned.

TYPICALLY, January is the coldest month of the year in North Texas. It has been known to drop into the teens and snow flurries are not unusual. That wasn't the case in 2013, but there were a few chilly days hovering around the freezing point.

A few weeks earlier, Christmas Day brought a surprise that we had never seen on that holiday in Texas.

It snowed.

Not just a few light snow flurries dancing on a sunlit day. A steady blitz of plump clumps of snow took little time to delicately blanket the landscape. Barely an accumulation, yet there was enough depth that kids eagerly embraced it. Merely the sight of snowflakes always had Texan kids scraping the ground to make snowballs and snowmen, and using cardboard boxes for makeshift sleds to slide down the slightest snow-dotted slopes.

Sasha was no different from any kids ready to run out the door without proper winter attire. We always let her hair grow out during the winter months for protection from cold weather, but that offered little protection from exposure to snow. She was so captivated by snow that like kids, she could stay outside playing for hours if we'd let her. She loved to chase snowballs and run in circles with Sydney through the snow. It was always their best outdoor play time.

Whenever snow began to pile high—high for small dogs, that is—I'd toss snowballs for Sasha and watch the icy toys disappear into snowdrifts. She would pursue swiftly, bouncing like a bunny through the snow, diving headfirst to pounce on her frozen prizes. Every time, she would resurface with her face bearded like Santa, ready to fly like Rudolph to the next snowbank.

Communion

Okay, c'mon ... keep 'em comin'.
Toss another snowballie!

Early in her life, it only took a few of these wet winter days to see that Sasha would need to wear a coat when snow was dropping in droves. She would come into the house drenched and undoubtedly chilled to the bone. When the snow was heavy and wet, she became a living snowman. So many snowballs accumulated and hung from her neck, body, and legs that she could hardly walk back to the house. I'd put her in the tub to defrost under a warm water spray. It was a small price to pay. She loved every minute in the snow. And when dry, she was ready to go out and do it all again.

Sasha was our snow dog.

A few years back, during a shopping mall holiday clearance, we found an incomparable cover-up for her winter romps. It was a petite pink parka, including a hood, with tiny Playboy bunny logos all over it. We had to have it for Sasha. Her favorite TV show to watch with Mama was *The Girls Next Door*. Whenever the glaring theme music—"Come On-a My House"—began to play, Sasha ran in great haste to obey, and to see "the *pups* next door." The show often featured lots of growl-and-lunge-worthy doggies and kitties (not to mention the "bunnies") gamboling all around on our big magic screen.

If a blizzard came calling, and snow was falling, Sasha donned her sexy snowsuit. She wasn't too excited about it. As each front leg lifted into a sleeve, a fierce growl let everyone know—especially her brother—that this preparation, although tolerated, was not exactly acceptable. The message to Sydney was perhaps, *Don't you even think about commenting on this*. Then they were off on a chase through the snowscape as Sydney chuckled under his breath.

Sydney didn't always escape the cold weather preps, though. During our winter visits to Michigan, all the dogs suited up in knit sweaters to brave the chilly trips to tinkle. My mom always had a profusion of pullovers for her pets over the years, so finding a suitable color and fit for each of our pups was like a trip to the department store fitting room. Sydney was regal in deep red, Millie, pretty in pink, and Sasha wore rows of rainbow colors. It didn't matter whether she stepped into sleeves or went headfirst into a turtleneck, Sasha always let everyone know this was not a laughing matter.

I'll wear this stupid outfit, but I'm taking notes. I'm talking to you Sydney. You better watch out! is the one-sided conversation we wanted to hear in translation before she charged at her similarly dressed sibling.

Sydney was such a good boy. He always had to take the brunt of her harassment, but he always knew the tough talk was never brutal.

That's just my big sis telling me how it is, was his typical reaction, sometimes with a teeth-baring snap in return, as he'd ride like the wind out the door, Sasha hot on his heels.

While those two made a mockery of the sweater-wearing procedure, Millie calmly squeezed into her sweater knowing she'd be back out of it in a matter of minutes. Millie and cold weather never went well together—even when she was snuggled in a warm sweater. A few quick steps out the door were just enough to take care of business. Then she would hightail it back to the house—a mad dash through the snow—faster than if she had heard the dinner bell. The sweater was more or less ceremonial for Mil, but there was never a complaint.

On our Texas white Christmas, Sasha donned her pink Playboy parka for a few frolics in the snow. Sydney enjoyed a few dashes around the deck and Millie tried to avoid going out altogether. Jazzy found the playful allure of snowflakes satisfying, certainly worth braving a few minutes of cold feet every now and then.

It was a weather day for our record books and a holiday we will always remember.

After the holidays, I checked the clearance sales at local pet stores. I have often found a great selection of dog toys at greatly discounted prices, so I would stock up for future gifting occasions. That year was no exception and I found many bargains, including a couple of wraparound dog sweaters.

With January temperatures bordering on freezing, and in her fragile condition with little protection from muscle and flesh, these sweaters would be warm and comfortable for Sasha during bathroom breaks. Covering her back and sides (where she needed it most), these were quick and easy to wrap her up, unlike the suiting routine required for her pink parka snowflake antics.

A quilted sage green wrap cut the chill dramatically, but it did look as if she were walking around in a sleeping bag. The other sweater offered less cold weather protection, though in winter-appropriate dark plaid, it was much more fashionable. With a quick securing of Velcro straps, she was warm and ready to go in a snap. For a few weeks, these protective garments curtailed the cold temps during outdoor excursions.

To counter the few January days of freezing temperatures, many days were above normal. The last weekend of the month was unusually warm. Our guest bedroom, vacant after recent use during the holidays, also served as my music studio. With just a daybed to constitute a bedroom, lots of floor space sat empty, waiting for music equipment. Specifically, my drums.

In recent years, I had used a small four-piece drum kit in my bands or for home practice. My entire drum kit consisted of eleven drums and as many cymbals. This large configuration had remained in storage since we moved to Texas. Attending recent live concerts and my continuing desire to explore further music opportunities inspired me to unpack, clean, and reconstruct my full drum set in the music room. The combination of warmer weather, empty studio space, and free time to do it coincided nicely on that Saturday afternoon.

The dogs had grown accustomed to moving things around over the years, so Syd and Mil essentially ignored my leisurely afternoon and evening drum cleaning and building session. Sasha needed to know what was happening, so she made numerous trips to sit and watch the jungle gym of stands, skins, and cymbals continue to expand in what she had recently known as the guest bedroom. She always wanted to help.

If a project was pending, Sasha was first in line to participate. Building shelves, painting walls, moving furniture—these tasks were far more interesting to her than they were to me. If the project came in a box, she started on top of it, quickly moving on to opening and unpacking it. She took inventory of the contents as I searched for tools. She sat near as I assembled. She gave her final approval as we found the appropriate space to display our newest masterpiece.

When I recorded bandmates in the space my drums were slowly filling, Sasha was my studio assistant, alternating tasks between performance cheerleader in the studio and mixing engineer in the control room. As drum domination became our newest focus, she sat by to make sure I didn't forget anything. We worked in rhythm and shared our beats; I provided the drumbeat, and Sasha, the heartbeat.

The other pups made an occasional visit to check on my work in progress, mainly to remind me to break for their dinner prep soon. For Sydney and Millie—and most dogs, I imagine—the path to the heart starts at the stomach. Sasha never refused a meal or a snack, but spending time with people always came first. She would abandon her meal in a heartbeat if someone came to visit.

Before Millie lapsed into starvation, we took a doggie dinner recess. They gobbled the goods as I returned down the road to rhythm. Sasha ate her dinner and appeared to be in as good health as she had been all month. Throughout the evening, I carried her around the house between positioning and tuning drums, while rockin' out to a selection of greatest Rush tracks pulsating over the studio loudspeakers.

"The Spirit of Radio" echoed through the house as Carol returned home from work and Sasha expressed her typical upbeat enthusiasm. All seemed normal and my slow-paced drum renovations continued well into the night. Around five in the morning, when I finally finished, Sasha came to see me again. I held her for a few minutes while we sat behind the restored and sparkling, fully assembled eleven-piece drum kit. A few years earlier, I had sat with Sydney behind my much smaller drum setup, and Carol had snapped a few photos. I wish we had done the same with Sasha behind the drums on this final early Sunday morning of January.

Nevertheless, the picture remains a dynamic beat, forever in my heart.

SASHA RETURNED to the bedroom and fell asleep in front of my pillow while I shut down equipment and turned off lights before preparing for bed. I was moments away from settling into bed when I saw her start to have a seizure. I had helped her through dozens of seizures (or fainting spells), but it had been two months since she'd been through a similar episode.

This seemed the worst of all.

Like many times before, I was within mere steps when she tossed her head backward and started crying out for help. I immediately picked her up to calm her, holding her close against my chest, interrupting the attack. However, unlike previous times, she was very slow to recover. Carol woke up in the midst of this spell and we stayed with Sasha throughout the morning and the rest of the day while she showed only slight signs of feeling better. Her breathing problems also returned and were worse than usual. She found it increasingly difficult to lie down or remain comfortable.

By mid-afternoon, she began licking the bump on her leg. It had started to bleed lightly and she was keeping it clean. We were becoming extremely distressed. I called the vet clinic to see if Dr. Nowlan was working that afternoon. She often worked Sundays and we hoped she would be there for an emergency exam. No such luck. She was scheduled to work the next morning, however. We could have taken Sasha to see another vet, but we decided to make a morning appointment with Dr. Nowlan.

We cleaned Sasha's leg and applied antibiotic on the bump. I wrapped her leg in gauze and a bandage once in the evening and again at two in the morning. She still had an appetite and ate a good portion of her dinner on Sunday evening. She had good bowel movements. She seemed to be slowly recovering once again from the terrible CHF symptoms that continued to randomly appear and persistently plague her. She rested well for a few hours, and finally, so did I. But around six o'clock on Monday morning, her breathing problems returned.

I held her close as we walked slowly through the house for a while. I had not been in any hurry to take down the Christmas tree, but had not turned on the lights since the first week of January. Sasha always liked to see the twinkling lights on the tree, so in the darkness, I plugged in the lights and we walked around the living room. Blue, green, red, and yellow filled the holiday tree, while softly beaming to points on the walls. A galaxy of colors washed over the ceiling.

Sasha rested in my arms while my thoughts raced back through Christmases past with her. How she waited with her siblings, like a child, in great anticipation each Christmas morning to find and open her packages. How she went back and forth between Carol and me, checking out every present as it was opened. How she would play for hours with her new toys, until she could no longer keep her eyes open and a nap—belly-up under the Christmas tree—was imminent.

And then the reality of the moment set in and I had to catch my breath, knowing this slow dance in the dark, lit only by Christmas lights, would perhaps be her last time to see the colorful lights and experience a joyful holiday memory.

"Look at all the pretty lights."

I could barely get the words out, my voice cracking, as we paced the room.

While I hoped she enjoyed the sights and appreciated the gesture, she felt too bad to acknowledge it and remained still and quiet in my arms. After a few moving minutes, with tears in my eyes, we turned away.

And turned off the pretty lights for another season.

SASHA WAS UNABLE to rest comfortably as the minutes of the morning ticked by ever so slowly. It seemed her nine thirty exam could not arrive soon enough. I encouraged her to take her heart medicine, but she would not eat the other cheese-covered pills.

She fought bravely against her unsettling symptoms while we counted the minutes and got ready to go see Dr. Nowlan. Though calm, she struggled harder than she ever had before. I knew she felt extraordinarily bad; when we finally left the house, she did not show the same sort of enthusiasm she had always expressed when we were about to go for a car ride.

She sat on Carol's lap and panted lightly while I drove to the vet clinic. Upon weigh in, we discovered Sasha had lost another quarter-pound since the last visit and was down to her lowest weight as an adult dog, seven and one-quarter pounds. At her heaviest, she had tipped the scales at just over eleven pounds. In one year, CHF had claimed roughly one-third of her weight.

I sensed that Dr. Nowlan, while happy to see Sasha,

immediately noticed a worsened health condition. Upon examination, Sasha showed discomfort in her abdomen, indicating the advanced decline of her vital organs, and her gums had become pale. Dr. Nowlan recommended an injection of diuretic for immediate relief. Sasha had responded well to this during previous exams. Her right forearm (still wrapped in the bandage) showed signs of continued bleeding and needed tending as well.

Sasha did not struggle or object when the attending vet technician carried her from the examination room to administer the diuretic and bandage her leg. She never did. For her entire life, although I'm sure she felt concerned, she trusted my judgment if I allowed someone else to take her from me; she assumed they would be tending to her needs and would never do anything to hurt her. When I caught her glance this time, however, she gave me a much different impression.

Please don't leave me here, radiated from her dispirited eyes and echoed deep in my heart.

Carol sat quietly while I paced the room. Muted barks echoed from beyond the walls, the cries of unwillingly kenneled dogs waiting for the miracles of health care to cure their ills. We continued to pray for one of those miracles. Sasha had made it through a dozen similar vet visits for over a year. We remained optimistic that she would once again recover. But this time, we knew matters were much worse.

When Sasha was brought back into the examination room and handed to me, though not showing it as she would have in healthier times (tail wagging and happily panting), she was unmistakably relieved to be back in my arms. But even that was a bit too much for her failing body. She quickly became restless and wanted to stand on the examination table, a place she had never chosen to be. With a heavy dose of diuretic to reduce fluids and help her breathe easier, and a clean bandaged leg, Sasha was ready to go home for much-needed rest and recuperation. Carol had the day off and our plans were to stay home with her.

Once we left the clinic, we ran a few errands so we could be home the rest of the day. Sasha was riding comfortably on Carol's lap, looking out the window for most of the ride home. As I stopped at each location to take care of business, Carol and Sasha waited in the car. I'd return to see Sasha looking out the window as she always did, intently anticipating my return to the car. She seemed to be feeling better and was relieved to be going home.

When we arrived home, something was different. Sasha did not exhibit the usual happy aggravation with Sydney that she typically expressed while he ran through the house showing his excitement for our return. She was unusually calm and quiet, and no longer showed her typical reactions to the regular routine at home.

Although she seemed in better health and spirits during the ride home, she was suddenly uncomfortably detached from the norm. She held her head up to allow easier airflow to her lungs. She had to sit or walk around; if she made any attempt to lie down, that put too much pressure on her chest and she'd start to cough. Holding her caused the same reaction.

We still expected time would heal and she would see much-needed relief from the booster shot of diuretic. But her symptoms were not getting better. They were unlike anything we had seen to date and she seemed to be in rapid decline.

THROUGHOUT THE AFTERNOON, we took Sasha outside where Carol sat with her on the deck, trying to keep her comfortable, while she continued to show the same symptoms. Sydney and Millie were always nearby to keep her company and relish the mild winter weather. Unlike the freezing temperatures we had recently experienced, this was an unusually warm January day (in the seventies), yet it was overcast with gray clouds and windy.

The breeze blew Sasha's hair and ears from her face while she continually held her head back and neck extended, allowing the air to pass into her nose and mouth. This seemed to help her breathe. Upon coaxing her, she occasionally walked down into the yard, sometimes to sit, other times to consider going to the bathroom. She had only relieved her bladder once all day.

After about ten minutes outside, she decided to return indoors (on her own and through the dog door), finding a place in the kitchen to sit and continue her struggle to be comfortable. Every now and then she found a more secluded spot to sit, like her dog kennel, under Carol's makeup table, or in the shower stall.

She likely was looking for a place to die.

I began to grapple with those inevitable thoughts. I continued to question myself as I kept a watchful eye on Sasha.

How much longer could we possibly wait for the relief she desperately needed? Previously, relief had *always* come after trips to the vet, and after countless episodes of suffering the symptoms of congestive heart failure.

Should we return to the clinic? Would there be anything more Dr. Nowlan could do?

And the most gut-wrenching debate of all ...
Is it the *time?*

Months earlier, after bouts of fainting spells and seizures that came on quickly (and in those moments seemed too terrible for Sasha to recover from), I had a discussion with Carol about the inevitable. Not just any *bad* symptom, *the* bad one—the *final* one.

"What if something should happen to Sasha when you're at work? How could I possibly tell you over the phone? Do I wait until you are home?"

We could never come up with a satisfactory answer. We were finding it equally difficult to decide what to do that afternoon. Sasha was our baby girl. But she was suffering worse than she ever had before. But she was a fighter. We knew she could get through this again. We were with her to help her get through it again.

We wanted to believe.

AT ROUGHLY FOUR THIRTY-FIVE, Sasha was beginning her seventh hour since visiting the vet. Carol, tired and distraught, had taken a position on the floor in the hallway near the guest bedroom. All the pups gathered around. Sasha sat near for a while, then mustered the strength and took the lead, as usual, to climb into Carol's lap.

I was nearby in the kitchen during this entire display of attention and affection. Our terrific trio was etching another picture destined only for memory.

Sasha sat calmly, wanting to be close, trying to hide her concerns, but her joyous smile of ten years had fallen silent.

After a few moments in Carol's lap, Sasha decided to

walk over to her kennel. I took that opportunity to go to the bathroom. I soon realized that Sasha had followed me into the bedroom to sit near the bathroom doorway. As I stood by the sink, washing and drying my hands, I looked at her looking at me with her head held high, still extending her neck to breathe easier.

She sat quietly, devoted and faithful, her deep brown eyes focused, while I could no longer contain my sorrow and indecision.

I felt compelled to express my concerns and apologies to her about her failing condition. I would begin a brief conversation with Sasha that gave her "permission" to move on to a better place, far from the suffering she had been enduring not just that day and during the previous thirty-five hours, but for the past couple of years, no doubt.

"I am so sorry. I have done everything I can, but your body is just too frail. You have been so strong, and have fought this disease, but I don't want you to suffer anymore. It is all right. You can go."

Sasha continued to look into my eyes, never looking away. I felt the pain confronting her, not just of body, but of mind and spirit. She was suffering much more than we could possibly imagine, but she continued to be strong for us.

She did not want to leave us.

She was a loyal companion and did not want to disappoint us.

Repeating the most painful sentiments I ever had to say, I choked back the words, only a few escaping, telling her once again, "You can let go."

"Oh sweet girl, I ... I don't want to see you hurting or suffering anymore."

Our moment of communion was brief, the message explicit. For me, it was a heartrending confirmation of the inevitable. For her, it was a clock-stopping validation that the time had come. Within minutes, the profundity and immediacy of our understanding became devastatingly clear.

Sasha moved to an adjacent position underneath Carol's makeup table and chair, still sitting since she was unable to lie down without experiencing severely troubled breathing. It had been a half hour or so since we were outside, so I told her that we'd go out for a bit. I went to the kitchen to gather her sky blue doggie bath towel we had been using all day for her to sit on while we were out on the deck. I thought about placing the towel on the deck before going to get Sasha from the bedroom, but the strong breeze would have blown it away. I kept the towel with me, folding it into a soft cushion to carry her outside.

"Let's go outside to see if you need to tinkle," I said, as I lifted her onto the folded towel.

The towel was comfortable, but she needed to sit to keep pressure off her chest. We went outside to the deck, closest to the yard, where I gently set her down while she remained on the towel. Without hesitation, she took a small step down to the yard and promptly sat in the grass, next to the deck. She rested in that spot for a moment, taking in the fresh air of the persistent breeze.

Feeling distressed and defeated, I turned away from her to face the southwest skies, still gray with heavy clouds that raced briskly to the northeast, and exclaimed in desperate frustration, "If she's not able to recover from this, then take her now! I don't want her to suffer anymore! She is so strong and has put up such a fight, but she cannot take it anymore!

Please take her so she will no longer suffer!"

I had prayed to these same skies during starlit nights for months, asking that angels be sent from heaven to watch over Sasha, allowing her to stay with us another day, another week, another month, another year. We had passed all the specific events I'd so hoped Sasha would be with us to enjoy. I was grateful that she had remained in relatively good health and each holiday had come with wonderful celebration. My prayers had been answered. But day after day, I still continued to pray for Sasha's good health.

Every day was precious and we were forever thankful, but I knew that any day could very well be her last. When it became evident on that urgently windy gray day that Sasha's condition was not going to improve, and it had become just too unbearable to see her enduring in a way that was so physically demanding on her frail seven-pound body, I had no other prayer to ask except that she be taken to heaven and not made to suffer in this world anymore.

As I turned back to Sasha, still sitting in the grass near the deck, head in the air and little body strongly pulsing with every beat of her severely enlarged heart, she decided to walk a short distance to the edge of the yard. She assumed the usual position to poop. It was immediate and quick—one tiny plop. She had no strength to stand and instantly sat down right where she had pooped. I rushed over, lifting her gently to clean her off. Surprisingly, nothing had stuck and her rear was clean. I moved her a few feet away to the center of the yard to see if she also needed to pee. She sat down in the tall verdant grass, which was in an unusual growth spurt despite the recent freezing temperatures.

I returned to the deck to let her decide if she needed to

continue her bathroom break. It had only been a minute or two since I pleaded to the heavens, and another few minutes since we'd been inside having the heart-to-heart discussion about her suffering, and ultimately, her mortality. I never assumed that while she sat briefly in the middle of the yard, she was having more difficulty than she had minutes before. Maybe she wasn't, but she continued to sit.

I thought for a moment that it might be nice to gather the towel and take her to a bench toward the back of our yard to sit with her for a while. As I began to return to her, I decided it was probably better to return to the same spot where we had first sat. I spread the towel on the deck for her to sit on and walked over to her in the center of the yard. I gently lifted Sasha and carried her back to the deck.

Upon placing her and without delay, she rolled onto her left side, collapsing on the towel.

"Oh no! Sasha!" I cried out.

Her body was beginning to convulse and her breathing was unstable and rapid. I tried to steady her while thinking about running to the door to call for Carol to come out. But during that same split-second thought, I decided it was best to scoop her up with the towel and run inside where I placed her on our kitchen island. I called out to Carol (who had fallen asleep on the floor where her final comforting embrace with our sweet girl—Sasha's goodbye to Mama—had occurred fifteen minutes earlier). She rushed to the kitchen as we began to sob uncontrollably.

By that time—just seconds after she had collapsed on the deck—Sasha was lying calmly on her soft blue towel on our kitchen island and her breathing was declining rapidly. Each subsequent breath was further away from the previous one.

Sasha was nearing her final breath and there was nothing we could do except lament, calming and comforting her with loving praise through tearful words.

"It's okay. It's okay. You can go. We don't want you to suffer anymore. We love you so much!"

My heart was heavy, tugged in anguish, desperately wanting her to live, yet also relieved for the release of her burden. I felt helpless and overcome with guilt.

"Oh, my sweet girl, I'm so sorry. I'm so sorry. We love you so much!"

I could only encourage her to be free, away from the pain and doubt, to move toward the peaceable kingdom that awaited her arrival.

"Go into the light. It's okay. We love you so much!"

We caressed her limp, languid body, comforting her through a stream of tears we continued to shed. Expressions of our everlasting love for her would be the last words she would hear.

"We love you so much!"

In less than a minute, and with one final, short, and tiny cry, Sasha took her last breath on this Earth and passed on to a much more wonderful place, a divine dimension safe from harm, pain, and discomfort.

At 4:55 PM on Monday, January 28, 2013, our little Sasha—our sweet girl, Sasha—was gone.

She did not want to go. She loved her life in our family far beyond the limits her body could survive. But time had taken her away. Much too soon.

Carol and I stayed at her side, with aches to the core that

numbed all senses. We were drowning in emotions that flooded those final moments. As we gasped for breath, we grasped for each other.

The air was still. Ten years of exuberant energy rippled spontaneously away from our home. Life as we knew it, spilt from us all.

We were devastated.

Devastated, we were not defeated, for without faltering, Sasha's loving spirit would fill us and comfort our hearts.

It was our turn to be strong.

Rest in peace, dear Sasha girl.

We will miss you very much and we love you more than words can describe.

You are our sweet, sweet girl.

♪♫

chapter nine

faith

Sweet Girl

Faith

With impetuous evanescence, her personality and physical expression of individuality escaped this mortal existence, exiled to the memory of those fortunate enough to have experienced and witnessed her life form in all its unique magnificence.

The universe, as known to our family, changed forever as Sasha's lifeless body lay before us in a space reserved for happy family times. We shared the furthest emotion from happy as Sasha left this world calmly with a single, almost imperceptible cry. Unable to move or breathe, beyond the point of no return, it was her last effort to voice concerns.

Help me!
I don't want to go.
I'm afraid.
I'll miss you.
Goodbye ...

I could sense all these sentiments in that split-second syllable. Final words, before her spirit was forced to leave the weary shell of flesh and bones she had fought so long to inhabit and animate.

At that moment, she slipped from my grasp. She tried with all her might to hold on. She wanted to stay with us. And I could no longer help her.

A moment so difficult to grasp.

And that was it.

In an instant, Sasha was gone.

THE CENTER OF OUR UNIVERSE, our bright shining star burst like a supernova, slowly scattering her life force into the heavens, her radiance no longer physiologically restrained.

Two minutes earlier she had been walking in the yard, albeit, uncomfortably.

Two hours earlier she had posed for what became her final photographs.

Two days earlier she had been rock-'n'-rollin', keeping the beat as I set up my drums.

Two weeks earlier she had been sporting a new winter vest, delighted with a light snow.

Two months earlier she had enjoyed a holiday at home with our visiting niece.

Two years earlier she had been in her prime, yet to suffer the relentless symptoms of congestive heart failure.

Within two seconds of her death, time stood still, and her life began to flash before our eyes.

IN A FROZEN TRICE of grief and sorrow, our normally bustling kitchen had become jarringly vacant. Carol and I found ourselves alone. Our consolations, through tears, sniffles, and crestfallen embraces, must have alerted our household pets to leave this moment for us. Sydney, Millie, and Jazmine were nowhere to be seen. I did not realize this for several minutes, as I continued to caress and pet Sasha's tranquil body, trying to wrap my mind around what had just transpired.

Carol was facing the kitchen clock when Sasha passed, and noticed that it was five minutes to five. By the time I thought to look at the clock, it was 4:59, changing to 5:00 PM as I watched. I was already beginning to think ahead, deciding what we needed to do next.

From the time, roughly two years earlier, when Sasha had begun to have mild seizures and fainting spells, I had contemplated this eventuality we were suddenly facing.

How would we be prepared—emotionally *and* logistically—to handle her passing?

Would we face the question of euthanasia?

What would happen if she died at home?

Her death was now a reality, eliciting a vast outpouring of emotion and requiring immediate action on our part.

My mind was lost in emotion while trying to think clearly enough to make decisions that would impact us for the rest of our lives. We had spoken with the vet on an earlier occasion about options for cremation. A backyard burial was out of the question; the heavy clay soil was difficult to penetrate to a significant depth (as I found out firsthand when digging out our pond). While we did not want to rush any decision, we needed to act soon since the evening was upon us, and while the veterinarian's office was still open.

The time between a pet's passing and the "arrangements" for the body is one of the most difficult to confront. It's usually strictly limited, full of unyielding emotion, and with no freedom to honor the representation of what was, just minutes earlier, a beloved family member. Sasha was five days shy of ten years in our home, and, suddenly, in a matter of minutes, we had to arrange the removal of her physical presence from us forever.

Without pause, my first concern was brushing her hair, cleaning away a few spots of dirt and grass that had stuck from the yard. The hair on her face had dried remnants from weepy eyes. I used a fine-tooth comb regularly to keep her face clean and she always hated that. Sasha did not like having her face messed with. I'd grasp her hair behind the comb to reduce tugging on her skin, meticulously combing through gloppy eye goobers while she tried to be patient, eventually pulling her face away from me.

When done, I'd say, "Got it!" and Sasha would jump on my lap, kissing me on the face. It didn't seem to be a thank you for getting the mess off her face, but rather a thank you for stopping that nonsense altogether. On this final occasion, she could not resist my efforts, and her face was combed free of all unsightly debris.

"Got it," once again, but no kisses this time.

BRUSHING AND COMBING her hair was not one of her favorite pastimes. Her hair was so fine, it easily matted and clumped together the longer it got. Combing through matted hair is difficult at best, and when it caused unintentional tugging, Sasha did not like that. Baths hadn't been so bad. She enjoyed having the hair dryer treatment after a good massage-like towel drying. But she would have much preferred to avoid attention to her hair altogether. Sasha was a tomboy and primping was unnecessary, if it were up to her.

It wasn't up to her, though. To facilitate her grooming needs, we often left the details to the professional. Once every couple of months, Sasha visited a groomer for the chic treatment: haircut, trimming toenails, expressing of her anal glands, bath, blow-dry, and topknot styling. Ironically, she could not have been better behaved, unlike her acts of clear disapproval for such hogwash at home. Never a bad attitude for the groomer, but I'm sure she was secretly longing to just get done with it as soon as possible. Upon returning home, she always strutted around showing off her new do, which included her topknot decorated with a fashionable ribbon. She came across as proud and pretentious in front of Sydney and Millie, seemingly to hide her embarrassment.

Yes, I had a bath and a haircut. I smell nice. Yes, that's a bow in my hair. I look and smell much better than you filthy rascals, were the words I imagined she'd say, head held high, curtailing attempts by the other pups to make fun and diminish her dignity.

For the first few years of her life, we waited to see her hair grow long, flat, and silky white, according to the Maltese standard. Her coat never did become as straight and long along her topline as we had hoped; however, her hair did grow long on her head, ears, and tail. Her apricot puppy ears eventually changed to white, although upon close examination, a hint of light tan tint remained throughout her life. For coat reasons alone, Sasha would never have met the breed standard requirements in a dog show ring. That did not preclude the fact that she was indeed a true Maltese. It would have been unfair to classify her as "standard" anyways. Sasha was always a maverick, extraordinary and unique.

When she was about three years old and we determined that her hair had reached maximum length, the issues of frequent matting and Texas summer heat made the decision to cut it off all the easier. Trips to the groomer had usually included instructions to give her a puppy cut and only a trim to the head, face, ears, and tail.

We were fortunate to find Terri, a terrific dog groomer and wonderful friend, when she and Carol attended Bible study classes together in 2006. For Sasha's final few years, we were able to establish an exceptional routine for grooming. Carol would stay and visit with Terri while Sasha underwent her regular makeovers.

Grooming became a crucial consideration as Sasha's health began to decline. Never knowing when a seizure or fainting attack might occur, it was necessary for us to be close at hand to help Sasha through those times. A stressful occasion like a drop-off for the day at the groomer's salon might have triggered an unfortunate event that we were not willing to risk had it not been for Terri's accommodating schedule. Sasha sat patiently with Mama in her sights as her hair was sheared clear during a duet of hairdresser dialogue. With the selection of a colorful ribbon for her topknot, and a tie of the bow, Sasha was ready to go home, fresh, fit, and free.

Though she did not like the process, she did enjoy the finished product. Ever since her first professional grooming, she always preferred short haircuts. Afterwards, she felt comfortable and was always proud to show off her firm, athletic physique.

HER BODY, much too lean and failing much sooner than her radiant wits had desired, was now suddenly still, in eternal rest. A few final strokes of the brush through her medium-length coat rendered a proper final grooming for a body that had been unable to keep up with her spirited mind.

A blue pair-of-doves plastic hair clip always replaced the groomer's bow a few weeks after grooming. Every few days, I would take it out to comb her hair, replacing it properly to keep her long, flowing bangs from covering her face.

She wore it most of her life.

I removed the blue barrette from her hair for the final time and closed her eyes.

Having noticed the unusual absence of animals nearby, my attention was drawn to the whereabouts of Sydney and Millie. Syd had retreated outside to a favorite spot along the fence, searching for signs of his Jack Russell neighbor. I called him inside and picked him up, telling him Sasha had died. I took him over to her body so he could see. I wanted him to know what had happened to her, that she was in a better place and no longer suffering, and to let him know that he was all right. He could sense our sorrow and instinctively understood she was not alive.

I found Millie in the bedroom, resting in her dog bed. After I repeated the same sentiments and viewing for Mil, she offered a final nod to her big sister.

Jazzy, always more difficult to find than the others, came in through the doggie door at that moment and I lifted her to see. She let out a meow of sadness, sharing the condolences of all the siblings, *Our big sister, our friend, is gone.*

Finding a box to carry Sasha's body to the vet's office was conveniently quick. An Avon shipping box with a removable lid remained from the holidays. It was tidy and the perfect size. I prepared an old, clean bath towel in the bottom of her makeshift coffin, resting her body comfortably on the cushion. It had been a half hour since her passing. We still had many decisions to make.

For as long as I can remember, through all the deaths of dozens of pets in my family, my belief stayed firm about the separation of body and spirit. When all signs of life had escaped the fun-loving, friendly frame of a beloved companion, I always believed that the essence—the true spirit—was safe and far removed from the troubled shell that remained.

Burying or cremating a pet's body as soon as possible was the proper means of disposal. A tribute would be in spirit. So, I decided we would deliver Sasha's body to the vet's office and pay the minimum fee for a communal cremation, a proper procedure. At nine o'clock that evening, that is what we did. After all, we would have many ways to honor her memory at home.

Sometimes, especially in haste, overwhelming emotion, clouded thoughts, or plain stupidity, a regrettable decision is inevitable. Fortunately for me, even after a few short hours of sleep and continued grieving, I began to think more clearly.

A communal cremation?

How could we rightfully surrender her body to some random mass incineration?

How would that possibly honor the memory of our beloved Sasha?

Yes, it was "just a body" now, but it was Sasha's body, a body we had loved, nurtured, and protected for ten years. It was our sweet girl.

What had I been thinking?

These thoughts began to tear at my very core. I was kicking myself for making such a rash decision as every minute of the morning ticked by and I was waiting for Carol to awake.

"I've been having second thoughts about Sasha's cremation," I told Carol.

Having had much better sleep than I did, she was now out of bed and preparing breakfast.

"I don't know what I was thinking. We should have a private cremation for her," I continued.

A private cremation was just that. Sasha's body would be isolated, her ashes collected and placed in an urn for us to keep. The cost was about three times what we had paid for the communal cremation. We were already on a tight budget, but, at that point, cost was not a consideration. It didn't matter. Doing the right thing was all that mattered.

I asked Carol, "Why don't you call the vet's office to find out more details about changing the arrangements? I hope it's not too late."

We knew that the cremation was handled through another company on the outskirts of Fort Worth, and it would likely be a day or two before it happened, but we needed to confirm these new arrangements and pay for the changes. The vet's staff could not have been more caring and accommodating, promptly issuing the necessary instructions to all concerned to reflect our change of heart.

To further investigate my modified plan, I looked at the website for Smoke Rise Farm, a renowned pet cemetery in Azle, Texas, where the cremation would take place. I discovered many options, more than the few services offered through the vet's office. In addition to a private cremation, we could schedule and attend the cremation, have a funeral service, so to speak.

I felt as if I had unearthed a buried treasure.

A wave of different emotion, opposite from the gloom I'd been drowning in, washed over me. I was filled with tremendous elation and relief that our time with Sasha's physical presence might not be finished and forgotten. We had another chance to see her. Her dismissal did not have to be so painfully abrupt. We could honor her whole being, tending her body through to the very end, to ashes, to dust. For our sweet girl, *this* was the proper procedure.

After my heedless decision the night before, I finally felt joyfully redeemed. Carol phoned Smoke Rise Farm to offer details about Sasha, arranging our private appointment for her "funeral" Thursday morning at nine o'clock, two days away.

That was perfect.

It would give us a day to collect ourselves and be in a better frame of mind. We could rest assured that Sasha's remains would be handled with care until we saw her again. We were still filled with sorrow, but the stress all but disappeared. In my mind's confusion of circumstance, my underlying faith prevailed. We were undeniably guided to the right course of action by earthly angels when my own judgment failed.

I felt better about the arrangements, but it remained difficult to sit still. Doing so only invited memories of Sasha to flood my mind and strain my equanimity. I had to continue moving. I had to think of other things.

I packed away most of the Christmas decorations that continued to adorn our living room and vacuumed the entire house. I spent time with Sydney and Millie, continuing to show them how much we loved them and that everything would be all right.

I set out three doggie plates as I began to prepare their dinner. Force of habit. I'd catch myself doing that for the next few days.

Tuesday evening, Becky and our friend, Seena, came by to take us out for dinner for a change of atmosphere. I was reluctant to go, but they insisted and it eased our grief substantially.

Later that evening, it felt right to assemble a photo collage and short "obituary" to post online to notify friends and family of our loss. An abundant outpouring of sincere sympathy filled our inbox for days to come, touching our hearts and easing our minds.

AFTER ANOTHER near-sleepless night, Wednesday morning arrived and we had to resume our "normal" schedule. Carol prepared a nice Aussie-inspired "brekkie" for us: scrambled eggs, sautéed mushrooms and halved tomatoes, fresh kiwifruit, and orange segments. She would soon be off to work and I had a few errands to run.

We were still mourning, but that did not seem unusual. We felt ready to face the world again. We hadn't been outside during daylight hours since Sasha's passing. We didn't expect that to elicit unusual feelings, but it did, dramatically. My impression of the proverbial world I'd always known changed to something oddly different.

It was sunny, yet chilly, in the early afternoon when Carol left for work. I followed shortly thereafter, my destination being the post office, noticing something curious along the way. Everything—roads, trees, houses, buildings, people driving—was familiar, yet seemed strangely sterile and foreign.

Boundless winter rays washed out the customary azure, creating a pale backdrop for a smattering of wispy clouds billowing swiftly, merely to fade away. A golden hue suffused the environment. The ambient tone seemed ethereal.

I became transfixed, almost hypnotized, observing this otherworldly atmosphere. It occurred to me that I wasn't in a hurry—I was driving much below the speed limit—and I continued at a slower, relaxed pace, just taking in these eerie feelings. As I viewed life through the windshield, everything seemed routine, unemotional, and oblivious; it was a mechanical world moving like clockwork as I drifted through it. (I was reminded of *The Matrix* movie, when the main character becomes able to see "the matrix," the world defined by scrolling columns of green digital codes, a computer program creating simulated reality for an assimilated society.)

Was it a spiritual awakening?

Was I suddenly seeing things on a different celestial plane?

Was I experiencing an alternate universe?

This "new" universe is one without Sasha. Does that mean the "normal" universe continues with her still in it?

I arrived at the post office and the strange sensation continued. It didn't occur to me until a few days later that I drove an "old" route to the post office that day, a path not taken for several months since a new, more direct road had opened. It seemed I was on autopilot, following a predetermined course, which allowed me to observe and absorb my surroundings more easily than usual.

I also stopped at Walgreens to return one of the doggie sweater gift sets I had purchased for Sasha just after the holidays. It did not fit her and was never used. I took it to the counter for a refund, explaining that the sweater was just too small.

Unexpectedly, the older woman clerk said, "You should

get a smaller dog."

I blithely replied, "Yes," hesitating to say anything about the unfortunate truth. She handed me the cash refund and I exited to the anomalous milieu.

Once I returned home, the strange feeling outside became omnipresent. Inside, I began to experience a whole new sensation of "different." While it was bright and methodical outdoors, indoors was dark and disconcerted. I was seeing everything from a skewed perspective.

It was all just there.

Nothing of interest.

Simply material objects.

It seemed as if the house had been spun in circles, rotated to face another orientation. My sense of direction inside the house gave me a distinct feeling that the outside perspective had changed.

Very weird.

Everything was out of whack. I felt trapped in some kind of time warp, somewhere between Sasha's dying, when emotional time came to a halt, seemingly caught in hazy perpetuity, and the apathetic clockwork world moving unstoppably forward in so-called real time. I could not sit still. I had no desire to watch TV. Even sitting at the computer seemed wrong. I had to keep moving. This was not my typical behavior.

I phoned Carol to see how she was doing, telling her about my newfound feelings. She had had similar sensations during her commute to work. Everything felt different to her as well. Of course, she was busy with her work and could not reflect upon her experiences to the extent that I could.

As unusual as everything seemed, I tried desperately to

stay in touch with those feelings. The more I relaxed my mind to embrace the sensations, the more supernatural they began to feel, and even from a different universe to that which I'd been accustomed. Everything physical and material seemed superficial and irrelevant. I had no interests or desires, except to be in touch with the spiritual world around me.

And with Sasha.

I WAS UP AT SIX THIRTY on Thursday morning, an hour before we needed to leave so we'd arrive at Smoke Rise Farm by nine o'clock. It still felt strange in the house, and especially odd outdoors again, on a cold, clear day. It was nearly seven thirty when Carol woke up, still sleepy, but she quickly got ready to go. We told the pups we would be back in a few hours as we headed out at seven forty-five.

We'd been to Azle to visit friends many years ago, so I was sure my memory of the highway route would serve me well. I merely noted the address and roads near our destination. While we were driving, Carol input the information into her phone's GPS as well, so I wasn't concerned about the route. That is, until unexpected chaos began to cloud our travel.

We were in the midst of morning rush-hour traffic heading west and the sun was starting to beam furiously from behind. Our conversation centered on the odd feelings and strange perceptions we were having—our "golden matrix." I'd driven that stretch of highway to Fort Worth dozens of times, but that day felt unlike any other. The eerie sensation was similar to the day before, but much greater in intensity.

As we neared the southwest side of Fort Worth, I knew we'd need to exit north soon, so I asked Carol to check the GPS to confirm. The highway we wanted nearly circles the city, so confusion ensued and I became lost in translation.

I exited to a familiar highway that I incorrectly assumed was the one I had hoped to take. It would lead us in the right direction, but with many stop lights along the way. We were already beginning to run late after an earlier stop-and-go session, inching along the freeway to get past a fender bender a few miles back. To make matters worse, upon taking this exit, we were directly swallowed up by a massive construction zone that ironically became, in and of itself, a spectacular escapade.

The world once again felt extremely bizarre as we drove through a new highway construction area that appeared more like a quarry. The partitioned roads were wicked and narrow, weaving through canyons of bedrock and stone, sometimes winding high with deep drop-offs and no shoulders, clearly not typical of Fort Worth terrain.

(I later found out that this unintended route would become a section of a new highway—the Chisholm Trail Parkway. This revelation seemed both uncanny and relevant. Like the drovers in the late 1800s, delivering Texas longhorn cattle on their long, arduous, final journey through canyons and badlands, we were on our own long and difficult journey—to Sasha's final deliverance.)

The peculiar, bright golden hue that presided in the atmosphere seemed amplified during those few dusty miles. Looking beyond the construction, the landscape was familiar, but the sometimes excavated, sometimes elevated, barren route made it seem as if we were driving on another planet.

I marveled at this oddly alien environment, and tried to be receptive to all the strange sensations we had been encountering. I wanted to understand why I was having such an unusual perspective on the world.

It was so bizarre, but I liked it.

It had a calming effect on me when I would allow myself to meditate on those feelings. Unfortunately, time and reality began to dominate all my other thoughts, and the end of the construction zone alerted me to our continued delay.

"How many miles till our next turn?" I asked Carol.

She checked the GPS and determined where to turn northwest toward Azle.

"It's about six more miles," she said as the car clock changed to a quarter to nine.

With over fifteen miles and several stop lights between us and our destination, I suggested that she call to let them know we were running late. I was becoming increasingly frustrated, knowing we should have left earlier and I should have confirmed my route ahead of time.

"I did not want to be late," I said in a bitter tone.

I had been letting the spiritual calm of the recent odd sensations fill me, making every effort to cast away undesirable attitudes and emotions during this time of sorrow and remembrance. But it was just almost too much for me to bear that we were going to be late for Sasha's service.

"I just can't believe it. I knew this would happen. I'm sure I'll be late for my own funeral," I said as we continued driving farther away from the populous urban outskirts.

At five minutes after nine in the rural countryside, we turned down a long gravel road, marked by a sign that proclaimed SMOKE RISE FARM in capital letters. Our attention was drawn to our left, beyond a split-rail fence, to a pleasingly-maintained pet cemetery lined with gravestones honoring hundreds of beloved departed pets and statues of Saint Francis of Assisi gazing peacefully in the morning sunlight. These sights gave me solace and eased my tension.

Directly ahead, in a small office building, we would meet the gracious, caring proprietors who were prepared to welcome us in the manner of any respected funeral home. As we pulled into the parking lot, we noticed that we were the only visitors. Our slight tardiness was of no consequence. Regretful thoughts of my outbursts of frustration became instantly consumed by the serene calm that I had hoped to maintain during our time of mourning.

SMOKE RISE FARM, a full-service family owned and operated pet cemetery, has provided respectful cremation and burial services since 1982. The Operations Manager (OM) and an office assistant greeted us at the door and offered their sincere condolences as we introduced ourselves. After a few moments to catch our breath and collect our thoughts, they asked if we were ready to see Sasha.

Although expected, those words seemed surreal, but that *was* the reason for our morning rush-hour journey. The focus of our visit came rushing back to me in an emotional avalanche as we were kindly escorted to the crematorium, a few steps outside the back door.

Adjacent to the main office, a pole barn-type building housed several crematories, each intended for different arrangements. Large crematories could accommodate several isolated corpses, for separate private cremations. A smaller crematory was for an individual private cremation, if a separate private cremation was not acceptable. And a large outdoor crematory chamber was used for communal cremations, with no way to identify individual cremains.

When we discovered the unique differences between the cremation procedures, I was once again thrilled and relieved to enter the part of the building that housed the small crematory. We were led straight ahead to a table where Sasha's body rested on a large towel. Our first glimpse, two and a half days since we had handed her over to the vet's office in our delicately-prepared corrugated box, was cue to skip the breath we just caught and scatter our collected thoughts into an emotional flurry.

Sasha had been carefully prepared for our visitation; her hair was brushed and she rested on her right side, slightly concealing her still swollen, unwrapped front leg. The OM told us to take as long as we'd like and left the building, giving us several precious minutes to spend with our sweet girl one final time.

Immediately following her death at home, as I brushed her hair and set her body gently in the cardboard coffin, I had not experienced the same sense of serenity that I now felt her body and spirit had attained as she lay before us.

Sasha was at peace.

Illness and struggles were left far behind.

Her spirit was free and far removed from these magnificent remains.

Carol and I took turns stroking her side, her pure white hair so soft and delicate. That was the feeling we'd find so hard to release. The physical touch of our sweet girl meant so much, and now, it would only be a treasured memory. One to add to the cornucopia of memories created and shared every day from within that compact treasure chest of flesh and bone: her spirited personality, her unique individuality, and her delightful physical presence in our lives.

Several months before her passing, during one of her beauty sessions, we had saved some of Sasha's hair clippings in anticipation of the day we would no longer see her snow-white coat. We decided to do the same thing one more time. Carol brought styling scissors for a snippet of Sasha's hair. We would keep it with her ashes in loving memory.

Carol said a little prayer for Sasha, and for our family, and we said our final goodbye to our sweet girl.

We summoned the OM back inside where he began to explain the cremation process. He demonstrated what would happen with the crematory, which was just to our left. He asked if we had any final questions or comments, and then proceeded with the cremation preparations.

I reached out to pet Sasha one final time, commenting, "Her hair is so soft."

He nodded and gently lifted her body to center it inside the crematory. Our eyes began to well with tears as he pressed the button to fire the furnace. We could hear it ignite behind the back panel. The front door panel slid shut, shielding Sasha's peaceful body from view, allowing the main burner to start the cremation.

The furnace roared. Our hearts sank to the pits of our stomachs. Sasha's spirit soared safely far and away.

With a mournful sigh, and wiping the tears from our eyes, we departed the crematorium.

In two hours, we would return to collect her ashes.

I ASKED THE OM if there were any good breakfast restaurants nearby. He suggested a hometown diner, popular with the locals. The Azle Café was exactly what we were looking for. We knew we'd be in for a treat when we saw a sign near the door, "Biker Babe Parking Only." (I don't think it was a joke.)

There were only a few customers remaining after the morning rush. We chose our seats in the booth labeled with a street sign that said, "Elvis Presley Blvd." Carol sat under a large '60s-era photo of a leather-clad Elvis, while we studied a menu of abundant breakfast choices. Carol settled on a Southwest egg scramble with hash browns and a biscuit, while I ordered a ham-and-cheese omelet with hash browns and a single pancake.

I asked our waitress, a sprightly young woman, "How large is the pancake?"

"Oh, it covers the plate," she said in a matter-of-fact tone.

I chuckled at her exaggeration.

When my omelet and hash browns arrived on one plate, I found out she hadn't been kidding. I could only assume there was a second plate underneath the hubcap-size flapjack she scooted across the table.

"Can I get you anything else?" she asked.

"Maybe a few hours to eat all of this!" I said, with a glancing double take at the gigantic pancake. But I was now ready to savor and slowly devour our morning feast.

After all, we weren't in any hurry to eat. We enjoyed the quiet breakfast while reminiscing about the earlier days of Sasha's life. The pancake recalled memories of our road trips when the pups looked forward to hotel stays, a sure sign that mornings would include treats from the breakfast buffet.

The most favorite morning morsel was found only at pet-friendly Texas La Quinta Inns & Suites: a Texas-shaped waffle that Sasha conspicuously spied from the bed, stretching and straining to reach it while we dined at the adjacent desk. Hotel rooms were thrilling adventures for Sasha. She loved to bounce from bed to bed, digging, tunneling, and rolling around in all the fluffy pillows. She always chose the best pillow to snuggle in for a good night's sleep, in anticipation of waking to Mama's room-service breakfast the next morning.

An hour and a half into our leisurely breakfast, we were bursting at the seams and ready to return to Smoke Rise Farm. It would be another emotional few minutes while we drove, knowing our sweet girl had completed her physical journey on this Earth. We arrived a few minutes earlier than scheduled, so Carol decided to nap briefly in the car.

My fingernails were in need of a trim, so for some odd and unknown reason, I had thought in advance to bring clippers, something I rarely carried with me. I took the opportunity to step outside the car to the gravel parking lot and began to clip my nails. The office assistant noticed our return and came out to tell us that Sasha's cremains were ready. I acknowledged, saying we'd be there in a moment.

I wanted to finish my impromptu manicure. With hundreds of pets laid to rest just beyond the fence in front of me, an interesting thought came to mind as I littered the ground with tiny, indecipherable fingernail fragments. I was leaving a part of me on those grounds, just as an inevitable fraction of smoke and ash from Sasha's cremation would forever grace that location. It was a comforting thought. Even as we would go home with Sasha's ashes, the tiny bit of her that remained would not be left alone so far from home without a trace of her family left behind as well.

Maybe the notion to grab my clippers that day wasn't just because I needed a trim?

WE JOINED THE OFFICE ASSISTANT inside to find a small rectangular cedar box sitting on her desk. A brass nameplate adorned the top, engraved with a filigree design and "SASHA" in caps. The hinged lid remained closed with a small padlock in the front hasp.

"Would you like to see the ashes?" she asked as she prepared to open the padlock.

"Yes, of course," we said without hesitation.

"Some people would prefer not to see," she explained, "so I always ask first."

We appreciated every care and concern expressed and demonstrated by the personnel at Smoke Rise Farm that morning. It was their business to be caring, but we could still sense genuine empathy for our difficult loss and much heartfelt sympathy.

The office assistant proceeded to remove a pint-size zip-top bag from the cedar urn, roughly one-quarter full with Sasha's grey ashes. She went on to explain that it was impossible to collect every bit of ash, but what we had was most of what remained.

Not very much. (That also confirmed my earlier thoughts about Sasha's residual ash that would inescapably rest forever at Smoke Rise Farm.)

Her ashes were an early concern when I was making rash decisions about her cremation. I confidently separated body and spirit. I could release the responsibility of protecting her in the physical world. But that would fundamentally extend to her cremains. She was gone. Her spirit was safe. But with a private cremation, we would still need to look after her ashes.

Throughout this entire process—with a leap of faith to do the right thing—I was uplifted with confidence in having made the right choices, expertly guided by many angels along the way.

From the caring attention and accommodations at the vet clinic, to the empathetic embrace from pet cemetery undertakers we'd never previously met, Sasha's remains were always in good hands. I felt reassured when her final cremains had returned to our loving possession. It was our responsibility. It would be our choice.

We would find the perfect resting place for her ashes.

WE SAT IN THE OFFICE chatting for a while, sharing stories about Sasha and listening to the office assistant describe similar, yet unique instances with pets in her own family. After several minutes, I felt confident I could share my story of Sasha's final communion.

With a lump in my throat and a brief hesitation to contain my overwhelming emotional state as I began to think of what I was about to say, I described my last few minutes with Sasha. (Specifically, the moment when I told Sasha that I did not want her to suffer anymore, that it was all right to let go—and then minutes later, she was gone.)

My eyes began to well with tears again, but it felt good to share this story. It was during those few days between death and cremation that reflections on those exact moments of communion kept hitting me like golden bricks from heaven.

Sasha's was an important story to tell.

A defined purpose suddenly appeared clear to me, much more than anything else ever had before.

I had struggled for many years, trying to find the meaning of life. I had lost faith in daily routine. A few close relationships—family, friends, pets, and God—had remained loving and hopeful. But faith in understanding any overall purpose had continued to dwindle.

From next to nothing, hit with the terrible loss of our sweet girl, came this growing point of light illuminating the path out of darkness. It was my tiny companion, my best friend of ten years, nonjudgmental and overflowing with unconditional love, suddenly guiding me from beyond, toward ways I couldn't see on my own.

In life, Sasha gave me the glimmer of hope to continue, and now in death, she restored faith in my direction.

WE DROVE AWAY from Smoke Rise Farm, following the road home through the golden matrix. It was all beginning to make sense.

It was an epiphany.

Almost ten years to the day earlier, we were on a long drive home with our cute little bundle of love resting peacefully on Carol's lap. We had no idea what to expect from the relationship ahead.

It just happened to become the most spectacular, rewarding ten-year relationship I've ever known. It defined my life in more ways than I'll ever realize.

Once again, we were on another long drive home with our cute little bundle of love resting peacefully on Carol's lap.

This time, however, it was a cedar box urn with our sweet angel guiding us from heaven above.

♪♫

Sweet Girl

chapter ten

signs

Sweet Girl

PARANORMAL is an adjective that means "not within the range of normal experience or scientifically explainable phenomena."[2] Statistically, a death in the family occurs infrequently and, therefore, is outside the range of "normal" experience for most people. So, I suppose strictly by definition, the loss of a loved one could be considered "paranormal" activity. However, it is usually the unusual, inexplicable activities occurring after a death that become classified as paranormal, assuming a supernatural identity.

COINCIDENCE is a noun that means "a sequence of events that although accidental seems to have been planned or arranged; the state or fact of corresponding exactly at the same time or in the same place."[2] Unusual alerts to the senses—precisely familiar or oddly apropos—after the passing of a loved one may be regarded as coincidence, warranting relatively little attention.

WHEN IS A PRESUMED COINCIDENCE significant enough to note? And if, upon further investigation, it just seems too specific (or unbelievable), then how do we explain it?

Does an unusual coincidence subsequent to a death suggest paranormal activity? Perhaps, if one believes that inexplicable phenomena are spiritual sensations.

What does it matter? A label is not required.

But in the minutes, hours, days, and weeks following Sasha's passing, there were plenty of odd events worth noting.

So for the record:

It ...

Just ...

Happened.

WHETHER SIMPLY STRANGE, *soundly spiritual, something supernatural, or subtle signs from Sasha, several scenarios set the scene, summoning our skeptical, yet susceptible senses.*

I've always believed we are guided and visited by spirits. Consciously, subconsciously, or in our dreams, people and animals no longer with us in this world often send us messages, especially when we seek hope and faith. We simply need to be accessible to the communication, sometimes in ways we least expect. Our vulnerability during emotional times may be just the reason we can tune in to these spiritual broadcasts.

My greatest awareness of a clear spiritual message came during the vision of my departed grandparents, shortly after my grandfather's passing. Before that, a few deceased pets made ghostly appearances days after their passing. In similar instances, I sensed their presence as I slept, waking me as they approached and nudged the bed. The sensations were always distinctly different from dreams, with strong messages conveying peaceful calm. Interestingly, these paranormal communications did not occur with every pet that passed, and often with those I would least have expected.

I wanted to believe that if any pet would attempt such communication, it would be my closest canine companion. During her life, I had always felt a closer connection with Sasha than I had with any of my other pets.

Sasha was my animal soul mate.

There were countless instances of extrasensory perception. A simple glance into her eyes might suggest several different intentions—to go outside, to fetch a toy, to look for Mama—but she always knew what I intended before I said a word.

It was reciprocal.

She would often come to me, stop, and look straight into my eyes, and I knew exactly what she wanted. It might be as simple as "I need to go potty" or "It's dinnertime," but the communication was clear and unspoken.

If any pet could traverse psychic dimensions, I hoped Sasha would try.

I supposed that the most joyous interaction might be in a vision, as I had experienced with my grandparents. I would be happy just to have Sasha visit in my dreams. Eventually, that would happen, but contact came in a much different form and in many more ways than we could have imagined. The message would not be clear and precisely defined, but the communication was evident.

It wasn't the expected "I'm okay and at peace" declaration I was hoping to experience. Instead, the feeling was always a sign that she was near; her spirit was with us. I could, therefore, confidently assume that through these "messages," she was trying to let us know that she was okay and at peace.

After delivering her body to the vet's office (four hours after her passing), we stopped to pick up In-N-Out burgers and fries. As the sad events of the day played out, we hadn't taken time to eat, so we just wanted something quick.

The fast food aromas filled the car as we patiently waited to consume our meal, with only a few nibbles of french fries on the way home. As the sweet smell of indulgence followed us into our kitchen, the deep-fried fragrance was summarily replaced by the scent of our sweet girl. In two specific areas—first, close to where she had passed away in the kitchen, and a short time later, next to our computer desk in the bedroom, a place where she often slept while we worked—there was a strong sense of Sasha.

She did not normally exude an "animal perfume" unless recently bathed and groomed, and then she would sport a bouquet of cleanliness. Maltese dogs do not smell like dogs with fur. Of course, if they're dirty, a stench is likely, but Sasha rarely gave off a filthy dog odor.

She had, however, been in need of a bath, so she had been presenting a distinct scent in her final days. It was barely noticeable on her, but when we returned home that evening, that unmistakable aroma was in the air, strong and specific. It was evident for only a few moments before it vanished forever, but long enough for us to take notice. An overwhelming olfactory anomaly was Sasha's first reminder that although her body was gone, she was still very much with us.

After our burger dinner, I didn't hesitate to continue Sasha's late night quest for bunny sightings. While Sasha was with us in spirit, Millie was pleased to join the search that first night when we promptly spotted a rabbit in our front yard. Not unusual, but rare. Most sightings occurred in the large neighboring yard.

The nightly bunny hunt gradually became more random, but Sydney and Millie always enjoyed a late night look. We'd see rabbits on several occasions, sometimes two or three at a time, then after two weeks, the sightings abruptly stopped. Undoubtedly, Sasha continues her celestial quest, amongst more bunnies than she ever imagined from the edge of our terrestrial yard.

As briskly moving clouds continued to sweep overhead into the overnight hours of that gloomy Monday, I accompanied the dogs—sadly one fewer than usual—to the backyard for their final bathroom break before bedtime. While Syd and Mil tended to their business, I stood on the deck as I had when praying to the heavens night after night for many months. I watched the clouds race by, covering every angle of the midnight sky. I talked to Sasha, telling her we loved her and missed her, and that we were glad she was no longer suffering.

Then, as if on cue, a small break in the clouds formed directly above with one bright star shimmering through. Alas, the fleeting look lasted less than a minute, fading behind the billows. It was a brief visual moment in our time, but an eternity in significance.

The cloud-covered skies could not hide that Sasha was

already shining down on us.

This same scenario—overcast skies and the same single bright star with no other stars in sight—occurred two more times with special significance: one week to the day after her death and two weeks to the day after her death.

Probably a coincidence. Perhaps paranormal?

ALTHOUGH I HAD HOPED for Sasha's blatant starring role in my dreams, the few hours I did sleep in the nights leading up to her cremation were devoid of dreams, or there was nothing to note. It was the mysterious golden matrix that awed our imagination, filling time between the grieving thoughts and treasured memories of our sweet girl.

We continued our trek home from the pet cemetery, Sasha's ashes in cedar, cradled by Carol, who dozed while I drove. I replayed the events of the morning in my mind, over and over, while soaking in the pervasive, enigmatic atmosphere. Over halfway through the hour-long drive, it dawned on me that I was not listening to music, so I turned on the radio. As a repeating refrain faded, the first full song began to play, an '80s classic I hadn't heard in years.

Cyndi Lauper's "Girls Just Wanna Have Fun."

Coincidence?

Sasha was sharing her message through song.

FEBRUARY 3 marked the tenth anniversary of Sasha's adoption. To celebrate this occasion, she did not fail to make her presence known. This time her message was rather mischievous.

It was Super Bowl Sunday, so I fed the dogs their dinner before the game started. As halftime approached, I noticed that we hadn't seen Jazzy in a while. She usually sauntered in during the pups' dinner, but not that evening. I decided to look in the backyard, but she was nowhere to be found. I checked the house again, looking under the bed and in every possible hiding place. I searched the yard once again with no luck.

Jazmine had disappeared.

It doesn't seem unusual for a cat to leave a yard surrounded by a wooden stockade fence, but it was unusual for our cat. When Jazmine came to live with us as a kitten, she quickly assumed she was one of the dogs. Everything the dogs did, she felt the need to do as well. When she watched the dogs pass through that magic flap to the outside world, she knew it was her door to the land of enchantment. Once through that passage, there was no turning back. If she was going to spend time in the backyard, I had to have a plan to keep her there. I did not want our cat to roam the neighborhood.

I started with trimming her claws. Most cats—at least the cats I've known—hate to have their paws messed with, especially to have their claws cut. Not Jazmine. Jazzy always sat calmly on my lap while I held each paw and clipped the needle-like tip of each claw. She would start to show a bit of impatience by the time I got to the last foot, but she always tolerated my efforts to keep her claws blunt. This made it slightly more difficult for her to climb the fence, but it certainly would not stop her from trying and, ultimately, succeeding.

We blocked the dog door for a while, but that did not sit

well with the pups. Before Jazmine could fall down that rabbit hole—her portal to adventures—we would need to implement some sort of barrier to keep our curious kitty corralled to the confines of our home range oasis. I needed a simple, quick solution.

I was racing the clock while our confounded cat was disappearing in a mad dash around our kitchen, growing restless waiting for wonderland.

After looking at several containment options, I decided the best method to see our cat grin was an invisible fence. I strung the single electric wire around the perimeter of our fence and placed the detector collar on Jazzy. If she tried to climb the fence, the collar would give a static shock and she'd retreat. Just a few attempts curbed her desire for additional test runs. The miracles of nature in our yard kept her entertained and engaged, so she was happy to stay put.

Soon after I implemented this system, I thought we had a failure. It was late one night when I could not find Jazmine, indoors or out. I circled the yard several times, checking under bushes and in trees, calling her name. The dogs had gone to bed and I was about to do the same, leaving the doggie door open just in case Jazz was hiding outside and decided to come back in.

Suddenly, with explosive force, an orange blur burst through the door. I jumped back, nearly knocking over a chair, when Jazmine ran past as if a coyote were on her tail. Her hair stood in a ridge along her back, her tail spiked like a bottlebrush. She slammed on the brakes when she saw me standing near, and started walking around my feet, wanting to say, *Hey, what's up? Just another normal night, huh?*

She was filthy, splotched with pine tar, and her collar was

missing. I assumed smelly cat breached the system, climbing over the fence and into the woods. I grabbed her and headed straight to the bath tub, closing the bathroom door behind us. If she happened to get away from me, she wasn't going to go far.

Holding the scruff of her neck in one hand and the shower sprayer in the other, I began to wet her down. As I traded the shower spray for a bottle of shampoo, Jazzy started to sing her sad cry of great displeasure. This was her first bath, in the middle of the night, and she wanted no part of it. She squirmed a fair amount while her wretched cat song continued to crescendo into the coda.

A few minutes later, without a scratch to my bare limbs, Jazz was wrapped in a towel, looking only a slight bit happier. When I opened the bathroom door, I discovered Sasha sitting there filled with curiosity about what I was doing to that cat. Whatever it was, she knew the cat deserved it. This was a midnight feature she did not want to miss.

After a good night's sleep, I discovered Jazzy's collar in the yard, near one of our pine trees. Apparently, she had been in the evergreen, too embarrassed to let me know she could not get down as I searched for her. She had mustered the courage to leap, knocking her collar off before scrambling to the house and right into the unexpected late-night soaking surprise.

When she went missing on Super Bowl Sunday, I checked all the trees thoroughly, and every other hiding place I could imagine. It was after dark, so with flashlight in hand, I decided to take a look over the fence, into the woods. I shined the beam along the back of the fence and, lo and behold, about twenty feet away, Jazmine was crouched, collar still secure, staring back at me in bewilderment. She seemed as surprised as I was that she was on the wrong side of the fence.

After fourteen months with no escapes, Jazzy defied the shock treatment and found her way out of wonderland and into never-never land.

Once back in the yard, I checked her collar and the battery was dead; it had been a risk-free, simple escape. The battery had just happened to fail and Jazzy tested the system just days after Sasha's passing—*on Sasha's tenth anniversary*.

I think Sasha was having a little fun with us. She wanted us to know that we could just get rid of that kitty. Distractions were no longer needed.

Especially on her special day in our life.

SHORTLY AFTER THE KITTY RESCUE and back in the house, I noticed a slightly wavy line, about eighteen inches long, drawn in the carpeting. Displayed near the bedroom doorway, it could not be missed. It caught my eye on the spot due to its size, shape, and location; however, the origin of the impression seemed peculiar and difficult to discern.

I tried to imagine what could have caused such a distinct symbol. (I had an idea, but resorted to rationale before jumping to paranormal conclusions.)

Nothing nearby could have left such a thin line had it been dragged across the floor. I tried to simulate the imprint using the pointed tip of a wooden skewer to part the short pile carpet. The result was vastly different from the curious crop circle that had appeared.

The mysterious mark wasn't a circle, though. It was a narrow curved line shaped as a backward "S". Then I noticed Sasha's most recent favorite red ballie against the wall, just inside the door, the closest object to the harrowing hieroglyphic.

Since her death, the toy had remained untouched inside the bedroom, but a fair distance from the door. Sydney or Millie must have moved it, but maybe through an extrasensory suggestion? The timing seemed rather suspicious.

Coincidence?

Or a nice little sign from our sweet angel?

The spiritual signature had vanished without a trace within a few hours.

AS THE EMOTIONAL TOLL slowly lessened, and the days gradually got better and the nights continued to promise more uninterrupted sleep, it would still be a long road to feeling "normal" again. It was not the same without Sasha. Signs of her presence were exciting and inspiring, yet controversial. Were we simply projecting hopeful messages onto these random coincidental events?

Although I hoped for substantial proof, something more tangible than speculative circumstances, I wanted to believe these events and strange occurrences were all Sasha's doing. Every night I'd go to sleep anticipating a revelatory dream, but no such luck. Weeks later, I'd remember Sasha had been in my dreams. Her presence always had been incidental, striking me as neither surprising nor unique.

I began to pay attention to Sydney's and Millie's sleeping

patterns, looking for anything unusual. Millie was known to snore and make all sorts of noises while she slept. Sydney was always whisper quiet. It was most unusual when I noticed Sydney moaning often in his sleep. There's no way to know for sure, but my guess is that he was having dreams about Sasha. I wouldn't doubt that Millie dreamt about her, too.

They missed Sasha more than we'd ever know.

She was the leader of the pack, and as much as she enforced that status like a drill sergeant, she was still Sydney and Millie's loving big sister and good friend.

ON MONDAY, February 4, one week after Sasha's passing, I stepped on the scales and was stunned to see that I had lost seven pounds. I hadn't lost my appetite, but I was eating less than usual. Then it dawned on me—another reminder of our loss. I had lost seven pounds in two ways: my own weight and Sasha. (She was just a few ounces over seven pounds the day she died.)

Around four o'clock I felt a strong need to take a nap. The time marking one week since her death was approaching and on my mind as I lay down on the bed. Convenient time frames—one day, one week, one month, one year—seem significant when related to life events. They are noteworthy markers to measure, remind, and remember.

I fell victim to the belief that those dates could be the basis for something supernatural to occur, the best chance to deliberately observe odd conditions, grasping for potential messages my dearly departed Sasha might be trying to convey. But I wasn't going to wait up to see. I felt fatigued

Signs

and needed a nap. If she were going to leave me a message, it would have to be in a dream. She did not disappoint, but the communication was not in a dream. It was something completely different.

The message was once again emphatically simple to interpret; it was a reminder that she was still with us. The method of delivery could not have been more complex, though. It was a matter of timing and mathematics, almost too ridiculous to consider and admit, but too coincidental—too *paranormal*—to dismiss.

At erratic times for several years, an electronic glitch in our heat pump thermostat would cause it to jump to 90°F. It would happen whether set to heat or cool, but it was a rare occurrence, and when we noticed it, I'd simply reset it to the correct temperature. It was obviously easy to detect during the cooling season. Hot air should not be coming out of the air vents when the system was set to cool.

The temperatures were mild for a Texas winter during the week following Sasha's death. Our digital atomic kitchen clock displayed 70°F outside and 72°F in the house on the afternoon of my nap. The thermostat was set to heat, but the moderate temperatures rarely caused the system to start. I had recently changed the batteries and set the time on the thermostat to match the kitchen clock.

Carol remembered specifically looking at the kitchen clock when Sasha passed. It was 4:55 PM. I looked at the clock at 4:59, seeing it change to 5:00 PM. A week later I was napping through the same time period, and although I had hoped differently, without dreaming of Sasha. When I awoke abruptly, I looked at my bedside clock, bearing in mind the timing of her death exactly a week earlier.

But it was 5:03 PM.

I thought, *So much for the one-week measure of remembrance, huh?*

As I lay in bed in silence, sadly thinking how calm and quiet our home had become, my nerves were startled, peace disturbed, when my drumbeat ringtone rattled my phone. I picked it up to answer, noticing the time was 5:05 PM. Carol was calling to let me know she was on her way home.

While we talked briefly, mentioning that we just missed the time marking one week since Sasha's passing, I felt warm air blowing from the bedroom ceiling vent. It seemed much too warm in the house for the heat to come on, and then it dawned on me, *I'll bet that stupid thermostat jumped to ninety degrees again!*

I checked the thermostat and sure enough, it was set to 90°F. I looked at the time on the thermostat—it was 4:59, and in that instant, it changed to 5:00 PM. That's when it hit me like a psychic snooze alarm—something strange was happening again. I immediately looked at the kitchen clock and it was 5:10 PM. The thermostat clock had somehow lost ten minutes. I started to do the math in my head, thinking specifically about the times I had been noting during the previous few minutes.

I woke up just in time for Carol to call at 5:05 PM, mentioning that it was just past a week since Sasha's passing. At that instant, the thermostat jumped to 90°F, causing the heat to come on, and precisely reset its clock to 4:55 PM—*the time of Sasha's death*. After a couple of minutes on the phone, the warm air alerted me to go to the thermostat, specifically noticing the time change from 4:59 to 5:00 PM, just as I had noticed the week before.

Although the actual time was different—precisely ten minutes—the conditions setting me up to notice the relevant times were uncanny.

Coincidence?

I don't think so.

Sasha's spiritual energy utilized an extraordinary set of circumstances—an aptly-timed phone call, a temperamental thermostat, the impossible-to-ignore inappropriate warm air, the recalling and mimicking of the exact change of time on a digital display—to let me know she was still with us. She knew that the systematic conveyance of her message would undoubtedly catch my attention.

A chill ran up my spine as I reset the thermostat to a more appropriate temperature. I didn't bother to change the clock; I'd continue to compare the time with the kitchen clock for days and weeks to come (it never altered from the ten minute discrepancy), remaining captivated by the remarkable scenario surrounding those settings.

All the strange "coincidences" we'd been noticing at random throughout the week were promising signs, convincing us that they were paranormal and indeed from our sweet girl.

When Carol arrived home, I explained the confusing details of my "thermostat encounter." It was spooky and enthralling, the closest event yet that I had experienced to having "proof" of a message from Sasha.

Of course, it was only proof for me.

But she wasn't finished.

She had a similarly unique sign to send to Carol.

Our evening would become even more electrifying.

When we returned home from Sasha's cremation a few days earlier, we had to determine where we would place Sasha's cedar urn. It seemed appropriate to keep her close to the areas where she most often relaxed: the computer desk and the bed. Conveniently located between the two, a bedside table was the perfect spot. Her cedar box, sitting directly under the side table lamp, would symbolically remain unlocked to honor her free spirit. Sasha would always be near when we worked or slept.

Still in a state of wonderment that something supernatural had indeed occurred, we sat down to a leisurely dinner, remembering our sweet girl, in disbelief that a week had already passed. We wanted to see a show on PBS at nine o'clock, so we decided to watch in the living room, something we hadn't done since days before Sasha's passing. She loved to sit with us to watch television and that was a memory we were yet to revisit. When the show ended a few minutes before ten o'clock, Carol went to the bedroom to work on the computer. I had turned on the side table lamp (over Sasha's urn) earlier in the evening.

While Carol sat at the computer, the light bulb in the lamp started buzzing loudly and then burned out. I could hear the electrical commotion from the living room.

Carol shrieked and called out, "Did you hear that? The light just went out."

I noticed the kitchen clock was at exactly ten o'clock as I went to the bedroom. With the only illumination coming from the computer monitor, I flipped the switch for the ceiling light as I entered. A heavy electrical odor was dissipating throughout the room.

"What happened?"

"I was working on the computer and the light started buzzing and flickering like crazy. Then it just burned out," she repeated.

"That's a fluorescent bulb. Those are supposed to last for several years. That one can't be more than a year old," I remarked in surprise.

I'd only known compact fluorescent bulbs to simply quit working (and that usually happened when switching the light on), never to spurt and sputter, fizzling out in a blaze of glory.

"Sasha wants you to know she's there with you," I told Carol confidently.

I touched her urn, running my fingers along the smooth cedar top. "We miss you, girl," I said, as we looked on in amazement, trying to grasp what had happened. This stunning spectacle once again caught us by surprise, but we were delighted at its pertinence as I went looking for a replacement light bulb.

The lamp had been on for several hours before this occurred. The light bulb burned out after Carol entered the room, sitting at the adjacent desk. Sasha's cedar urn sat directly below the lamp. It was a week after her death; the same time we had returned home to her unmistakable "aroma" exactly a week earlier. And now there was a strong electrical "aroma" in that same space.

Yet another coincidence?

I think not. The timing was critical.

Earlier, beginning at 5:05 PM, the message was for me. At 10:00 PM, *exactly four hours and fifty-five minutes later*, the message was for Carol.

4:55—the time of Sasha's passing.

The proof seemed undeniable.

Sasha wanted us both to know that her energy was still present. Her spirit was steadfast. She continued to be with us and would always be near.

WE GRADUALLY FELL BACK into our routine over the next few weeks, with each day a little easier than the one before, but we still missed Sasha tremendously. Sydney and Millie knew that nothing would be the same anymore, no more fierce competition for attention, no close camaraderie to fill the hours when Carol and I were away from the house.

They had each other, but with Millie, that left a lot to be desired. She was satisfied to be alone for endless hours in a warm, cozy bed. Sydney was not as easily contented. He was incontestably dependent upon companionship. Of the two, he more noticeably felt the pain of Sasha's absence.

Over the years, when the pups had been left alone in the house, it was rare, yet inevitable, that one might not have been prepared to hold her or his water (or other contents) long enough. For that reason, they were always constrained to the kitchen where cleanup was easiest.

They were never reprimanded for such an accident. They always did their best to avoid that situation, but in some instances, it was unavoidable. Needing to use the bathroom, yet being forced to wait, without knowing when the opportunity might come is an awful feeling. And that's what indoor dogs endure time and time again.

Our pups always did their best to comply. But when they couldn't, Sasha was probably the guilty offender most times. She had much less bladder control than the others, especially as she entered into her prescribed diuretic discipline. She assumed we knew it was never intentional, so although she would have preferred to go outside, she was never ashamed if she could not hold it any longer. When I would discover the evidence of such an occasion, it was usually within a few steps of the back door.

Valentine's Day marked two weeks since Sasha's cremation. It was another convenient measure in time, another holiday to reminisce. I was home with the pups, Millie was sleeping on the bed, Sydney nearby, when I discovered in the most inappropriate and irritating way—foot to flux—a large puddle on the kitchen floor. It was transparent and difficult to see, appearing to be water, but in the middle of the floor, away from any water source. It was also where Sasha was known to have had an occasional "accident." This notion immediately occurred to me, and as much as I wanted to believe that I had stepped into the twilight zone, I knew that this doggie deluge did not inscrutably appear from the great beyond. It had to have been Sydney's doing.

When I began to wipe up the clear fluid, I noticed a surprisingly clean aroma. It was not urine. It could not have come from one of the dogs. The only reasonable explanation was that it came from our dishwasher, a few feet away. But the water was in the middle of the floor with no evidence of leaking to that location.

When this continued to occur at random times for several days, I was able to determine that the dishwasher was indeed leaking; not while running, but after the cycles had finished. The puddle of clean water always trickled to the middle of the floor, with hardly a trace of moisture along the way, exactly to the same spot where Sasha had occasionally had an accident. I couldn't discount that these unusual leaks began on Valentine's Day—her first holiday as our new puppy—always a favorite occasion for Sasha.

Was she once again reminding us that she was still here with us?

Or was this just another coincidence?

Later that same evening, when this first occurred, the thermostat kept jumping up to ninety degrees again. And it was set to the "off" position.

She was not finished with having something to say.

A FEW DAYS LATER, February 18, marked three weeks since her passing. I remained cognizant of these weekly measures of time, remaining open to unusual sensations or strange pulses from any electronics.

The occasion and my awareness did not fail me.

I sat down to work on the computer, near Sasha's cedar urn, just after four o'clock in the afternoon. At 4:39 PM, roughly the same time I had my heart-to-heart talk with Sasha exactly a fortnight and a week earlier, a strong aroma of freshly cut wood surrounded me for less than a minute. The phenomenon alerted me to note the time, recalling once again the time frame of events leading up to her passing.

In tribute, I marked the time of her death in silence at the kitchen island. I flinched, slightly startled when the refrigerator came on at that moment. While I stood there in the same spot where I had stood when she passed away, I remembered those final moments, the time that had passed since, and how much we'd been missing her.

This setting spontaneously metamorphosed into an unlikely séance when a noise like nothing I'd heard before screeched from the refrigerator. It cried out, almost voice-like, as if straining to speak, three brief sixteenth note patterns:

ai–is–ou ...
i–iss–oou ...
I–miss–you!

The mimesis of words seemed ideal, but the inspirited sounds were very real.

A random clunk from the ice maker was not unusual, but I had shut that off earlier in the day. The icebox shrieked a uniquely different language that afternoon and I have not heard it speak since.

I turned to watch the kitchen clock change from 4:59 to 5:00 PM once again. This time the digits seemed to change in cinematic slow motion with a resounding thud. A sudden stillness filled the room as I returned to continue work at the computer. I was noting these occasions and occurrences in a journal-like timeline, updating it as often as needed while specific details were on my mind.

About an hour later, I was listing many of Sasha's traits when the faint aroma of firewood returned. It was the smell of cut wood, almost like burning timber, but distinctly the odor that remains when a hot spinning metal blade cuts through fresh lumber. The aroma lingered for a few minutes while I searched to find the source. It didn't seem to be coming from anywhere. It was just there. And then it dispersed as quickly as it had materialized.

Through all this, the significance of her wooden urn did not go unnoticed.

I'm still with you.

Sasha's silent, yet powerful, message continued to echo clearly.

And I'll always be near.

AS THE WEEKEND APPROACHED, Carol began to have flu symptoms. She had received a flu shot earlier in the season, sickeningly, to no avail. She was lucky to see a rapid recovery. I had not received a flu shot, so within days, the symptoms hit me hard. I caught the worst flu I could ever remember, and to make matters worse, a strange rash and body itch decided to join the fun. Four days between bed and the bathroom coincided with four weeks, then a month, since Sasha's death. If anything unusual occurred, I was too subdued to notice.

For that short while, drifting off into a dream world was more likely to happen. Around that time, Sasha started to appear in my dreams. Never to share a specific message, never a feeling of special significance, she was merely there in ordinary circumstances. I never awoke to emotional highs or lows. I was just aware that she was sharing in my slumbering exploits.

As my flu symptoms subsided, the itching persisted. It would continue for several weeks, perplexing my doctor and keeping me busy with cream and lotion applications. For lack of a better explanation, I'm sure the stress that had been subconsciously building in me throughout Sasha's illness and recent passing was finally exploding free, being released in chaotic bursts of tickle and irritation all over my body.

It had been a trying time, living through Sasha's turmoil,

maintaining her happiness, praying for her survival. Nearly three years of random symptoms, watching our sweet girl slowly suffer, fight bravely, endure pains we could not imagine, and tolerate drugs I would painstakingly count and administer. A noble death, she was devoted to the end, sharing messages of serenity, hope, and inspiration with us. A trying time indeed was taking its toll on us emotionally, mentally, spiritually, and physically; however, it was time to keep the faith and time to heal.

ON FRIDAY, March 1, I received a voice mail from Dr. Nowlan. She apologized for not calling sooner, but she wanted to express her condolences and make sure we were doing all right. She also announced the dismal news that she would be relocating out of state in one week. We wanted to see her once again, so we promptly scheduled an appointment for the next day. We loaded our pet menagerie into the minivan and were off to see the doctor one final time.

In addition to a thoughtful sympathy card following her passing, the vet clinic provided a casting of Sasha's paw print as a token of remembrance. We appreciated the memento and thought how nice it would be to have the same from Sydney and Millie. Why wait until they were no longer with us?

That was one reason to visit the vet, but more importantly, we wanted to introduce them to Dr. Nowlan. Besides Sasha, the doctor had only met Jazmine (also going, for annual vaccinations). It was a final farewell from our family, a time to thank Dr. Nowlan for her wonderful care and attention throughout Sasha's CHF, and to wish her well as she was about to embark on a new chapter of her life.

As I told her how much we sincerely appreciated her continued dedication to maintaining Sasha's health (including consistent follow-up phone calls), we all choked back a tear or two. It was yet another sad day to see her go.

Dr. Nowlan was an important element in the final chapter of Sasha's life. Not only was she important, I believe she was destined to help Sasha.

I always respectfully referred to Dr. Nowlan by her title and surname, but fact be known, her first name is Melita.

Upon our first meeting, I was curious about her name. It was intriguing and delightful. For over a year, I had thought nothing more of it. It wasn't until several months after Sasha had passed (and Dr. Nowlan had moved across the country) that I happened to look up "Maltese" online. I had researched this information when we first adopted Sasha, but ten years had passed and the details had long ago escaped my memory.

What I rediscovered blew my mind.

"The breed name and origins are generally understood to derive from the Mediterranean island nation of Malta; however, the name is sometimes described with reference to the distinct Adriatic island of Mljet, or a defunct Sicilian town called *Melita*."[3]

I could not believe what I was reading.

I checked several sources to confirm. How could I have missed this during the entire course of Sasha's treatments?

Why didn't Dr. Nowlan casually mention that her first name and Sasha's breed name were historically linked?

Although curious at first, I never looked up the name. Apparently, I wasn't supposed to find out its significance until after Sasha was gone. We were never to be influenced by this knowledge.

Need I say it again?

Coincidence?

This was yet another sign from Sasha—*a sign from God*—long before she passed away. Dr. Nowlan—Melita—was *supposed* to be Sasha's doctor for her final year on this Earth.

It was fate.

It was destiny.

We were guided by angels all along, and all that time we didn't have a clue. I had to learn more, so I contacted Dr. Nowlan to inquire about her first name.

She shared that her father always liked it; it was his teacher's name. She knew of a correlation to Malta, but in fact—and despite her profession—had never made the connection to the Maltese breed.

We were all astounded by this late revelation.

As we counted the days, weeks, and a month without Sasha, we were adjusting to her absence, but it did not seem to get any easier. Just as we would begin to feel better, memories would come flooding back, causing great sadness. Carol thought often about the nightly return from work, how Sasha always longingly anticipated the welcome home. These memories made some nights incredibly difficult for Carol to come into the house without crying, leading to an exhaustive emotional breakdown.

I continued to talk to Sasha during my evening prayers, gazing into the starlit skies, "We love you and miss you so much. I want you here so badly. I miss your touch. I miss holding you, petting you."

Knowing that we would eventually meet again, at another time, in another place, in another dimension, was only slightly reassuring. It remained difficult to accept the fact that she would no longer be with us physically in this world.

In mid-March on a Saturday morning, Carol awoke early for work. She mentioned dreaming of Sasha, but like my dreams, there was nothing enlightening. Her morning schedule required a few errands, so she enlisted her coworker friend to accompany her. Carol talked about her dream, sharing her thoughts about missing our sweet girl. When they happened to be driving past the North Texas Humane Society, her friend suggested that Carol should see a melancholic, but friendly Spaniel-type dog she knew was inside and in need of a home.

We were not looking to adopt a dog.

We had not discussed it.

We were trying to get into our new routine and adjust to a two-dog household again. Sydney and Millie needed time to adjust as well. At some point, maybe in a year or two, we could entertain the thought of possibly adopting another Maltese puppy. But six weeks after Sasha was just too soon. Bringing a new puppy into our house of sorrow and remembrance was not something we were prepared to do.

It was just before ten o'clock and the Humane Society was about to open. Out of curiosity, Carol was tempted to indulge her friend's whim, so they stopped. As they walked the aisles of dog- and cat-filled cages toward the intended pooch, a small white dog caught Carol's eye. It nervously waited in a cage occupied by a much larger tan mutt.

The Humane Society worker asked Carol if she'd like to

see the Spaniel.

"Actually, I'd like to see the Maltese," Carol said, pointing to the sad little pup, lying on the concrete floor against the wall, nose pressed through the chain-link fence.

She wasn't sure it was a Maltese. Its hair was cut short, similar to a Toy Poodle, but she thought it could be a Maltese with a puppy cut.

"He just arrived last night. No one else has seen him," the worker reported as she opened the cage.

The timid pup gladly received Carol's warm embrace. His kiss to her cheek was all it took.

Carol was in puppy love.

When he snuggled in her arms, nuzzling her neck, resting his paws over her shoulder, she knew in her heart that this warm little guy needed to come home with her. But she also knew a phone call was in order. Much to my surprise, I became privy to the morning's events through texts, photos, and her heartfelt story. She could not bear the thought of letting her newfound love return to doggie confinement.

"If you're sure you want to do this—if you think he'll be all right with Syd and Mil—if you really feel in your heart that he is the right fit for our family, then go ahead and get him," I told Carol over the phone.

During the adoption process, five other people expressed interest in the soon-to-be newest member of *our* family. Carol's timing was impeccable.

Synchronicity. (Or perhaps, paranormal?)

He was indeed a Maltese, roughly a year old, background unknown. He had to wait for Carol to return after work before coming home to meet the rest of his new family. When they arrived late in the afternoon, I went to greet our new pup in the car. As I sat down in the passenger seat, he hopped over from Carol's lap to see me.

"Hi, little guy. Welcome to your new home," I said as I cradled him in my arms, stroking his short, soft, wavy white hair.

I remembered my most recent conversations with Sasha under starlit skies, "I miss holding you, petting you."

I was doing that again.

It wasn't her, but it was her touch.

It was a remarkable rendezvous, absolutely unplanned, utterly unexpected, but meant to be.

The road to our recovery was irrefutably in the works, littered with sweet signposts along the way, always part of the master plan. And undoubtedly, signs "at the paws of" our sweet girl.

Sasha was at it once more.

♪♫

chapter eleven

hope

Sweet Girl

Hope

As I LOOKED into a twinkling pair of joyful brown eyes, I immediately knew a new chapter of our life was beginning. Every fear, every question, every apprehension, every concern about once again growing our family was quickly put to rest, overshadowed by the bundle of loving spirit Carol had been inexplicably drawn to that morning. The glimmer of light that continued to guide us through grief suddenly grew bright as we began to emerge from the black hole that had engulfed us. Our six-week void, an ordeal of sorrow, confusion, and revelation, began to fill with the true possibility of hope.

For weeks we had grieved for Sasha every day. She was such a huge part of our lives. But life goes on. The music still plays, but our music was minus the melody. My greatest fear was that life would start to feel "normal" without her.

Inevitably, when schedules resumed and the presiding golden hue dissolved to blue, a feeling of normalcy did return, just not the normal it had been with Sasha. I could only characterize our life at that point—our everyday routine—as the "new normal," never again to be the "old normal."

The transition to our new normal would spontaneously leap forward as our new puppy propelled rousing new energy throughout our heartbroken home. All at once, it was all right for our old normal to reside in memory, a very happy melody to recall at will and sing in praise. But a new song was about to be written.

SIMPLY UNBELIEVABLE we thought as our new puppy instantaneously settled into our household. He took up right where Sasha left off, only he was nine years younger and in great adolescent health.

And, of course, he was no girl.

Before other considerations, that was my first concern when Carol called to tell me about her dog pound discovery. Sydney was always good around other male dogs, but he never lived with one. Even at Mom's, it was a house full of girls.

After ten years of masculine independence, and assuming top dog position in the chain of command, I wasn't sure he would gladly welcome a little boy dog into his domain. He missed his sister as much as we did, so the last thing I wanted to do was threaten Sydney with youthful XY chromosome competition as he was learning to live without Sasha.

With much curiosity and through playful exchanges, Sydney and Millie decided in short order that this strangely familiar-looking dog should stay with us. Jazmine did a double take on first glance, seemingly perplexed at Sasha's return. She would soon discover she had a new chase-and-wrestle buddy in our "Sasha look alike."

His haircut was different, notably his ears and no topknot, and his build sturdy, with prominent breastbone and Chippendale front forequarters, but our new puppy did resemble Sasha. It wasn't just a Maltese thing, either. I'd seen many Maltese dogs that didn't look anything like Sasha, but this one distinctly did. His personality was unique, but not far removed from Sasha's personality; his temperament was strangely similar.

We were astonished how he seemed to be instantly

familiar with his new surroundings: the layout of our house and the boardwalk paths of our backyard. This dog we barely knew was full of love to share and excited to be with his new family.

It felt as if he had simply come home.

Nevertheless, through all this sudden familiarity, we never confused our newest family member with Sasha. We never felt as though we were "replacing" her. That was never our intention. It would have been an impossible task anyway. But we did share a strong belief that his arrival was meant to be, as if the entire event had been orchestrated and overseen by our sweet girl.

Without much contemplation, our new puppy's name also came to me as if signed, sealed, and delivered by Sasha. She never gave birth to puppies, but if she had, our little guy could easily have passed for one of her own.

Son of Sasha.

"Sonny" it would be.

We momentarily tossed around "Alex" as a potential name before "Sonny" was revealed. Out of curiosity, I later researched the history of these names, starting with "Sasha." Once again, I was astounded to learn that "Sasha" and "Alex" are diminutives, or nicknames, of Alexandra and Alexander.

Without realizing it, we considered essentially the same name for our new pup.

This was just a little too close for comfort as I can imagine Sasha's thoughts on the matter, *Don't name him after me,... but you can call him my son.*

We complied.

SASHA EXPRESSED unique abilities and traits that defined her individuality, characteristics she would staunchly defend. At home, she displayed fierce courage toward an unfamiliar animal passing at a distance, but out of her surrounds, she remained shy and cautious.

She showed competitive spirit toward her siblings, vying for attention, but not for love. She always had so much love to give. Her mantra could have been, *You can share your love with others, too. That will not change how much love I have for you.*

Sasha never met someone she didn't try to befriend straightaway. She always felt a kinship with people. She thought she was a person.

I do not believe she knew she was a dog.

Her vivacious reception was overwhelming for many people. She truly expected a core of warmth and goodness from everyone. She was rarely wrong, often evoking unexpected emotions from unlikely victims of her loving assault.

She scaled the front side of our family and friends with pure passion, never to discriminate, and often to our embarrassment. Laps were always an open invitation.

Sasha relished the opportunity to hop up and down and over a reclined Sarah. She gently pawed at Becky's hair, returning a caressing favor. She danced figure eights around band members during a rock-and-roll jam session. She wasn't content until seated precariously on my mom's shoulder or perched under her chin. She leaped into Lynne's arms. She was a perfect princess on Lauren's lap. She posed for Anne's photography.

She kissed too many faces to count.

She pranced back and forth over the bishop while he visited Carol, who was recovering from minor surgery, during days that Sasha was sustaining her own difficult medical issues. She came to calm attention when he offered healing prayers.

Carol's mom was the first in our family to meet Sasha and Sydney. She embraced Sasha's loving welcome, a greeting of perpetual joy so unlike any other. During a visit with us in Texas, we found Sasha's twin in a plush toy for her to take home and keep in Michigan. It remained a special adornment and reminder of the love our sweet girl always had to share.

Most encounters required the complete candy cane treatment. With token held tight, her body swayed in a circling dance until a lap was available for the one-two bounce up to the face for a candy cane kiss. In her typical snorkel-hold fashion, Sasha loved to press her candy cane to my mouth in light little taps, affectionate kisses, too many for her to keep contained.

In the midst of her emotion, I'd say, "Give me five," and she'd start slapping my open palm with her paw. She didn't want to stop at just one, though. I'd count, "Five, ten, fifteen, twenty, twenty-five,…" as she continued to pat my hand.

She easily could have been counting the number of ways she celebrated life.

Sasha shared special relationships with her siblings and other animals, but in much different ways than with people. She had much less patience and more intolerance with animals, but still conveyed loving affection.

She and Sydney grew up together, they shared a kennel while we were away, they played together, they ate together, they fought each other, they chased each other, and they were the best of friends. However, for Mama or Daddy's attention, Sydney was left in her dust.

She loved Millie, an old soul and easy spirit to adore, often sharing a gentle kiss on her ear to encourage participation in pet-friendly family activities. She showed similar fondness for Jazmine for a while, only later becoming annoyed by the kitty's independence.

When Sasha stayed at Grandma's as a puppy, she crawled onto a resting and trusting Hannah's backside, a posh living Sheltie cushion for compassionate companionship and blissful relaxation. She was respectful and considerate around an ailing Sophie, her elder of the same breed.

She welcomed puppy kindergarten playmates to her yard for playful romps, but remained reticent, attentive, and courteous amongst the group during weekly learning sessions.

Along with Syd and Mil, she loved to explore new territory at Becky and Tracy's house, running around the backyard with their dogs and joining the eclectic troupe for neighborhood walks.

And then there were all the television creatures randomly appearing on those screens in our home; she never reserved judgment when expressing her concern or displeasure at their unwelcome arrival, trampling over every obstacle to swiftly meet those flat-image representations head-on.

Though quick to defend her territory if necessary, the common denominator was happiness, a loving thread running through every relationship of which Sasha was a part.

Even through stressful times (medical issues), aggressive exchanges (sibling rivalry), or cautious defense of impending threat (those darn TV animals), she was always quick to rebound with a cheerful disposition.

Bringing love and joy was her life mission.

She made every accommodation in pursuit of that purpose. There were no obstacles too large, no tasks too trivial. Whatever we asked of her, whether to wait for hours with her brother in a kennel, indulging our decibel-driven music or movie madness, or tolerating daily doses of heart medication for over a year, Sasha complied with kisses and a wagging tail.

ON CHRISTMAS EVE in 2012, I gathered the pets for a last-minute portrait, all decked out in holiday garb even they knew was absurd. As I positioned one after another side-by-side in front of the Christmas tree, I was amazed that they continued to sit still without trying to remove their reindeer antlers and elf caps—including Jazmine in snowman attire.

With a few quick clicks of the shutter, I captured an adorable Christmas memory of our one-of-a-kind motley crew. Sasha, frail and unknowingly in her final weeks, sat patiently posing for my camera in a Santa hat, undoubtedly teeming with the spirit of the holiday.

She understood and cherished the joy of the occasion, allowing the miracle of the season to temporarily overcome her illness. Her positive, loving spirit kept her going when her body was too stressed to continue.

She desperately wanted to live and she did live every day to the fullest.

A new day meant another great reason to celebrate life.

WE DID EVERYTHING within our means to see that she would continue to live a fulfilled and happy life. We were always inspired by the abundance of love Sasha freely expressed every day, and we did our best to reciprocate.

"Sasha's journey was an unusual one. I have yet to see any owner take such great detailed care of a family pet. I cannot say enough about how fortunate she was to be embraced by such love. I took inspiration from your desire and determination to keep her from knowing that she was sick," Melita shared with us when reflecting on Sasha's struggle with CHF.

"That was the ultimate goal: keep her from knowing anything's wrong, right up until that final day."

Sasha's heart was the core of everything. She had a heart full of love to share, a loving body full of heart to restrain. She never let physical limitations stifle her positive spirit. She was a true inspiration in the fight against all heart disease.

My father died from complications of heart disease. Carol's father endured his final years fighting heart disease. Carol has worked closely with the American Heart Association for over twenty years, developing hundreds of recipes for their cookbooks, food recommendations for a heart-healthy diet. Matters of the heart have been close to our hearts for decades.

Whether person or dog, heart issues are not discriminatory and can be difficult to overcome. Learning to make necessary adjustments in diet, exercise, and medicine is the first step. Keeping a positive outlook can be the most challenging step, though. Sasha always met that challenge with honor, dignity, and the greatest desire to survive.

She felt obligated to survive.

It was her duty as a faithful companion.

Sasha stood by me when I couldn't stand on my own.

She brought constant joy, even when times were not joyful.

It was my duty, and my greatest desire, to stand by her, and provide a loving, nurturing environment during her much-too-short life.

By nature of domestication, dogs are dependent upon their owners for their well-being. It is a grand responsibility and a matter of choices, no longer determined by their natural instincts. They are members of the family, expecting that we will cater to their needs, ultimately shaping the quality of their life, forever devoted and grateful. I always responded, ensuring a good, fun, and healthy-as-possible life for Sasha and her siblings.

In response to the news of Sasha's passing, our friend Martin Yan offered poignant words of wisdom:

"Sometimes, it is not about life and death, but the pleasure and the experience. We love our animals and they bring us great joy."

THERE IS SO MUCH to learn from our relationships with animals, especially our pets.

We're so busy doing what the world wants us to do.

We get lost in the things that matter the least.

We lose the big picture.

Dogs are here to help us see the big picture, to live in the moment, to remind us what is most important:

Love.
Devotion.
Friendship.
Compassion.
Kindness.
Respect.
Faith.

IT WAS NEVER a matter of words, rather daily acts, vignettes of our family life—before, during, and after the ten years we were privileged to share with our sweet girl—that chronicled her story in ways, until pieced together, I never thought of as significant.

Therein suggests the miracle.

The sum total of experiences in each life is always significant. For collectively, they paint the big picture. It is our task, our choice, to unlock the meaning.

By sharing similar and relatable moments familiar in diverse ways to all life on Earth—whether corporeal, cerebral, spiritual, or emotional—I find hope that we are all inexplicably bound together for the greater good in this incomprehensible, yet overwhelmingly loving universe.

Although I may not understand the meaning of life, through the telling of this story—the life and times of our sweet girl—Sasha may just have helped me find the meaning of *my* life.

♪♫

Hope

To Our Sweet Girl Sasha

We celebrate ten wonderful years with you.
You are a remarkable, unique, gentle spirit and a loyal companion.
Your unrelenting, unconditional love continuously touches our hearts.

Your effervescent energy is contagious and inspiring.
Your unbiased willingness to share enthusiasm for all others is unparalleled.
Your star shines brightly in our hearts and in our minds.

While you are no longer with us in this world, your spirit will be with us forever.
The memories of your life with us will be cherished for the rest of our lives.
You have forever changed our lives for the better.

In our mourning, you remind us to be positive.
You are the inspiration for us to move forward.
For all things good and exciting, all things comforting and loving.

We hold you close, you will never be far.
We are so fortunate to have been chosen to share in your life.
In your death, all the memories are ours to keep forever.

We miss you so much and we love you dearly.
This is not goodbye, rather simply, until we meet again.
It will be yet another time for great celebration.

Rest in peace, play in peace, you are our sweet angel.
Remember all the great joys of your life with us.
We forever will.

— *Your loving family*

Sweet Girl

postscript

Sweet Girl

Postscript

Between two and three in the morning on October 13, 2013, something was upsetting the dogs terribly. It wasn't unusual that I was awake, busy with paperwork in our home office. It was unusual, however, that Carol was up, also working on a project late that Saturday night. Music filled my workspace, but not loud enough to prevent me from hearing Carol calling to me from another room.

"The dogs are outside and they won't stop barking. I think you should take a look."

I could hear the barking faintly beyond the undulating speakers. I did not like it when the dogs rushed outside after midnight in a vocal rage, but fortunately, it rarely occurred. They were usually responding to the barks and howls coming from neighboring dogs. And those late night callings usually resulted from noises beyond the fence, warnings about creatures of the night lurking in the woods. This scenario was not unusual and no cause for alarm, but they were much too loud, much too late, so I went to the patio to call our dogs out of the uproar.

By the time I got outside, Millie was the only one still barking. I quietly called to her first, but that was enough to get the attention of Sydney and Sonny as well, so they all trotted back to the house. The night once again became still as I resumed my work while the rest of the house drifted asleep. I didn't think twice about the dogs' overnight disturbance, not until something seemed horribly wrong the next afternoon.

A MONTH EARLIER, Jazmine had turned two years old. She had become a beautiful cat, her calico coat soft and sleek. She was shy around people, except me—the one who kept her bowl full of surf 'n' turf cat food nibbles. She would let me hold her and often snuggled close in bed, and she would let Carol pet her, but that tested the limit of her human connections. She adored the dogs; they were her best friends. In typical cat fashion, she would brush up against Sydney under his chin. He would try to look away before her tiger-striped tail smacked his face as she breezed by. She would playfully bat her ivory paws at Millie, an easy target waddling by as Jazz rolled around the floor. And although usually pinned to the mat, she loved to wrestle with Sonny, a worthy opponent of the same age and weight class.

Jazzy had become comfortable with a lifestyle of dog-door access to the backyard, roaming at will within our fence for nearly two years as well. She was a free spirit kitty, always excited to explore the nooks and crannies around trees, bushes, and herb gardens, chasing geckos, grasshoppers, and butterflies day after day. More often than not, those chases ended with captive creatures Jazmine zealously brought into the house to show us. Dragonflies, cicadas, and baby snakes were top trophies, but she shared her *pièce de résistance* with us before dawn one morning as I was closing up cybershop and Carol was prepping for work.

"Oh my God! Jazzy just brought in a mouse!" I heard Carol yell from the kitchen.

Well, she had half of that right.

When I looked in the kitchen, I was instantly taken aback when something the size of a softball with fur and eyes stumbled—dazed and confused—in my direction.

Postscript

"Oh crap! That's no mouse, that's a rat!" I blurted out as the mutant monster slowly wandered under the oven.

Jazmine sat by in delirium, snickering in delight.

The dogs had come running, too, but were clearly as confused as the weary rodent and kept their distance as I grabbed the broom. Jazzy evidently had injured the little, uh … large fella, so it was content to stay hidden while I racked my brain for its speedy exit plan.

Carol gladly made her speedy exit to work and I finally coaxed the cautious critter out of hiding with a yardstick, guiding it with the broom out the back door and, ultimately, out of the yard before Jazz could reclaim her prize. She wouldn't dare follow it beyond the fence.

She learned very early that an attempt to climb the fence gave an unwelcome static shock from her collar. She wisely avoided further attempts, except the one strange instance on Sasha's tenth anniversary when the battery in her collar died.

Jazmine never tried to remove her collar. If snagged on a branch, the quick-release clasp separated easily to avoid choking her. The collar fell off regularly, usually because she'd accidentally bump the bulky plastic compartment that housed the electronics. It never bothered her to wear it, essentially allowing twenty-four-hour access to the backyard, but it looked as if she were prepared to deliver brandy to snow-stranded mountaineers.

Once a week or so, I'd notice her collar was missing. I'd see Jazzy sans neckband, often sleeping in her favorite cat hammock, so I'd be on a scavenger hunt for her lost golden ticket to adventure. It was usually outside and not always quickly found, but always recovered. Many times, Jazz followed me outside during the search, without her electronic restraint, yet without any evident escape plan. After more than a year, I considered leaving the collar off for good. She knew her boundaries. She was content in our yard. She was happy to be "one of the dogs."

ON THE NIGHT of the backyard hullabaloo, I assumed Jazzy was once again "one of the dogs," prowling in the yard as she did every night, while the dogs vehemently defended our property. At midnight, I saw her curled in a ball, sleeping on the Saint Bernard-size dog pillow in our living room.

Sonny discovered his kitty buddy in that vulnerable position, so he decided a wrestling match was in order. When I saw him disturbing Jazzy's nap, I told him to leave the kitty alone. He offered me a quick glance and came to see what I wanted. Her sleep interrupted, Jazmine decided to head outside, collar intact, for a usual moonlight retreat.

That was the last time I saw her.

Jazzy almost always waited until our household became quiet for the night before she came in and settled in her cozy hammock. In the morning, I would usually see her sleeping as the house brimmed with activity.

That October Sunday morning, she was not in her hammock. When she didn't appear by noon, I had a terrible gut feeling something was wrong. As I looked throughout the house, under beds, behind furniture, and in every closet, thoughts of the overnight commotion came to mind. I began to search the backyard, by then having a strong feeling I would not find her there. I circled the property three times, looking under every bush, up in every tree.

Jazzy was nowhere to be found.

Postscript

The woods beyond our fence grew dense with wild brush and thorn-covered mesquite trees, not an inviting environment for adventurous trail hikes. I looked over the fence and into the woods, hoping for evidence of Jazzy's apparent departure. If she had jumped over the fence, surely her collar would have dropped off. For the first time ever, her collar was also nowhere to be found. Wherever she had gone, her collar had gone with her.

Cats are known to disappear for days, weeks, even months, before returning home as if nothing out of the ordinary had happened. When Jazmine was nowhere to be found, I knew in my heart that she was gone forever. I was afraid it would not be a happy ending. We never found evidence that anything bad had happened, yet a perfect storm of dreadful circumstances seemed to have occurred that would indicate otherwise.

When the dogs were outside late at night "crying wolf," they were likely "crying coyote." The nights had become cooler, nocturnal animals were more active, and there was a higher likelihood that transient predators were out searching for prey.

For reasons we will never know, Jazzy decided to test the fence that night. Catastrophically, her collar must also have quit working. And, unbeknownst to her, something sinister was waiting in the woods. Only the dogs heard her cries of despair and tried in earnest to warn us. A very bad, very sad scenario, beyond our fence, beyond our control.

Not knowing what happened leaves us wondering, *What if ...?* But the circumstantial evidence (or lack thereof) confirms for me that Jazmine's short time with us was just another part of the master plan, a literal postscript to Sasha's story. The state of affairs leading to Jazzy's arrival coincided with a critical time in Sasha's life.

Jazmine was Sasha's kitty.

I cannot dismiss the thought that Jazzy's alleged tragic demise was only for a better purpose. Undoubtedly, she is once again with Sasha, over the rainbow, chasing bluebirds and neon butterflies in a summery breeze through boundless verdurous grasses and a wide spectrum of radiant wildflowers bursting forth, scented of sweet jasmine.

Her free spirit is truly free at last.

The dogs remained concerned that their kitty—they all assumed proud friendship with Jazzy at one time or another—never returned through the doggie door. Sonny seemed to suffer the most. He loved to chase Jazzy, often resulting in a mutually playful embrace. Traces of her existence—hammock, cat tree, play tunnel, toys—were all gradually removed as we adjusted to yet another "new normal" at home.

WHEN SONNY JOINED our family, a perfect new sibling for the pups and kitty, memories of Sasha became treasured gifts to reminisce about and life moved forward much more easily than we had ever expected. The recurrent signs of Sasha's spiritual presence culminated in Sonny's adoption.

Sasha was forcing us to move forward.

I began telling her story to the computer screen, word by word, chapter by chapter, reflecting on the wonderful pet adventures in my life.

When I was a young child, I hoped for real magic. As I grew older, I began to compose the unique drumbeats of my

Postscript

life. My heart lovingly welcomed devoted pets along the way.

Then Sasha came along.

She presented real magic. She provided the pulse for my rhythms. She embodied the meaning of love and devotion. Sasha captured and comprised the essence of my life.

Sasha's remarkable story was an extension of my own, a tale of the circle of existence along united paths in time and space. It is a story never told if not for an impetus to express and share, based on Sasha's everlasting inspiration, a guiding light toward the meaning of life.

For it is Sasha's legacy.

Her inspiration is the true gift. It does not answer our question "Why?" But during times happy and sad, and times when things happen that we just do not understand, her loving spirit offers comfort and peace.

Once again facing an unexpected change in our family, I did not become consumed with sadness or guilt or regret, wondering *Why did Jazzy leave our lives so abruptly?* Instead, I felt comforted that she fulfilled her place and time in this world, a significant piece of the big picture, and now she rests and plays with Sasha in peace.

A few nights after Jazmine's disappearance, I returned to the space on our deck where many of my prayers to the heavens took place. Under overcast skies, not unlike those on the night Sasha had passed, my attention was drawn to the only break in the clouds.

It revealed two stars shining brilliantly.

> If a man does not keep pace with his
> companions, perhaps it is because
> he hears a different drummer.
> Let him step to the music which he hears,
> however measured or far away.
>
> *– Henry David Thoreau*

Sweet Girl

Epilogue

THE 2013 HOLIDAY SEASON, sadly our first without Sasha eagerly waiting to celebrate the Christmas spirit, brought gifts of deeper meaning that I have yet to fully understand. December 5 marked the eleventh anniversary of Sasha's birth; her first birthday postmortem. As we fondly remembered and honored our sweet girl that day, an evening television event caught my attention.

For the first time in over fifty years, NBC was airing a live broadcast of a Broadway-style musical. In and of itself, this show would seem interesting to me at best. But given this production—*The Sound of Music*—was occurring on Sasha's birthday, it sparked an unrelenting curiosity guiding my undivided attention to the history of this musical; a musical originally introduced to me (and a worldwide audience) on the big screen during my early childhood.

I remember, through countless repeated listens and memorable sibling sing-alongs, wearing out the vinyl grooves of what was likely my first music album, the soundtrack to *The Sound of Music* motion picture. It was also likely the first movie experience of my life as well, coupled with a grocery bag full of home-popped popcorn, seated between my parents in the front seat of our ember red '64 Chevy Impala at the local drive-in theater.

I ALWAYS ENJOYED the film, through decades of TV reruns and even owning a DVD copy to view at will, but, admittedly, it has never struck me as one of my most favorite movies, or musicals, for that matter. (I much preferred *The Music Man*.) I became forever linked to one of the child characters by given name, and as a child, I was never fond of that connection. But memories aside, I decided to research and look further into *The Sound of Music*, unexpectedly discovering interesting facts that began to uncannily tie many events of my life together with an almost prophetic common thread.

The Sound of Music originated on Broadway, and two years later—the year of my birth—opened at The Princess Theatre in Melbourne, Australia. Forty years and five days later, during our interstate travels in Australia, Carol and I attended the *Mamma Mia!* musical at that same historic theater. We had first seen *Mamma Mia!* earlier that year in Chicago, and then a year later at the Winter Garden Theatre on Broadway. (Carol was a huge ABBA fan!)

In the year of Sasha's birth, we were just coming off a two-year Broadway overload. Our attention was focused on our new little "Princess" whose first sound of music was the motion picture soundtrack of the musical *Chicago*, heard repeatedly while riding with "Mamma" as we traveled along Interstate 45 to adopt her Australian-Breed-Brother—Amen!

Anecdotal and purely coincidental occurrences (or are they?), but they're amusing juxtapositions nonetheless. A common thread intertwined through a tapestry of events hard to ignore.

Through this recent attention to *The Sound of Music*, I was inexplicably drawn to one song: "Edelweiss."

Epilogue

All my years, I had remained ignorant of and oblivious to the meaning of that oft-thought-to-be-authentic Austrian folk song. Although pleasant and appealing, it was never of remarkable interest to me (and not authentically Austrian—it was composed by Rodgers and Hammerstein for the musical). However, I suddenly felt the need to know.

Referring literally to *edelweiss*, a beautiful small white sunflower of the alpine winter garden, the lyrics to this song instantly spoke metaphorically to me.

Memories of our sweet girl, snow white and always welcoming, blossomed from the delightful theme of that song, once again recalling the sweet melody of her life. Connecting the dots, like constellations in the night sky, continues to tell (and foretell) a story I could never have imagined.

As this story continues to unfold, it should not be a surprise to learn that the word *Malta*—the island where the Maltese breed originated—derives from the Greek word *meli*, "honey." The ancient Greeks called the island *Melitē*, meaning "honey-sweet." (The Romans followed, calling the island *Melita*.)[4]

In retrospect, clues abound throughout our lives. As we collect all the random pieces (many of which seem at the time to be unrelated), it is our task to decipher the message, to assemble the puzzle, to see the big picture. Every acquaintance, decision, and journey we make links us to a timeline network, which defines our individual path while it discloses our purpose along the way, on our collective stellar voyage.

IN YET ANOTHER unexplained coincidence, the name *Sasha* came to me long before I learned its origin—Slavic *and* *Greek*—was based on several meanings: sunshine, gentle, soft, defender, helper of mankind, truth, and true.

Words that inherently describe our honey-sweet girl from Malta.

All these meanings were germane and indeed true, following the common thread of truths throughout my timeline voyage, and exemplified in the gentle guiding love and heartbeats of one little dog that I unwittingly, yet confidently, named "Sasha."

The spirit of Sasha continues to shine brightly. Her miraculous melody resonates in a pure and joyful voice as her special life song is heard in perfect harmony. Celebrating her magnum opus is a provident gift during the holiday season, and, as time goes by, a true gift to cherish every season.

Sweet girl Sasha will forever be my sweet sound of music. And now, she is a welcome blossom that blooms forevermore, for all to behold in the garden of life.

Epilogue

Sweet Girl

[1] Maltese breed description based on information in the books:
   A New Owner's Guide to Maltese, Vicki Abbott, T.F.H. Publications, Inc, 2002
   The Complete Dog Book, 19th ed, Official Publication of the AKC, Howell Book House, 1998

[2] Definitions of "paranormal" and "coincidence" based on information in:
   Merriam-Webster's Collegiate Dictionary, 11th ed, Merriam-Webster, Inc, 2004
   Webster's New World College Dictionary, 4th ed, Wiley Publishing, Inc, 2004
   Webster's Third New International Dictionary, Merriam-Webster Inc, 1986

[3] Wikipedia contributors, "Maltese (dog)," *Wikipedia, The Free Encyclopedia*,
   http://en.wikipedia.org/wiki/Maltese_(dog) [accessed 12-25-14]; emphasis by author

[4] Wikipedia contributors, "Malta," *Wikipedia, The Free Encyclopedia*,
   http://en.wikipedia.org/wiki/Malta [accessed 12-25-14]

[5] At the website, select (click on) the music notes.

Sweet Girl

Photos by Anne Dixon:
Sweet Girl Sasha • book cover
Sasha: That's a Big Yawn! • book spine

And from the Ritchie family photo album:
Sasha: Stylin' on the Deck • title page
6th Grade Autobiography • 7
Kim & Tinkerbell • 9
Hocus Pocus • 9
Mickey & Tippy • 9
Yoda & Açúcar • 33
Sasha: Trinket of Sunshine • 59
Sydney, Sasha & Millie • 85
Sasha: The Bridge • 117
Sasha: Snow Dog • 147
Sasha: Patio Time • 175
Sasha: Sweet Angel • 203
Sasha: Spa Day • 237
Sonny • 265
Sasha: Santa • 295
Jazmine & Sasha • 309
Sasha • 325
Princess Sasha • 329
Sasha: Selfie • 329
Sasha: Eyes on Ballie • 331
Sasha: Candy Cane Dance • 335
Sasha: Sweet Angel • back cover
Sasha & Daddy • back cover

photos

Sweet Girl

acknowledgments

Sweet Girl

Acknowledgments

MANY THANK-YOUS to Robin Sullivan for her dedicated book editing skills. Her judicious methods to properly reorganize my thoughts and ideas have helped me tremendously in telling this story. She consistently made valiant efforts to rein in my overzealous attempts to use words in ways, which until now, may never have been known to the English language. And she has saved you, the reader, from my silly whims and an abundance of gobbledygook. In any case, I sincerely thank Robin for elevating my story—written to be informational and entertaining, and, at times, a tale difficult to tell—to prose that is above all, heartfelt and inspirational.

WITH GREAT APPRECIATION to Melita—Dr. Nowlan—for her continued support to provide detailed and accurate veterinary information and advice, throughout Sasha's ordeal and as I worked on this book. She remained ready and willing, always with a cheerful and optimistic disposition, to offer her medical knowledge without hesitation. Her professional skills and talent as a Doctor of Veterinary Medicine are exceptional. Dr. Nowlan's empathetic care and attention to Sasha's declining health was always above and beyond our expectations, and I will forever be indebted to her for the honest treatments and fearless compassion she dared show toward Sasha. Thank you, Melita.

THANK YOU to Spence, for trudging through an early manuscript of my book. His chapter-by-chapter commentary offered regular, entertaining correspondence and helped me eliminate several ambiguities long before anyone else could get lost in my locution. Thank you also to Carol, Kathy, Don, Lynne, Lauren, Sarah, Ione, Debby, Roy, Becky, Sue, and Melita for reading and listening to many passages of my manuscript as it transitioned through many versions, and for offering their insights and suggestions along the way. And special thanks to Martin, a good friend and mentor, always supportive with inspiring advice and words of wisdom.

A SPECIAL THANK YOU to Anne for the amazing cover photograph, capturing Sasha in an honest, true-to-her-heart, prime-of-her-life pose—one forever distinguished among all the photos of our sweet girl.

MY SINCERE THANKS to all the pet care professionals—veterinarians, groomers, puppy trainers, animal clinic staff, and the personnel at Smoke Rise Farm—who kindly tended to Sasha's needs during various stages of her wonderful life.

MANY THANKS to family and friends who were always a big part of Sasha's life. She could not wait to welcome them into her world and enjoyed every opportunity to spend time with them. And to Carol and the pups, I say a loving thank you for allowing me to share many of our personal moments with readers. I cherish the decade we had together with Sasha. It is not only a remarkable chapter in our lives, it is a story of eternal love and compassion that is an inspiration for all to recognize the good and beauty in all things and in all of life.

Acknowledgments

AND FINALLY, I would be inexcusably remiss if I did not thank you, the reader, for indulging my storytelling and immersing yourself in my memoir. If you have read this far, you are to be commended, and you undoubtedly would like to see more. I thank you and reward you with an invitation to peruse the Sweet Girl Sasha[5] scrapbook, with photos and images you'll likely recognize from stories in this book. The clues to Sasha's "Easter egg" start within the text of this paragraph, so happy hunting! The content and limited time frame to access this online addendum will be solely at the discretion of the publisher and may change at random. Once again, thank you, best wishes, and Godspeed!

OUR DEAREST SASHA, you are the inspiration. Your spirit lives on, with everlasting love.

♥

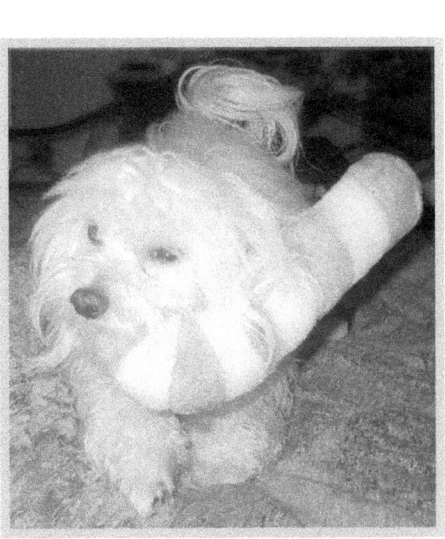

www.ingramcontent.com/pod-product-compliance
Lightning Source LLC
Chambersburg PA
CBHW022000100426
42738CB00042B/970